February 2009

Egon Zehnder International

EGON ZEHNDER INTERNATIONAL INC.
BROOKFIELD PLACE, 181 BAY STREET

SUITE 3920, P.O. BOX 810
TORONTO, ONTARIO M5J 2T3
CANADA
TELEPHONE +1 416 364 0222
WWW.EGONZEHNDER.COM

With Compliments of

Mr. David S. Ain
david.ain@ezi.net

Mr. Rajesh V. Gokhale
rajesh.gokhale@ezi.net

Mr. David P. Harris
david.harris@ezi.net

Ms. Valerie T. Spriet
valerie.spriet@ezi.net

Ms. Jan J. Stewart
jan.stewart@ezi.net

Ms. Pamela A. Warren
pam.warren@ezi.net

Mr. Rashid Wasti
rashid.wasti@ezi.net

GREAT
PEOPLE
DECISIONS

GREAT PEOPLE DECISIONS

Why They Matter So Much,

Why They Are So Hard, and

How You Can Master Them

CLAUDIO FERNANDEZ ARAOZ

John Wiley & Sons, Inc.

Published by John Wiley & Sons, Inc., Hoboken, New Jersey.
Published simultaneously in Canada.

Wiley Bicentennial Logo: Richard J. Pacifico.

For general information on our other products and services or for technical support, please contact our Customer Care Department within the United States at (800) 762-2974, outside the United States at (317) 572-3993 or fax (317) 572-4002.

Wiley also publishes its books in a variety of electronic formats. Some content that appears in print may not be available in electronic books. For more information about Wiley products, visit our web site at www.wiley.com.

Library of Congress Cataloging-in-Publication Data:

Fernández-Aráoz, Claudio.
    Great people decisions : why they matter so much, why they are so hard, and how you can master them /
Claudio Fernández-Aráoz.
        p.   cm.
    Includes bibliographical references.
    ISBN 978-0-470-03726-3 (cloth)
    1. Executives—Recruiting.   2. Executive ability—Evaluation.   3. Employee retention.
4. Organizational effectiveness.   I. Title.
    HF5549.5.R44F47   2007
    658.4'07111—dc22

                                                        2006101040

Printed in the United States of America.

10   9   8   7   6   5   4   3   2   1

To my beloved wife María,
the greatest people decision I ever made

To our beloved children Ignacio, Inés, and Lucía,
the greatest people decisions God
could possibly have made for both of us

Contents

The Make-or-Break Choice

*G*reat People Decisions will help you improve your personal competence at hiring and promoting great people.

Literally, *nothing* is more important. For almost every manager, personal success grows directly out of the ability to choose the right people for his or her team.

But making key appointments is *hard*. Few people get any formal training in this all-important activity, and no comprehensive tools exist to make up for that lack of training.

Great People Decisions fills that gap.

As you've already discovered in your own career, organizations are all about *people*. It doesn't matter how high-tech, stripped-down, decentralized, offshored, outsourced, or automated your organization is (or, more likely, *thinks* it is). At the end of the day, your organization is still all about *people*.

Managers lose sleep over lots of things: poor cash flow, impending lawsuits, a failing strategy, mergers and acquisitions gone awry, a competitor making a direct move against a profitable product line, and so on. What successful managers *mostly* lose sleep over, though, is people: *How do I get the very best person in the right job?*

People are the problem, and also the solution. How does a manager go about fixing a serious problem? Usually, he or she goes out in search of *great people*, whether inside or outside the organization.

Organizations that are skilled at solving the "people puzzle"—finding, recruiting, hiring, promoting, and retaining the very best people for the job—tend to thrive. (Jack Welch has told me that in his years with GE, he spent more than half his time getting the right people in the right positions.) Those that are bad at it tend to fail in the long run.

But the truth is that organizations don't really solve puzzles. *People* solve puzzles. Within every organization, a surprisingly large number of individuals—probably including you—have to make crucial people choices.

You may be part of a Human Resources (HR) group, formally tasked with making these kinds of decisions on a daily basis. Or you may be a member of the board of directors, who—once or twice in your tenure on the board—will be asked to participate in choosing a new CEO or other senior executive. More likely, though, you're part of a much bigger group in "the middle"—that is, the group of managers who are occasionally called upon to make a personnel-related decision for their division or functional area.

These are vitally important decisions. And by *important*, I mean two things.

It's Vitally Important to *You*

First (and this is the main reason why I've written *Great People Decisions*), *people decisions are important to you, the decision-maker*. If you prove to be skilled at solving "people puzzles," your career prospects will almost certainly get brighter. Conversely, if you repeatedly fail to get the right person in the job, your career prospects will suffer. Think about the experiences of people you've worked with. Do you agree that good people-finders move up, while others move out?

The problem is that very few people get any formal training in finding and choosing good people. Business schools, especially at the graduate level, tend to downgrade Human Resources Management (HRM) issues in general, or at best focus on HRM as just a minor one of a half-dozen functional areas; they rarely get down to the level of *skill-building* that is required.

Sometimes I use an investing analogy to make this point. Would you like to be as successful an investor as, say, Warren Buffett? I would, too! Would you like to get there without any relevant skills or experience? Me, too—but that seems like an unlikely goal. In order to become as good at people finding as Warren Buffett is at investing, you have to become an expert. You need the right tools.

Great People Decisions puts those tools in your hand. It is a comprehensive toolkit for managers who want to improve their personal competence at hiring and promoting people. This is not an art; it's a craft that *can be learned*. And it's important to you that you learn this craft.

It's Vitally Important to Your Organization

My second point is that *making great people decisions is vitally important to your organization*. Getting the right CEO, for example, is of paramount importance. And yet, about a third of all CEOs who leave their positions are either fired or forced to resign. *What are we doing wrong?* The same holds true at other levels of the organization. According to one study in which I participated, where we looked at thousands of executives in leading companies around the world, roughly a *third* of the executives we assessed turned out to be in the bottom half of the competence curve with respect to their peers at other companies in their respective industries.

In other words, even at great companies, the wrong people wind up in the wrong jobs. *Can't we do better?*

My Background

Before proceeding any further, you should probably ask what my own qualifications are. Who am I to be telling you what's important?

I've been in the profession of finding great people—and growing great people—for two decades. I was trained as an industrial engineer at Argentine Catholic University in my native Argentina, where I graduated first in my class, and then earned an MBA at Stanford, also with honors. I worked for McKinsey & Co. in Madrid and Milan, and in 1986, I joined Egon Zehnder International (EZI), a leading global executive search firm. Today, I am a partner with this firm, and a member of its executive committee. While I live with my family in Buenos Aires, my role is global, and I constantly travel around the world.

Maybe the phrase *executive search* needs some elaboration at this point. Executive search includes what some people call "headhunting," that is, hiring external candidates for senior positions both in for-profit and not-for-profit situations. I personally have led some 300 such searches, and actively participated in another 1,500 or so. These searches have comprised positions on the most senior levels (chairpersons, presidents, and CEOs) all the way down to first-time managers. I have served in this role for companies with billions of dollars in annual revenues as well as for very small ones, and for a range of nongovernmental organizations (NGOs), foundations, and not-for-profits. My personal success rate at hiring external candidates has been consistently above 90 percent, which is a very high percentage in light of the fact that external hires are typically made when times are particularly tough.

But executive search, broadly defined, also includes the activity of *management appraisal*, that is, assessing managers within a client's organization. This can be critically important in certain situations. In the context of a merger or acquisition, for example, the company has to decide how to allocate its management resources (even to the point of deciding who should stay and who should go). Or, to cite another circumstance, when a new CEO arrives and wants a rapid, professional, accurate, and independent assessment of his or her team, people like myself are often called upon. Management appraisals can also be very useful when a company faces a new competitive scenario, or when technological or regulatory changes suddenly rewrite the rules of the game. In all of these cases, my colleagues and I assess not just competence (the current ability to do the current job) but also the individual's potential to *grow*. We offer advice on promotions, assignments to new roles, development plans, and so on—all functions aimed mainly at *internal* candidates.

I led our Management Appraisal practice worldwide for some time. Recently, we went back and compared our assessments with the actual performance and evolution of the managers whom we had appraised. Again, our accuracy at predicting both performance and development potential has been on the order of 90 percent globally, while the accuracy of some of our client companies' internal assessments that we have analyzed have ranged as low as 30 percent.

I say all of this not by way of boasting, but rather to underscore two things. First, I have extensive experience with people decisions. I know the landscape intimately. Second, the prescriptions contained in this book cover the entire gamut of hiring and promoting—from both outside and inside the company.

I should add that I have an intense intellectual commitment to my field. In 1994, in addition to my search work, I became responsible for the professional development of consultants in our global network. Currently, I lead the development of our firm's intellectual capital for our network of 62 offices worldwide. In the 1990s, I led a major effort to upgrade our work methodology for our executive search practice, and have recently once again led a similar effort to become even better at helping our clients hire or promote the very best people in the world.

I have read literally thousands of books and articles pertaining to some aspect of people decisions. I've written articles for the *Harvard Business Review* and the *MIT Sloan Management Review*. I have also contributed a chapter to *The Emotionally Intelligent Workplace*, a book edited by Daniel Goleman and Cary Cherniss, and collaborated with Jack

Welch on his book, *Winning*, and with Jim Kouzes on the latest edition of *The Leadership Challenge*.

And finally, I have a *passion* for helping others improve their hiring and promotion decisions. I honestly believe that the world would be a much better place if hiring and promotion decisions at all levels, from the shop floor to the boardroom, could be substantially improved. I believe they can be improved. I believe that I have the skills, and therefore the *obligation*, to contribute to that improvement.

What You'll Find Here

In the first two chapters of *Great People Decisions*, I go into depth as to why great people decisions matter so much—both to you and your organization.

Next, in Chapter 3, I explain why great people decisions are so hard. Yes, part of the problem lies in the talent pool, but a bigger part lies in the "eye of the beholder." All too often, the people who conduct searches make one or more in a series of tactical mistakes, all of which combine to make a successful outcome that much more elusive.

Chapters 4, 5, and 6 address the *whens*, *whats*, and *wheres*: when to look, what to look for, and where you're likely to find what you're looking for. Throughout these chapters (and elsewhere in the book), I'll tell you how and when to engage outside help, and I'll explain why (at least in most companies) the decision to look *only* inside is a bad idea.

Most of the book is naturally about the *hows* of great people decisions: how to appraise, attract, motivate, and integrate the best people. Chapter 7 is devoted to the specifics of appraising people. Many people think this is self-evident: You bring the candidate in, interview him, and check his references. But in my experience, each of these tasks is more difficult than may appear at first. For example: How do you check references in an environment in which people are afraid of getting sued if they tell you the negative truth about a former employee? (The answer:

Dig deeper. I'll tell you how.) Should people "down the ladder" from the job for which a candidate is applying be allowed to appraise candidates? (The answer: *as a rule, no.*)

And as you've probably discovered on your own, it's not enough to find a great person. You also have to successfully recruit that candidate, with the right package of incentives, and then *integrate* her into her new organizational context. Despite the profusion of recent books and articles on the subject of integration, many companies still make the mistake of expecting a candidate to "sink or swim."

In the final chapter, I circle back to the question of *why this is important.* I believe high-performing organizations not only provide good employment and generate returns for their owners, they also make our society better. A great company—full of great people—raises our standard of living, raises our sights, broadens our horizons, and gives us hope for the future.

CHAPTER ONE

Great People Decisions: A Resource for *You*

It was mid-1986, and I was about to attend a very important meeting in Zurich. Over the course of the previous four days, I had made stops in London, Paris, Copenhagen, and Brussels. In each city, I sat for interviews with consultants from Egon Zehnder International (EZI), the international executive search firm. I had already completed some 30 such conversations, including sessions with a great variety of partners in the firm as well as its full Executive Committee.

But now, here in Zurich, I was about to meet with Egon Zehnder himself—the firm's founder, and at that time its chairman. I was keyed up, to say the least. (Even today, I can still summon up some of that long-ago nervousness.) I was well aware of the stature of the man in front of me who—having graduated from Harvard Business School the year that I was born—launched the executive search profession in Europe in 1959, and in 1964 started his own search firm, which he immediately began expanding internationally. He was, simply put, a legend.

I'm embarrassed to say that I don't remember many of the questions he asked me that day. For some reason, though, I *do* remember some of the questions I asked him. In particular, I remember asking him a question that went something like this: *Based on your experience of more than 25 years of executive search practice, meeting with both successful clients and candidates for high-level positions, what makes a person successful?*

1

I guess I was expecting him to respond with an elaborate success theory. After all, he was enormously successful himself. Already, I could see that he was a man of strong convictions and great integrity. So what did the great man say, in response to my question?

"Luck!"

I admit it; I was taken aback—*luck?* He continued along these lines:

Of course, all the successful people I have met are highly intelligent. They are also hard workers. They believe in preparation. They relate very well to others. But if you ask me to point to the most important reason for their success, I believe it is luck. They were lucky to be born into certain families, and to be born in certain countries. They were lucky to have some unique gifts. They were lucky to be able to attend good schools and get a good education. They were lucky to work for good companies. They were lucky to stay healthy. They were lucky to have opportunities for promotions. So, in answer to your question, the number-one reason for individual success is luck.

If I had been a little quicker on my feet (and perhaps a little braver) I would have regrouped and asked him what the *second* most important reason was. But the moment passed, and we moved on to other topics.

Since that long-ago meeting, I've had countless opportunities to revisit my question, and Zehnder's answer. Many times, I've had to grant the wisdom of our founder: Luck certainly played a role in lots of people's careers, including my own. But I've also tried to find some more systematic answers that might help someone take *action*. (Telling someone to "be lucky" is not enough, obviously.) So, when interviewing great candidates for a search assignment, when meeting impressive clients, when having conversations with executives who want to choose a new career path, when giving speeches to students at Harvard Business School, when looking at my own children, I've continued to ask my question: *What, exactly, accounts for compelling career success?*

It's now more than 20 years since that first meeting with Egon. In those intervening two decades, I have conducted close to 20,000 in-person interviews (about a thousand a year, or four per working day, throughout most of my career as an executive search consultant). I have traveled all over the world, whether to work on client assignments, train our colleagues, attend our executive committee or partners meetings, or give speeches. In the course of those travels, I have had thousands of personal, deep, touching conversations with managers and executives, discussing their careers, their lives, their glories, their dramas.

I have witnessed great success, but also dramatic pain. I got to know some outstanding examples of career and life management. Sadly, I also got to know a few wonderfully talented people who killed themselves—literally.

I admit that it's become something of an obsession for me. *Why do certain people succeed, and others fail?* I think I have an answer.

The Success Formula

First, as noted earlier, I don't disagree with Zehnder about luck. Luck can come to bear in all the ways he enumerated, and then some. In the extreme, bad luck can terminate your career, through death or other tragedies.

I believe, though, that the formula for career success includes at least four other factors. They are:

1. Genetics
2. Development
3. Career decisions
4. People decisions

I am convinced that these factors reinforce and build upon each other, and create a multiplier effect. I also believe that most of these factors have different weights at different stages of our life. The exception, of course, is your genetic inheritance, which, like your luck, remains relevant from birth to death. Development is also important throughout life, but it is particularly critical in the early stages. Career decisions become important when we reach our early twenties. Last (but not least) is what I call "people decisions."

I'll give you the punch line first: *I am absolutely convinced that, once you have completed your formal education and embarked on your professional career, people decisions are the single most important contributor to your career success.*

Now let's run through each of the factors in a little more depth.

Genetics play a big and continuing role. Your genetic makeup explains (for example) why some things are easy for you to learn, while others are extremely difficult. Genetics set limits on you, even as they open doors for you. But they are not exactly static. While until quite recently genetics were assumed to be a constant in the success formula, current research is showing that even one's genetic legacy can be considered dynamic. As Matt Ridley demonstrates in *Nature Via Nurture*, your day-to-day experience partially determines which genes switch on, which in turn determines which proteins are manufactured, which in turn shapes and reshapes the synapses between your brain cells.[1] In the debate over nature versus nurture, it appears that both sides are right.

Development, which is my shorthand for the formal and informal learning that occurs over one's lifetime, can be a powerful force for career success. Your ability to learn also depends in part on your career choices: What kinds of learning opportunities are put in front of you in the workplace? Do new things keep coming at you?

Obviously, a wise investment of time and effort in professional development can significantly enhance your level of competence, and therefore increase your chances of success. The best development experiences can have enormous impact.

But there are clear limits on the potential of development. As noted earlier, your ability to learn depends in part on your genetics. In addition, much as it pains me to say it, the ability to learn decreases with age.[2] Yes, you can teach an old dog new tricks; it just takes longer, and maybe not the entire trick is retained. So the costs and benefits of training shift in subtle ways over the years.

I'll let my friend Lyle Spencer summarize the potential of development, in his pithy way (he is a world authority both on selection and development): "You can train a turkey to climb a tree," Spencer says, "but I would rather hire a squirrel."

The impact of **career choices** on personal success should never be underestimated. For much of my working life, I've been struck by the dramatic differentials in the achievements of individuals who embark on their respective careers with roughly similar talents, but who choose very different work environments. My undergraduate classmates, for example, include a number of truly bright and talented people who made the mistake of joining unprofessional or intensely bureaucratic organizations; today, in professional terms, they are miles behind our similarly gifted classmates who took much better career paths and happened upon more enlightened employers. Simply put, good career choices multiply the fruits of your own development efforts, and therefore are a key factor for outstanding career success.

In her book, *Career Imprints: Creating Leaders Across an Industry*, Harvard Professor Monica Higgins tells how the "Baxter Boys" built the biotech industry in the United States.[3] Based on her study of 300 biotechnology companies and 3,200 biotechnology executives, Higgins concluded that a single firm—Baxter Labs—was the breeding ground for an astonishing number of successful biotechnology spinoffs and startups. This phenomenon—of one organization spawning leaders across a whole sector—has also been seen in other industries, such as Hewlett-Packard and Apple in high-tech hardware, and Fairchild in the semiconductor field. Obviously, putting yourself in a hotbed of innovation is better than putting yourself in a backwater, in terms of long-term career success.

For most of us, **people decisions** become important sometime in our twenties. In our personal lives, we make lifelong friends—at college, in graduate schools, and in church and neighborhood settings. We meet and marry our life partners. And, in the workplace, we start making decisions about people. We start deciding things about colleagues, clients, and vendors.

Once you become a manager, you start working through others, and therefore your people decisions become essential for your own unit's performance. As you take on larger responsibilities—from running the shop to running the ship—the stakes get higher, because the only way that you can exercise control is through the team of people you've put together. As you move from manager to senior executive and eventually to CEO or company chairperson, people decisions are both your highest challenge and your biggest opportunity.

Now I'll restate my punch line: After 20 years of practice, research, and reflection, I am firmly convinced that *the ability to make great people decisions is the most powerful contributor to career success*, as illustrated in Figure 1.1. And note that the farther along you get in your career, and

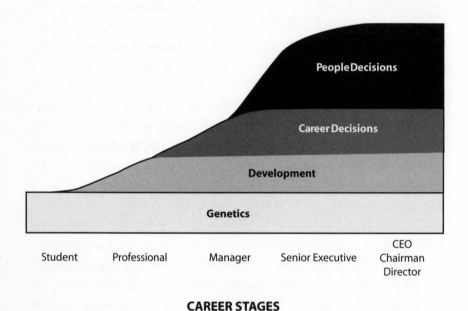

FIGURE 1.1   **Impact on Career Success**

the higher up the organizational ladder you climb, the more important these kinds of decisions tend to become—both in absolute terms and in relation to all other factors.

How to Get Honored by the Harvard Business School

Let's look at an example of this "success formula" in action. I don't think Egon Zehnder will mind if I scrutinize his own career in terms of this formula—even if I wind up suggesting that there was more than simple luck at work.[4]

In 2002, Zehnder received the Harvard Business School's Alumni Achievement Award—one of its most important honors. Established in 1968, this award goes to a very small number of distinguished graduates (one or two a year) who, throughout their professional careers, "have contributed significantly to their companies and communities, while upholding the highest standards and values in everything they do." According to then-Dean Kim Clark, the award winners "represent the best in [the School's] alumni body. Exemplary role models, they inspire all those who aspire to have an impact on both business and society."[5]

Exactly how did Egon Zehnder achieve this success? I think if you looked at the evidence, you'd have to conclude that genetics played their part. Zehnder has the genetic good luck of being tall, handsome, articulate, and intelligent in the traditional (IQ) sense. (In the sweepstakes of life, never underestimate the importance of a commanding physical presence!) At the same time, at least in my own experience of him, Zehnder is also a master of what is often referred to as *emotional intelligence*. (This concept will be expounded upon in Chapter 5.) Although one might debate which of these characteristics are determined in large part by genetics (I'd say many of them are), Zehnder is self-aware, full of integrity, and a man of amazing commitment, initiative, and optimism. He is a "natural-born leader," with all the attendant genetic implications. And as highlighted by Jim Kouzes in *The Leadership Challenge*, he is also a master at encouraging the heart.[6] I have no doubt that Zehnder's genetic makeup is privileged.

Reinforcing his God-given talents, Zehnder has also worked hard on his own development, literally throughout his life. His formal education ended with an MBA from Harvard, but he has remained a constant learner. An avid reader, and an astute reader of people, he learns from all kinds of characters and situations.

Development is also about finding ways to put what you've learned to work—for your own benefit and for the benefit of the organization. Zehnder worked hard—always six long days a week—and prepared himself with amazing thoroughness for every single event, meeting, or speech on his busy schedule. Maybe a personal anecdote is in order here. Before delivering a speech, he would practice for endless hours in front of a mirror, tape record it, and time it. I remember asking him once how much time he *really* needed for his speech at one of our new consultants' orientation sessions. The schedule allocated him one hour, but perhaps he wanted a little more time, or a little less. He looked at me in surprise. "I have one hour," he replied, "so it will *be* one hour." And it *was* one hour: not 59 minutes, not 61 minutes—it was exactly 60 minutes.

Let's agree that genetics and personal development got Zehnder into the game, and helped keep him there. I'd also argue that his career choices allowed him to jump to the next level of the success curve—first when he decided to move from law to business, and then again when he moved from advertising into the executive-search arena. In fact, he personally introduced this profession into Europe, launching his firm with a unique vision, comprising both an original consulting approach and exacting levels of professionalism.

You could also make the case that some of Zehnder's subsequent business decisions were also "career choices," including the decision not to go public, as well as the creation of a unique form of equal partnership, collaboration, and compensation system. He summarized this approach, which is still the envy of many professional service firms globally, in a *Harvard Business Review* article entitled "A Simpler Way to Pay."[7]

Yes, these were all wise (even brilliant) career choices. But (and you can guess where I'm going with this) the most important factor in Zehnder's personal success has been his ability to make great people decisions. Simply put, *he built a great firm by being personally involved in the hiring of every single consultant, all around the world, for the entire 36 years of his full-time work in the firm he founded.* That's why I was in Zurich, that nerve-wracking day in 1986. He was making a people decision, and to him, nothing was more important.

I was the rule, not the exception. In fact, Zehnder permitted *no* exceptions to the mandatory round of interviews by multiple people, in multiple countries. Even today, the firm requires that all consultant candidates be interviewed by dozens of colleagues from several different offices, in addition to the chairman, to make sure that they meet the firm's exacting global standards and represent a good cultural fit.[8]

To recap, yes, Zehnder has been a lucky guy—luckier than most. His luck extended to his genetic inheritance. He built on his luck and genes through development and hard work. He made great career choices (and even got to invent his own career, which is nice work if you can get it). Most important, though, is that he turned himself into a master at making great people decisions.

Note the active voice: *turned himself into a master.* How did he make great people decisions? In part by inventing a structure that drew upon the smarts and experiences of many of the brightest people in his organization. Yes, he had innate gifts when it came to dealing with people, but he also came with techniques for leveraging those gifts.

Making great people decisions is a *craft*, and it can be taught and learned.

What Successful Managers Look Like

Let's dig a little deeper into how individual success is defined.

In my view, one of the best analyses of individual success comes from researchers associated with the Greensboro, North Carolina–based

Center for Creative Leadership.[9] Having analyzed hundreds of executive selection situations, they concluded that executives are perceived as successful when they (1) deliver strong organizational performance, and (2) build good relationships, particularly with subordinates.

By this definition, at least, strong organizational performance (the subject of our next chapter) is a necessary component of personal success. But where does this strong organizational performance come from? It comes from people inside the organization having the ability to make great people decisions, one great person at a time. Yes, strategy counts for a lot, great products and services are key, and money in the bank is a great asset. But behind each of these assets—behind their creation and deployment—are great people.

What else can we learn from the management literature about what makes for great leaders and personal career success? One of the most significant studies of successful managers is summarized in *First Break All the Rules*, by Marcus Buckingham and Curt Coffman. Based on in-depth interviews by the Gallup organization of more than 80,000 managers in over 400 companies, this was one of the largest studies of its kind ever undertaken. One of the key conclusions of *First Break All the Rules* is that—contrary to our own opinions of ourselves—none of us has unlimited potential.[10]

What's the logical extension of this insight? I argue that if you can't count on personal development alone, then you have to hire and promote people who have the right stuff built in. You have to get the best people on board in the first place, and make sure that they are in positions where they can grow and develop, and then help them do so.

In his follow-up book, *The One Thing You Need to Know . . . About Great Managing, Great Leading, and Sustained Individual Success*, Marcus Buckingham discusses the four skills that you have to master if you are to succeed as a manager. He starts by emphasizing that managers must first select good people.[11]

After discussing the four basic skills of *good* management, Buckingham moves on to define the "one thing you need to know about *great* managing." And what's the single most important imperative in great management? In Buckingham's words, it is *Discover what is unique about each person and capitalize on it*. In other words, first you hire great people, then you assign the right person to the right job—both fundamental kinds of people decisions.

Buckingham's final prescription in this book concerns the "one thing you need to know about sustained individual success": *Discover what you don't like doing, and stop doing it*. Well, in order to stop doing what you don't like to do, you have to be able to delegate, which means that you have to have good people in place around you. And let's suppose that you have liked what you've been doing, but the years have gone by, and now you're getting bored. How are you going to move up? Again, you have to have good people in place behind you, in order to move up. Developing good successors is, in many cases, a prerequisite for promotion. For this reason, too, you need to become a master at hiring and promoting the best people.

Going Beyond the Obvious

Great people decisions, therefore, are extremely important in large and traditionally minded hierarchies. But even in companies where professionals manage a very small staff (as has always been my own case), the impact of great people decisions on personal effectiveness can be spectacular.

About a year after I joined EZI, I started looking for a new assistant. I decided that since I was an executive search consultant myself, it made little sense to hire an executive assistant employment agency. I would do it myself.

My first step was to sit down and think very carefully about what I *really needed*, rather than just assuming that I needed someone similar to the person who had occupied the post previously. I also discussed with some experienced colleagues what the ideal assistant should look like, and modified my thinking based on that input. In the back of my mind, too, was the example of Egon Zehnder, who hired his wonderful assistant Brigitte Jentsch when he founded the firm 43 years ago, and still works with her today.

So I undertook a search for my new assistant as if it were my most important client assignment. I didn't limit myself to people who were looking for a job. Instead, I investigated the best target companies and positions, and ended up considering close to 40 potential candidates, none of whom were looking for a change. I personally interviewed them, and secured references for the very best potential candidates from people I could trust. I agonized over the final decision, because I did not want to get it wrong—not only for myself, but also for the sake of the person whose life I would be disrupting in such a significant way.

As a result of this process, I hired Joanna Eden, who has been an outstanding assistant for the last 19 years, and has become a true corporate asset in our firm. She has dramatically improved my productivity and quality of life, while becoming at the same time a valued professional partner and a wonderful friend.

So literally every working day of my life, thanks to Joanna, I have been reminded that I have to focus with great discipline on the key people decisions. This has pertained not only to hiring from outside, but also to the internal deployment of resources. For example, whenever it fell to me to staff one of our internal teams, which in many cases are short-term, project-based affiliations, I tried to think very carefully about the skills and complementarities that the project called for, to research my available options, and to interview and check references in depth.

It was the same thing when it came to assessing external partners, such as training organizations. It was the same thing, quite frankly, when it came to choosing which clients to work for.

And it was the same thing in the nonprofessional aspects of my life, as well. I have tried to choose nannies and gardeners just as systematically. (What people decision is more important than the *nanny* decision?) When asked, I help other people apply this same kind of discipline in their own lives. A friend of mine suffered unnecessary pain and anguish for almost a full decade due to bad medical care—inaccurate diagnosis, and therefore inappropriate treatment. I helped my friend find the *right* doctor, with the right skills, and she's now on the road to recovery.

I like to think I'm good at this, but the truth is that I've simply learned a craft, over the years. You can learn it, too.

Forget the Myth: You Can *Learn* These Skills

"It's all in here."

I've heard this phrase far too many times, over the course of my career. Maybe you've heard it, too. It usually involves some self-satisfied person pointing at his or her stomach while he or she talks about people decisions. The implication, of course, is that great people decisions are based on one's "gut" instincts.

Lots of people believe that the ability to determine whether someone is a good candidate for a position is an art: the result of an instinct, an intuition, a gut feeling; something that you can't clearly explain; a talent that only some people possess, leaving the rest of us clueless. Curiously, lots of people who have no clear reason for believing in their gut still do so; that is, they think they are intuitive experts at making people decisions. I'm reminded of the fact that when surveyed, 65 percent of all drivers in the United States report themselves to have above-average skills.[12] Even worse, studies of several hundred engineers at two high-tech companies found that 32 percent of the engineers in one company and 42 percent in the other rated their own performance in the top 5 percent![13] This is what's known as "optimism bias."

Besides this being a mathematical impossibility (4 out of 10 engineers can't be in the top 5 percent), there are three things wrong with this thinking. First, there's that notion that we are good at assessing. (We are not. For example, people's beliefs about their ability to detect lying among others correlate only .04 with their performance.[14]) Second, there's that notion that it's *instinctive*. (It's not.) Third, there's that notion that you don't have to work at it, because either you've got it or you don't. (In fact, you *do* have to work at it.)

Let's dig a little deeper.

Amazing Experts!

Wait a minute (you may be thinking)—aren't there people who are *really good* at people decisions? Aren't there people experts out there?

Yes, some people are truly expert at assessing people. Not surprisingly, some of them work in executive-search firms. Our firm offers a case in point. (Other search firms would point to similar data, I'm sure.) In a recent study of internal candidates who were promoted at a number of our client firms, we compared actual people outcomes with our predictions about those outcomes, and also with the company's *own* predictions about those outcomes, where available. (In other words, we took our assessment of Internal Candidate A, the client company's assessment of Internal Candidate A, and the data about Promoted Person A's success or lack of success several years into his or her job, and compared the three sets of data.) It turned out that in those specific studies, the company's ability to assess its own people in terms of managerial competence and potential for further development was in some cases as low as 30 percent, while our comparable rate was about 90 percent.

In other words, we were *three times* as likely to be correct in our assessments of the firm's own people as they were, even though they had known them for years and they were dealing with them every day

Some people are *much better* than others at assessing candidates. While there is significant research on the accuracy of different assessment techniques (from astrology and graphology to different types of interviews, reference checking, assessment centers, testing, and other techniques that we will discuss in a later chapter), there is little research about the various levels of accuracy of different individuals applying the same technique. The limited research on this last point, however, suggests that some people are in fact significantly better than others even when applying the same assessment technique—and, of course, are *much* better when applying the best techniques. *The Employment Interview Handbook*, by Eder and Harris, looks at the question of whether some interviewers are better than others. Five out of the six studies reviewed confirm this hypothesis. In some of those studies, the best interviewers had predictive validities 10 times better than the worst interviewers.[15]

In fact, expert assessments (aimed at diagnosing present conditions or predicting future performance) are indispensable in countless dimensions of life and work. Choosing investments, diagnosing medical conditions, assessing legal risks, predicting candidates' performances—these are just a few examples of the kinds of things that experts can and should weigh in on. In *Blink: The Power of Thinking Without Thinking*, Malcolm Gladwell writes about John Gottman, an expert in predicting the success or failure of a given marriage. If Gottman analyzes an hour of conversation between a husband and a wife, according to Gladwell, he can predict with 95 percent accuracy whether that couple will still be married 15 years later. If Gottman observes a couple for only 15 minutes, his success rate is still around 90 percent. Sybil Carrère, a professor who works with Gottman, told Gladwell that if she and Gottman observed a couple interacting for as little as *three minutes*, they could still predict with fair accuracy who was going to get divorced, and who was going to make it![16]

So, yes, there are experts; but no, they're not simply acting "from the gut." They are highly trained and deeply experienced people (more on this later).

Forget Delegation

You might be thinking, *If these experts are so good, maybe the best strategy would be to simply delegate the job of assessing people to them.* (Have a tough people decision to make? Call in the experts!)

There are two problems with this strategy. First, it is in our *nature* to judge and classify people, even in cases where we are unprepared, and where we may make bad "snap judgments." It goes back to more than half of us being better-than-average drivers: When it comes to judging people, we want in. Most of us would hesitate to make a complex financial decision or a major technological investment based on inadequate data and without the right advice; but when it comes to people, we're less humble. This is a reality that has to be recognized and dealt with.

Second, while many organizations boast people who are better prepared than others and more experienced in making people decisions (including many Human Resources managers), senior executives often want to be personally involved in these decisions. And rightly so: You shouldn't delegate these key people choices any more than you should delegate your marriage choice. As Larry Bossidy and Ram Charan have stated it, "Having the right people in the right place is the job no leader should delegate."[17]

In many cases, though, this means that those who have the knowledge don't have the power to make people decisions, while those who have the power may not have the knowledge. That's not a good formula!

Knowing What to Look For

For many years (longer than I've been in the field), human resource decisions have been considered a soft, elusive arena. This is closely allied with the notion of the "gut"—either you've got it, or you don't.

This is simply wrong. People decisions, like many other assessments, can be systematically analyzed and greatly improved. To achieve his remarkable level of accuracy, for example, the abovementioned John Gottman (a psychologist by training, who also studied mathematics at MIT) has painstakingly analyzed in depth the predictors of marriage success or failure for three decades.

The first step is to focus on the relevant things to watch, which in

Gottman's case means what he calls the "Four Horsemen": defensiveness, stonewalling, criticism, and contempt. And of those four emotions, he explains, *contempt* explains most of it: the higher the levels of contempt being expressed between man and woman, the lower the likelihood that the marriage can succeed.

Malcolm Gladwell also tells the story of Brendan Reilly, who in 1996 was the chairman of the Chicago-based Cook County Hospital's Department of Medicine. One big issue that Reilly had to deal with was improving the hospital's ability to diagnose whether a patient was actually having a heart attack, or merely exhibiting (or reporting) troubling symptoms. This, of course, can be a matter of life and death, and a medical staff can err in either direction. According to Gladwell, between 2 percent and 8 percent of the time, a patient having a genuine heart attack in a U.S. hospital gets sent home.

There are also cases in which a patient appears to be having a heart attack, but isn't—a less life-threatening problem, but still troubling, since it ties up vital resources. Meanwhile, according to Gladwell, the threat of malpractice has made doctors less and less willing to take chances with a patient, with the result that only about 10 percent of those people admitted to a hospital on suspicion of having a heart attack are actually *having* a heart attack.

Faced with this situation, Reilly made an effort to isolate the few indicators on which the doctors should be focusing. This actually meant analyzing less information—but focusing more intensely on the most *useful* information—than they had in the past.

According to Gladwell, Reilly concluded that doctors ought to combine the evidence of the ECG with only three urgent risk factors (pain felt, fluid in the lungs, and systolic blood pressure). This simpler decision rule significantly reduced both types of errors: sending home those with a heart attack, or admitting those who were *not* having a heart attack.[18]

The point should be clear: These experts aren't checking their guts; they're *identifying and checking the key indicators*. You can do the same thing with people decisions.

Becoming Conversant

It turns out that it's not enough simply to figure out and check those indicators. Once you know *what* to focus on, you need to assign appropriate weight to those different dimensions. And after that, you still have to have the right vocabulary to discuss diagnosis and prognosis with others, in order to make a good collective decision. What if Brendan Reilly spoke no English, and the Cook Country Hospital staff spoke *only* English? It wouldn't matter how good his indicators were, or how effectively they were weighted.

Moving to a much less dramatic area of expert judgment—food tasting—Gladwell discusses how most of us, when presented with a very simple test such as tasting three glasses of cola (two of them from one brand and the third one from a second brand), would not be able to identify the odd duck. An expert food taster, of course, would always pass that test, and then some, being able to identify very minor differences from product to product, and even predicting how different consumer segments might like or dislike each product, and why.

Along the way to earning their status as experts, these food tasters have acquired an enormous competence at knowing and grading different dimensions of taste. They learn a very specific vocabulary that allows them to describe precisely their reactions to specific foods.

According to Gladwell, mayonnaise, for example, is evaluated along 6 specific dimensions of appearance, 10 dimensions of texture, and 14 dimensions of flavor. Each one of those specific factors is in turn assessed on a 15-point scale.[19]

Mayonnaise is no exception. *Every product on the market* can be analyzed along these lines. Over time, thinking and talking like this becomes second nature to expert food tasters. Once again, you can guess where I'm going with this. When making people choices, experts follow (at first consciously, and later more or less unconsciously) a process where they analyze the challenges at hand, identify the key competencies required in the candidate, measure them accurately, predict performance, and are able to properly discuss and decide on a hiring or promotion decision.

At the risk of stating the obvious, aren't people decisions more important than mayonnaise decisions?

A Little Learning Can Take You a Long Way

The point about all of this discussion is not to scare you about the complexity of assessing people. In fact, you don't need a deep expert knowledge about competencies and competency scales in order to become *much better* at your people decisions.

Going back to the marriage example, Gladwell tells how a group of psychologists took some of Gottman's couples videos and showed them to nonexperts. Not surprisingly, the ability of the nonexperts to predict outcomes was very limited. Then the psychologists asked the same nonexperts to try again, this time providing them with just a little help by giving them a list of the relevant emotions to look for. They cut the tapes into 30-second segments, and asked the nonexperts to look at each segment twice: one time focusing on the man, and the other time focusing on the woman.

"And what happened?" Gladwell asks rhetorically. "This time around, the observers' ratings predicted with better than 80 percent accuracy which marriages were going to make it."[20]

Time and time again, I personally have witnessed how just discussing with managers and executives a few basic concepts about people assessment has allowed them to become *much better* at it. But you don't have to take my word for it. There is ample evidence that you can learn a lot in this field, and apply that learning successfully. For example, an acquaintance of mine, Oscar Maril, enjoyed a very rewarding career as a senior Human Resources (HR) manager with Citibank, working in the United States, Europe, and Latin America, followed by an interesting stint in Saudi Arabia. Maril attributes his long and successful career in large part to his skill at helping CEOs make the right people choices.

He also emphasizes how helpful his initial HR training at Citibank proved to be. Several decades down the road, he still remembers some of his earliest training sessions. In those sessions, he interviewed a professional actor (playing a job applicant) and his trainer (talking to him through a tiny earphone plugged in his ear) instructed him in the techniques of behaviorally based questioning and probing.

If you *can* get better at assessing people, shouldn't you?

A Life of Focus Will Make You a Star

Sometimes we are tempted to write off great success to God-given gifts. But the truth is that even the great get much better with practice. In his book, *Winning*, Jack Welch tells that as a young manager he would pick the right people just around 50 percent of the time, while 30 years later, he had improved to about 80 percent.[21]

I believe Jack Welch is probably conservative in estimating his later-life accuracy at 80 percent. I have no doubt, though, that he not only achieved a high level of accuracy, but had the emotional strength to acknowledge when he had made a mistake, and then act decisively to deal with the consequences.

Let's look once more at the example of my firm. Egon Zehnder International is one of the largest and more respected executive search firms.[22] Our work is almost 100 percent focused on the myriad challenges associated with assessing people. So whom do we hire to perform these assessments—many at the highest levels of an organization? The answer may surprise you. The people we hire *never* come from an HR background, or from any other executive search firm. Never! Instead, we typically hire people from management consulting, or from a hands-on managerial career, on the assumption that they can understand the strategic issues and managerial challenges at hand.[23]

Yes, they always have a graduate—or professional—level degree, and the benefit of some rich international experience, and they tend to be highly competent along multiple dimensions. But my point here is that *we hire people who have absolutely no track record at assessing people.* We hire them and train them, and—based on this model—we have created an organization that succeeds solely due to its ability to assess people.

So these are *learnable skills.* I learned them, and you can learn them. And if you do, your career prospects will be immeasurably enhanced.

The Great Paradox

Great people decisions lie behind individual success, and ultimately, behind organizational success (the subject of our next chapter). Isn't it strange, therefore, that this is an area where very few people get any formal training at all?

As mentioned in the introduction, business schools, especially at the graduate level, tend to downgrade Human Resources Management (HRM) issues in general, or at best focus on HRM as just a minor one of a half-dozen functional areas; they rarely get down to the level of skill building that is required.

No wonder there is such a poor track record at making people decisions! *How can we expect people to solve enormously important—and sometimes very difficult—organizational problems, if they don't have reliable tools to call upon?*

In the introduction, I talked about wanting to invest like Warren Buffett without actually having the benefit of Buffett's wisdom and experience. That's impossible! Think about all the training we get in order to make financial decisions on behalf of our organizations. How many courses of accounting and finance do we take? (Answer: *probably too many.*) How much do we practice with exercises, cases, and simulations, in order to be able to master those decisions? (Answer: *probably too much.*)

Aside from the off-center emphases at business schools, there are at least two reasons for this strange situation. First, people-related skills become critically important only long after your formal studies have ended and you've become a manager. While you are studying, you may not be aware about the fundamental importance of people decisions. Why study something when there is no urgent need to know it? Later on, unfortunately, you will have even less time to learn, and you will be less disciplined about learning. Many of the bad habits you've picked up along the way, probably including the tendency to make snap judgments and indulge your unconscious psychological biases, will be deeply ingrained.

Second, as discussed earlier, people believe that this is an art, an area that still remains soft, rather than one in which you can get much better by learning and following best practices. That's not true, as we've seen. But here's the hard truth: *There is no other area where you will get a higher return on the investment of your development time and effort.* As Harvard professor Linda Hill explains in her book, *Becoming a Manager*, developing interpersonal judgment is an essential task of self-transformation, if you want to succeed as a manager.[24]

Here's another challenge: You don't necessarily learn from your experiences with people decisions, at least at the outset. In many cases, there's a lack of immediate and clear feedback on your people decisions. When you appoint someone to a position, his or her performance can be affected by many external factors, including macroeconomic and technological events, competitors' actions, and so on. In addition, it usually takes a long time to assess performance in a complex and senior job, where changes can't be designed, implemented, and assessed overnight. For these reasons, most managers don't learn much from their own experience in making people decisions—unless they also get some formal training and education in the basic tools of the trade.

While we may not learn from our experience, we still believe we are pretty good. In fact, we are *not*, and we are not even aware of our deficiencies. The best studies about self-perceptions show a very low correlation with reality. In the realm of complex social skills, where feedback tends to be occasional, delayed, and ambiguous, that correlation becomes extremely low (e.g., .04 for managerial competence, and .17 for interpersonal skills).[25]

In summary, we get little formal training in making the right people choices, both because of a lack of initial awareness about its importance and because of the false belief that this skill is not learnable. Then, when we're in a position to learn from experience, we often _can't_ learn from that experience. And to top it all off, we think we're far better at people choices than we really are.

From Success to Happiness

Up to this point, I have tried to appeal to your calculations of self-interest. I have tried to explain why mastering great people decisions is almost certain to have an enormous impact on your own chances of career success. I hope you are now convinced that stellar managerial careers are built not only on luck, genetics, a constant development effort, and good career decisions, but also (even _mainly_) on great people choices, beginning with your first managerial assignment and growing in importance as you grow in seniority. I hope you also believe by now that these are learnable skills. That's what most of the rest of this book is about.

But the following few paragraphs aim at a different part of your brain—or maybe, your heart. I want to explore something far more fundamental than simple career success: _personal happiness_.

Philosophers from all cultures, across all ages, have concluded that happiness is the ultimate goal of existence. Aristotle called happiness the _summum bonum_—the greatest good. Yes, we desire other things, such as money, power, health, or career success. But we desire them not for their own sake, but because we believe that they will make us happy (or content, or satisfied).

Happiness is a subject that has come under increasing scrutiny in recent years by people like Mihaly Csikszentmihalyi,[26] Dan Baker,[27] and

Martin E.P. Seligman. Seligman, former president of the American Psychological Association, is the leading proponent of the Positive Psychology movement, which focuses on mental health rather than on mental illness. In his book *Authentic Happiness*, Seligman presents a deceptively simple formula for achieving an enduring level of happiness.[28] According to him, while genetic factors may bound the range of your potential happiness, the remaining factors are very much under your control. Most important among these, he says, are your personal relationships and your level of satisfaction with your work.

And here's my final punch line for this chapter: *Mastering great people decisions will do both.* It will enhance and improve your personal relationships, and increase your professional satisfaction.

Making great people decisions is an essential life skill. It is the most decisive skill in determining your career success, and also your personal happiness.

■ ■ ■

Great people decisions are essential not only for personal success, but also for sustained organizational success—and this will be the subject of our next chapter.

CHAPTER TWO

Great People Decisions: A Resource for Your Organization

Let me start this chapter, too, with a longish personal sidebar, which I think winds up in the right place.

Following my graduation from college in my native Argentina, with an Industrial Engineering degree in hand, I started to work in our capital city of Buenos Aires. I had secured a job with a large wholesale market in the realm of logistics and operations: from my perspective, a choice assignment, and one that played to my strengths. Not only that, I was already happily married to my wonderful life partner, María. In short, I was on a roll. All I had to do now was enroll in one of the best business schools of the world, earn an MBA, and start my ascent into the upper reaches of the corporate world.

But there was a problem: I wasn't independently wealthy, and although I had graduated with high honors from my university, I saw almost no hope of getting a fellowship that would pay for my graduate studies abroad. Without much hope, I applied to the leading U.S. business schools, and also sent in the forms to the few granting programs that accepted applications from people in my situation. It seemed that I finally had bumped my head on a ceiling that I could not break through.

One evening in mid-1980, as María and I were returning to our apartment from a dinner with friends, we found by our door a bulky white envelope, the contents of which would change my life forever. Inside was a letter informing me that I had been awarded the "ITT International Fellowship"—one of the long-shot programs to which I had applied. Only one such fellowship was awarded every other year in Argentina. It would pay for two years of graduate study anywhere in the United States!

I chose Stanford.

Undertaking my studies at the Stanford Graduate School of Business (GSB) turned out to be quite a challenge. They used to say that students in the first year of the MBA program at the GSB went successively through the three "A's": from anxiety, to anger, to apathy. For better or worse, I never got beyond the first "A." I was all too aware of the high levels of anxiety that I was feeling. But I was less aware, at least at first, of something else that was going on in me. Each day, I was exposed to so many brilliant minds, including not only outstanding professors, but also exceptional fellow students, that I couldn't help but have my horizons broadened. And as my perspective became broader, I grew more and more curious about Big Picture issues. My anxiety subsided as my curiosity got the better of me. And it was about this time that my interest in the sources of *organizational* success started to emerge. What makes one organization succeed, and another fail?

Having spent the summer break between my first and second years at the GSB working in Spain for McKinsey & Company, I returned to McKinsey for three more years following graduation to work as an engagement manager in Spain and Italy. This management consulting exposure further fueled my curiosity about the true sources of organizational success.

As it happened, some of the best answers to this question that was now preoccupying me would be forthcoming, a few years later, from a handful of people who happened to be in Stanford at precisely the same time I was (either as professors or as fellow students, in my class and section) as well as at McKinsey and Harvard.

What Makes for Success?

One thing that I gradually realized in subsequent years, during my 25-year quest for answers about organizational success, was that very few people had looked at this question—What makes for success?—in any serious way.

The July–August 2005 issue of the *Harvard Business Review* (a special double issue focused on the high-performance organization) included a very good article by senior editor Julia Kirby about what it means to be a high-performance company.[1] Kirby made the somewhat astonishing assertion that for the first 1,000 years or so of business history, at least as business is practiced more or less as we know it today, no one appears to have asked the most obvious question of all: *What makes for success?* According to Kirby, a scan of the *Harvard Business Review*'s contents over 83 years suggested that the question first began to be raised in the early 1980s, around the time that Tom Peters and Bob Waterman produced *In Search of Excellence.*

Why the 1,000-year delay? Kirby pointed to inherent difficulties in defining the unit of analysis, who gets called a "winner," what constitutes a pattern, whether the answers are universal, and whether high performance is timely or timeless. She concluded, however, that the quest did not seem to be hopeless, and that there appeared to be prospects for a breakthrough in the near future. To support this assertion, she pointed to two excellent recently published books, the first by Jim Collins and Jerry Porras, and the second by William Joyce, Nitin Nohria, and Bruce Roberson.

Well, I knew several of these characters, either personally or by reputation. While I was anxious and struggling at Stanford, for example, one of my classmates was the very same Jim Collins. Collins at that point greatly impressed me, for two specific and unrelated reasons. First, he questioned our professors wisely, incisively, and courageously, which was not always true for the rest of us. Second, he was an avid rock climber, and you could often find him scaling the exterior walls of the GSB building.

At that same time, one of my professors was Jerry Porras. Years later, he became Collins's co-author of *Built to Last*, and was cited by Kirby as one of the major sources for her article. In his professorial role, Porras was one of the first persons who helped me start to deeply reflect on issues of organizational performance. We—his students— had to write a "reactions log" throughout the course, which Porras scrutinized at regular intervals. With Porras's prodding, I began to realize how much those "soft" factors—which, thanks to my background in the hard subjects of engineering and sciences, I had always scoffed at—had a direct and powerful impact on the success or failure of an organization.

A few years after his graduation from Stanford, driven by his unforgiving curiosity, Jim Collins went back to the GSB and began his research and teaching career, and soon received the Distinguished Teaching Award. After seven years in Palo Alto, he returned to his home town of Boulder, Colorado, where he set up a research laboratory in his old first-grade classroom. He became a self-employed researcher and writer. Against what for other people would have been long odds, he produced two bestsellers in a row: *Built to Last*,[2] coauthored with Jerry Porras, and *Good to Great*.[3]

Built to Last focused on the variables that distinguish leaders from laggards. In *Good to Great*, Collins and his research team carried that notion forward, describing a cadre of elite companies that made the leap to great results, and then sustained those results for at least 15 years. As Collins recently noted:

We employ a rigorous matched-pair research method, comparing companies that became great with a control group of companies that did not, and we make empirical deductions directly from the data. In *Good to Great*, we studied companies that made a leap from good performance to exceptional performance sustained for at least fifteen years in direct contrast to companies that failed to make a similar leap in performance, and we asked a simple question: what principles explain the difference?

For instance, when we studied Wells Fargo Bank to its comparison company during the era of deregulation, we found that Dick Cooley at Wells Fargo [focused on people first], and the comparison leaders did not. Instead of first developing a strategy for how to handle the turbulence of deregulation, he created the best, most adaptable team in the industry. "That's how you build the future," said Cooley. "If I'm not smart enough to see the changes that are coming, they will. And they'll be flexible enough to deal with them." Dick Cooley understood that in a volatile world, the ultimate hedge against uncertainty is to have the right people who can adapt to whatever the world might throw at you—like having the right climbing partners with you on the side of a big, dangerous, and unpredictable mountain.

The power of our research is the matched-pair method: we look at companies that became great in contrast to companies that failed to become great in the same environments. We can find pockets of greatness in nearly every difficult environment—whether it be the airline industry, deregulated banking, steel manufacturing, biotechnology, healthcare, or even in non-profits. Every company has its unique set of difficult constraints, yet some make a leap while others facing the same environmental challenges do not. This is perhaps the single most important point in all of *Good to Great*. Greatness is not a function of circumstance. Greatness, it turns out, is largely a matter of conscious choice, and discipline.[4]

Collins and his team found overwhelming evidence that *outstanding leadership* and *the ability to build superior executive teams* were the two essential and foundational prerequisites for remarkable corporate performance. As Collins summarized in this exchange, when a leader wants to build a great company,

> . . . the first most important decisions are people decisions. The corporate leaders we studied who ignited transitions from good to great practiced the discipline of "First Who": first get the right people on the bus, the wrong people off the bus, and the right people into the right seats and then figure out where to drive the bus. To be clear, the First Who principle is not the only requirement for building a great company—it is one of eight concepts we have discovered in our research—but it is the first principle in sequence. Until you have 90% to 100% of your key seats filled with the right people, there is no more important priority.[5]

In other words, *great people decisions* are the key. They are the foundation of almost all great organizational performance.

What about that second piece highlighted by Kirby in her article? In *What Really Works*[6] (a groundbreaking five-year study of the world's best companies), William Joyce, Nitin Nohria, and Bruce Roberson make (and, to my eyes, prove) the somewhat amazing assertion that *the choice of the chief executive of a company has an impact on profitability as large as the decision as to whether the company will remain in its current industry or move to another one.* In the wake of some recent corporate scandals, some people today are inclined to devalue or downgrade the importance of corporate leadership; not Joyce, Nohria, and Roberson.

Several other studies, such as those reported by three McKinsey consultants in *The War for Talent*, also make the point that the "best" companies, as defined by results and reputation, demonstrate significantly more discipline and skill at making the right people choices.[7]

You get the idea. An increasing volume of high-quality research argues strongly that the right people choices are a key driver of organizational performance, and are possibly the most important single factor for *top* performance.

It's *great people decisions* that make the difference.

The Few Things That Matter

Let's assume that you're willing to grant, or at least entertain, the hypothesis that great people decisions make the organizational difference. You may still wonder, however, whether there are other organizational levers or managerial practices that together or separately exert an even larger impact on company performance. Is it really "all about people," or even mainly about people?

When I started working with McKinsey in Europe, my first assignment was with a large retail chain, which was performing very poorly compared with its direct competitor. As was customary, we did all sorts of profitability analyses on the different stores. We found, to our surprise, that some stores in the chain had lost money every year since they had opened their doors. It seemed clear, moreover, that there was no chance that these losing operations could ever be made profitable, in part because they were located in cities that were too small to sustain them.

But other stores presented a more complicated picture. For example, one store we looked at was practically across the street from a competitor. Our client's store was languishing, and the competitor appeared to be thriving. Our client believed that more advertising was needed to increase customer traffic. "Wait a moment," we said. "Are you sure you have the right product mix and service?"

We decided to do a very simple analysis: We counted the number of people coming out of each of the two stores, and we also counted how many emerged with a shopping bag in hand. As it turned out, the foot traffic was not that different, but the "bag counts" were *hugely* different. Almost everyone who walked into the competitor's store bought something; almost nobody who visited our client's store bought anything.

In that situation, obviously, investing more in advertising would have only produced more frustrated visitors, most of whom probably would not have returned. The first priority, it seemed clear, was to fix layout, product-mix, and service-level problems. And in order to do *that*, top management needed to be changed. Why? Because there were obvious shortcomings at the corporate level (C-level), particularly in the commercial area (responsible for layout and product mix) and the operations area (responsible for service).

So it was not a strategy problem, nor a location problem, nor a macroeconomic problem. It was a people problem! The people at the top were not even able to perform a basic, simple diagnostic to figure out why they were doing so poorly, let alone execute properly. Those on the front lines, serving the customers, completely lacked effective leadership.

Unfortunately, that first experience with McKinsey was representative of my years as a management consultant, from beginning to end. Invariably, the problems traced back to the people involved. My last project was for a company that produced a huge range of laminated plastic products: from wall coverings to inflatables to floppy disks. They were losing *20 percent* on their sales, overall, and—due to union problems at a very sensitive time—could neither close the operation nor fire significant numbers of people. Since the business was part of a much larger conglomerate, they would have been happy just reducing the bleeding, if they could do so without any layoffs.

Once again, we did our basic analyses of profitability by product, client, and channel. The results were shocking. Some products had negative margins of 200 percent, meaning that it cost them $300 to produce a product that they sold for just $100! About a third of their production was brought to market by a company-owned distributor that was so inefficient that if they could have stopped using it, they'd have been better off—even assuming that they were to (1) keep paying the salaries of the distribution people to do absolutely nothing, and (2) suffer a one-third drop in sales volume. In that particular case, our recommendations included a CEO change, which was successfully implemented.

In almost every one of the major assignments I worked on while at McKinsey, this was a recurring pattern: The main problem was poor diagnosis and execution because *the wrong people were at the top*.

Maybe you think that these kinds of anecdotal evidence don't add up to a theory—that my personal experience was the result of a lousy client list. Is there any convincing piece of academic research that makes a compelling case that it is really "all about people," or even mainly about people?

What Really Works, the second piece highlighted by Kirby, addresses precisely this question, analyzing 10 years of relevant data on 160 companies and more than 200 management practices. The book's three authors come to the conclusion that only a *tiny fraction* of these 200 practices make any measurable difference in corporate performance. They summarize their findings in a "4 + 2" formula, arguing that there are four primary practices that must be followed, in the areas of strategy, execution, culture, and organization, and that any two of four secondary practices must also be followed. These secondary practices comprise the talent of employees, leadership and governance, innovation, and mergers and partnerships.

Looking at this work, I came to a further conclusion: that directly or indirectly, most of these practices (both primary and secondary) are mainly about people decisions. To my way of thinking, at least, execution, culture, talent, and leadership are *only* about people decisions. And what about those others—strategy, for example? Well, it's interesting to note that the premier strategy consulting firms now recognize *leadership* as a key contributor to successful strategy implementation, and even as the starting point of strategy.[8]

It's *great people decisions* that count.

Consulting a Legend

I think we can safely conclude that leading business theorists believe in the overriding importance of people decisions. But what about those people on the front lines of business? Do they consider people decisions as their first priority, and the key determinant of their success or failure?

Let's take just one case as an example. If you polled contemporary business practitioners to determine the most successful business leader in the second half of the twentieth century, I'm pretty sure that the number-one position, hands down, would go to Jack Welch, the former CEO of General Electric (GE).[9]

A few years ago, I had the opportunity to collaborate with Jack and his wife Suzy on the chapter on work–life balance in their bestselling book, *Winning*. In a couple of follow-up meetings at their home in Boston, we discussed my own plans for this book, and I sounded Welch out on my main theme. From what I knew of his career, I suspected that he was a firm believer in the critical importance of people decisions. What I *didn't* suspect was how deeply he felt about the subject. He talked at length, and with great passion, about the importance of getting the right people in the right positions. "You can have all the greatest strategies in the world," he told me, "but they aren't worth much without the right people."

In my experience, working with literally thousands of executives, Welch's views are the rule, rather than the exception. *Great people decisions make the difference.*

So it appears that both leading business theorists and those on the front lines agree that great people decisions are the number-one priority for corporate success. But perhaps you're still wondering how *important* this observation actually is. Is current practice really that bad? Is there really that much to gain?

The Road to Corporate Failure

The global press has inundated us, over the last decade or so, with an almost unending stream of stories about ineptitude, failure, and even scandal in the corner office. In the summer of 1999, for example, *Fortune* published a riveting (and depressing) cover story on CEO failure. The article featured literally dozens of cases of poor execution at the very top. It asserted that one of the main reasons for CEO failure was the profound difficulty that these failed professionals experienced when it came to making senior appointments.

"So how do CEOs blow it?" the *Fortune* authors asked rhetorically. "More than any other way, by failure to put the right people in the right jobs—and the related failure to fix people problems in time."[10]

Fortune got it right. Based on the many executive searches and management appraisals I have participated in, as well as the tens of thousands of managers and executives I have met and worked with, I have *no doubt* about the most important reason for major company failure: bad people decisions at the top. Putting the wrong people into key positions leads to corporate failure, which leads in turn to more individual failures. One bad decision (or two, or three) precipitates many more, in a cascade of failure.

Perhaps the most comprehensive view of the road to failure is contained in Sydney Finkelstein's 2003 book, *Why Smart Executives Fail.*[11] When analyzing the circumstances that are linked to corporate failure, Finkelstein points to four major business rites of passage: creating new ventures, dealing with innovation and change, managing mergers and acquisitions, and addressing new competitive pressures. All of these transitions might seem to be very different, on their face. But if you look one level down below the surface you can see that each is a situation that *requires new skills*, which in turn means that someone has to pay careful attention to the team that is in place. In other words, most corporate failures grow directly out of the organization's inability to *put the right person in the right place.*

In analyzing the causes behind executive failure, Finkelstein's list includes four components: flawed executive mindsets (including a distorted perception of reality), delusional attitudes (which help keep the distorted perception of reality in place), a breakdown in the communication systems needed to convey urgent information, and personal attributes (including deficiencies in leadership) that prevent the errant executives from correcting their course.

What's the common thread? Again, it's *people.* At least three out of these four contributing causes are people causes, while the fourth one (a breakdown in communication systems) can almost always be avoided if the right people are in place.

Why take this brief detour into the realm of failure? Because it's simply another way of asking and answering the question about the sources of organizational performance. What leads to organizational failure? Bad people decisions. What leads to outstanding organizational performance? *Great* people decisions.

Bad Batting Averages

In the opening paragraph of his wonderful 1985 *Harvard Business Review* article, "How to Make People Decisions," the late Peter Drucker emphasized the critical importance of great people decisions. "Executives," Drucker wrote, "spend more time on managing people and making people decisions than on anything else—and they should. No other decisions are so long lasting in their consequences or so difficult to unmake. And yet," he continued, "by and large, executives make poor promotion and staffing decisions. By all accounts, their batting average is no better than .333. At most, $1/3$ of such decisions turn out right; $1/3$ are minimally effective; and $1/3$ are outright failures." In no other area of management, he added, would we tolerate "such miserable performance."[12]

In the two decades since the publication of this seminal article, both the sordid record of public scandals and the bulk of related research have only confirmed Drucker's view of a very poor track record of people decisions, particularly at the top. In her 2002 *Harvard Business Review* article, "Holes at the Top: Why CEO Firings Backfire," Margarethe Wiersema noted that the trend lines were getting worse in recent years. In the 1980s, she reported, involuntary departures of CEOs hovered in the range of 13 to 36 percent, while between 1997 and 1998, that figure ranged as high as *71 percent*.[13]

Over the past few years, the consulting firm Booz Allen & Hamilton has published excellent research on CEO turnover, documenting both a very high level of comings and goings, and a large proportion of *involuntary* departures.[14] Interestingly enough, the Booz Allen numbers are very much in line with Drucker's 20-year-old educated guess of the batting average. He guesstimated that one-third of all CEO appointments were outright failures, which is exactly in line with Booz Allen's calculation of forced CEO departures.

Even worse, while there is a lot of press about CEO turnover being out of control, most evidence suggests that CEOs who stay too long can end up destroying value. One of the most consistent findings of the Booz Allen studies is that CEO performance in the second half of their tenure is significantly lower than that in their first half (and, in many cases, destroys value).[15]

Over the past years, my colleagues and I at Egon Zehnder International have assessed tens of thousands of senior executives, including CEOs, all other C-level positions, vice presidents, and directors, from all around the world and from every major industry. The results are consistently depressing. Even at companies with above-average performance and reputation, the wrong individuals are making it to the executive suite. Roughly a third of the executives we have appraised at these fine organizations are actually in the *bottom half* of the competence curve with respect to their peers at other firms in their industries.

When we analyzed CEOs against the specific competencies deemed critical for each particular job, the typical CEO was slightly below the target level. As a rule, the gap between an average senior executive and an outstanding one is so large that, even with the highest motivation on the part of the individual and the most sterling development efforts on the part of the company, getting to the required level of competence would be highly unlikely. And even if the gap *could* be closed, the process would take several years, which is time that most organizations simply don't have.

And finally, despite the urgent need to improve our performance in making people decisions, many organizations still lack effective succession programs, or indeed, any succession program at all. This sad story is recounted by Ram Charan in his recent article, "Ending the CEO Succession Crisis."[16] If your company is unwilling or unable to "grow its own," at least *some* of the time, that crisis can't possibly end.

Closer to the Top: Higher Risks, Higher Returns

But there's more. The longer the wrong people persist in the wrong career paths, the greater the potential for them to do real harm to the organization. This is because the more complex the job, the greater the difference between a superior performer and an average one. For example, while a blue-collar worker who is a standard deviation above the mean would be 20 percent more productive than the average worker, *this difference grows exponentially with the complexity of the job.* To cite an extreme example, one standard deviation could represent an increase in the order of 600 percent over the average for a high-complexity job, such as an account manager with a consulting firm.

Figures 2.1 through 2.3, adapted from my MIT *Sloan Management Review* article, "Getting the Right People at the Top," make two complementary points: (1) Organizations that hire or promote mediocre executives tend to suffer greatly, and, conversely, (2) organizations that are able to identify and appoint great people tend to develop a unique competitive advantage.[17]

Several studies have shown that the more complex the job, the larger the difference between a superior performer and an average one. For example, in Figure 2.1, a blue-collar worker who is a standard deviation above the mean would be 20 percent more productive than the average worker. It shows the typical bell-shaped, normal distribution of performance for simple jobs.

A worker in a more complex job (e.g., a life-insurance salesperson) who is one standard deviation above the mean would have a level of performance that is 120 percent higher than the average. For jobs of even higher complexity (e.g., an account manager of a consulting firm), one standard deviation could represent an increase on the order of 600 percent over the average. Figure 2.2 illustrates how this performance spread grows exponentially with the complexity of the job.

The performance spread offers substantial potential rewards. As shown in Figure 2.3, companies that are able to identify and appoint top

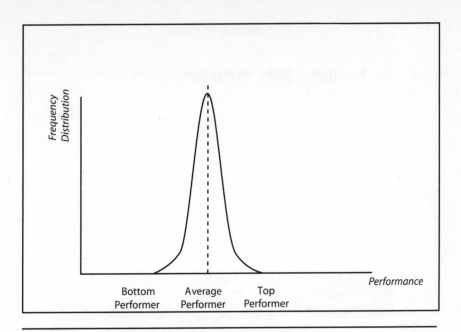

FIGURE 2.1   Distribution of Performance, Simple Job

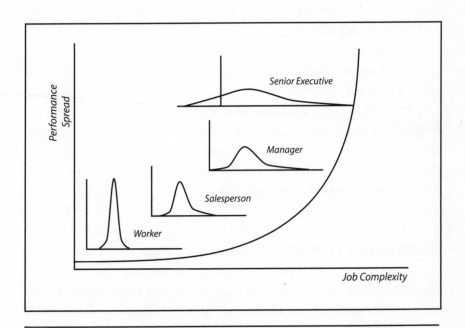

FIGURE 2.2   Performance Spread as a Function of Job Complexity

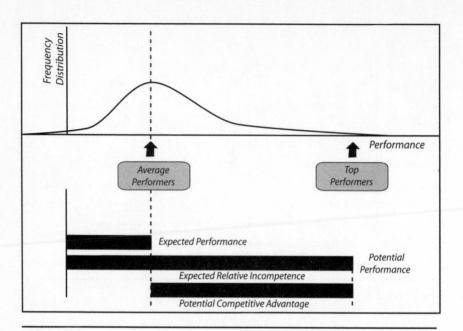

FIGURE 2.3   Potential Rewards of Great People Decisions

performers into senior positions will achieve a level of performance several times higher than that of firms that promote only average executives
into those positions. Put another way, organizations that hire or promote
mediocre executives will suffer greatly from the relative incompetence of
those individuals. Those who are able to make great people decisions,
however, will be able to achieve a very strong source of competitive advantage, as illustrated in the figure.

Quantifying the Expected Return on Great People

To summarize so far, organizations have a very poor track record of making the right people decisions, despite the huge potential value in meeting this challenge successfully. But how big is that value? Is there a way
to quantify the expected return on investing in great people decisions?

A study published by Wasserman, Nohria, and Anand provides the best answer I have found for this question, arguing persuasively that choosing the right leaders can have a dramatic impact on company performance.[18] In some situations, these three scholars contend, the "leader effect" accounts for up to 40 *percent* of the variance in performance or value. Let me underscore this point by stating it the other way around: There are other factors that can have an even larger impact than the leader effect, such as the year in question and related industry effects. But we can't travel in time to pick a better year, and most companies can't switch industries. So the leader effect not only is very large, but in many cases, is the largest of any actionable sources of company value. It may not be the biggest lever, but it's the biggest one you can pull.

During one of my visits to Harvard as a guest speaker, I met with one of the authors of the paper, Noam Wasserman, to make sure that I had properly understood the implications of the study, and to try to come up with a dollar value of what they call the leader effect. The answer really shocked me. Based on their findings, *even a medium-sized U.S. company could increase its value by $1 billion through better people decisions at the top.*

But is there a way to capitalize on this opportunity, given the difficulty of assessing managers? In order to answer this question, we need to move from the East to the West Coast, and from there to Australia in 1972.

Back when I was an MBA student, one of the elective courses I took was Marketing Models, which was taught by David Montgomery, now emeritus professor at Stanford, and a former Executive Director of the Marketing Science Institute. The course was populated just by a few PhD candidates and an even smaller number of MBA students, in part because it was known to be one of the most rigorous quantitative courses at the school. Throughout my professional career, my thoughts periodically have returned to a paper I read during that course: a seminal piece by Irwin Gross, published in the *Sloan Management Review* in 1972, entitled "The Creative Aspects of Advertising."[19] As I vaguely recalled the article, it attempted to quantify in quite an elegant way something that was very hard to measure: the expected value of specific advertising investments.

A few years ago, I finally did go back to my syllabus to find that article, and I wasn't disappointed. The article highlighted how consumer goods companies had discovered that smarter spending in advertising boosted their profitability, which enabled them to develop statistical models to quantify the expected value of a proper investment in the generation and assessment of advertising appeals. Digging a little deeper, I discovered that Gross's article was followed a few years later by another in the same journal by R.Y. Darmon, "Sales Force Management: Optimizing the Recruiting Process,"[20] which attempted to apply the same models in a way that would optimize a company's investment in its salespeople.

This got me thinking. While I will spare you the details of these complex models and calculations, suffice it to say that I have used them to calculate the expected value of investing in the search for, assessment of, and recruitment of the best potential managerial candidates. I believe that the results are dramatic: Even given very conservative assumptions about the validity and reliability of candidates' assessments, the return on such investments can easily be *1,000 percent or more*.[21] That's the dollar value of mastering great people decisions.

But can I say this categorically? To answer this question, let's take a number of cuts at people decisions, beginning with a geographical cut.

People Decisions Around the World

In Chapter 1, I described my job interview with Egon Zehnder, which took place in the summer of 1986. That meeting (and maybe some of the many others I participated in) apparently went well enough, because I was hired. Shortly after joining the firm, I moved back to Argentina, where the executive search profession was just being established.

One of the first clients I worked with, and then observed closely over the following 20 years, was Norberto Morita. Son of Japanese parents, but born in Argentina, Morita graduated first in his university class as a chemical engineer, and later obtained his MBA cum laude at Columbia University.

This outstanding academic performance was followed by an even more impressive managerial career. In 1975, he joined Corning Glass, where he worked successfully, and gained increasing managerial responsibilities, in the areas of finance, planning, and control (first in the States, and then in the U.K.). Six years after joining Corning, he was appointed CFO of the company's European Division, and two years after that he became the CEO of Corning Glass in France, its largest subsidiary outside of the United States.

In 1985, Morita returned to Argentina and became the CEO of Quinsa, a leading beverage company in the region. Quinsa was an interesting business, dominated by a single family, and then languishing in the wake of several failed efforts by the shareholders to force a professionalization of the company's management. Against this backdrop of frustration, Morita led a successful transformation effort, which made Quinsa not only one of the best examples of the professionalization of a family-owned company in Latin America, but also one of the most outstanding cases of systematic, managerially induced value creation.

Morita departed from Quinsa in 1997 to set up the Southern Cross Group, a partnership investing in private equity in Latin America. But he left in place such an outstanding team at Quinsa that the group continued to perform with remarkable results over the following decade, achieving the highest records of profitability in the group's history despite the dramatic crises in Latin America (and particularly in Argentina) over that period. Meanwhile, Morita has been incredibly successful in his private equity group, again despite the difficult times in Latin America.

I cite the example of Norberto Morita to make the point that the ability to make the right people choices is the key condition for success—in any business, at any time, and also across all geographies. I've spoken often with Morita about the reasons for his success, and I've observed him directly for 20 years. He has no doubt, and I have no doubt, that the key to his remarkable success has been his ability to pick the right people for each critical job.

My own experience, again, confirms this. In my internal professional development work at our firm, dealing with executive search consultants from 62 offices worldwide, I have consistently found that mastering great people decisions is the absolutely indispensable requisite for successful performance, all around the globe.

From Startups to Acquisitions

Is the *people factor* critical only for established, hierarchical, tradition-dominated organizations? Not at all; making great people decisions is important for organizational performance at all stages in the life of a business, from the business plan forward. As Harvard's professor William Sahlman (a top academic authority in the field of entrepreneurial ventures) puts it, "When I receive a business plan, I always read the resume section first. Not because the people part of the venture is the most important but because without the right team, none of the other parts really matters."[22]

Likewise, making the right people decisions is the key source of value in acquisitions. A recent *Financial Times* article, drawing upon findings from McKinsey & Co., concluded that *by far* the largest contributor to return in successful private equity deals was active management, either by changing the management team or by supplementing it with people from the private equity fund's own pool of talent. The contribution of a cheap purchase price, sector returns, or even the initial investment turns out to be minor, or even negligible, when compared to the people decisions' value in acquisitions.[23]

From the Boardroom to the Shop Floor

So it seems that people decisions are important no matter what the geography, and no matter what the sector or stage of corporate existence. But how about in the corporate hierarchy? Are people decisions important only at some levels, or at all levels?

Let's begin with the board, which is (or should be!) at the very top of the corporate hierarchy. Here are some commentaries on the importance of having the right people involved in corporate governance at the board level:

- The seminal 1992 *Cadbury Report*, which focused on U.K. board responsibilities in the realm of financial reporting and accountability, stressed the critical importance of high-caliber board members to all aspects of good governance.[24]

- In his *Harvard Business Review* article, "What Makes Great Boards Great," Jeffrey Sonnenfeld states that "it is not rules and regulations, but rather it's the way people work together" that makes for a board's greatness.[25]

- In their recent book, *Inside the Boardroom*, Richard Leblanc and James Gillies assert that board *process* and board *membership* are more important to board effectiveness than board structure.[26]

- Ram Charan, advisor to many boards, says that in his view, "60 percent of corporate performance depends upon the right CEO and succession," which is of course one of a board's main duties.[27]

- Colin Carter and Jay Lorsch believe that "while board structure is important and is the best place to begin thinking about board design, in our judgment the caliber and abilities of the directors is an even more critical determinant of a board's effectiveness. Good people—and people who are suited to the job at hand—will perform well even if the structure is less than ideal, but the opposite is certainly not true."[28]

But don't conclude from this list that people decisions matter only in the upper reaches of an organization. While people at the top obviously control more resources and have more authority, even the worker

on the lowest rungs of the ladder can exert great influence over an organization—both for good and for bad. The importance of choosing the
right people at *all* levels is a key theme in Stanford Professor Jeffrey Pfeffer's *The Human Equation*[29] and *Competitive Advantage through People*.[30]

Large or Small?

How about different *sizes* of organizations? During the last 20 years, I
have worked for companies ranging from little over $1 million in revenues to several billion dollars annually. In my experience, people decisions are critical across this entire spectrum.

In fact, you can make the case that although the absolute stakes
may be bigger at larger companies, the *relative* stakes are likely to
be bigger at small companies. GE could certainly survive one or two
poor C-level appointments, but a new venture might be done in by a
single bad decision in a critical position—and not necessarily the top
job, either.

While I was at Stanford, between 1981 and 1983, Silicon Valley
was already exploding with new ventures. As a result, one of the favorite
elective courses at that time dealt with new ventures and small business
management. The Bible for that course was a highly practical little book
by Stanford's Steven Brandt. Mimicking the real Bible, it included "Ten
Commandments" for small business survival. The First Commandment
is: "Limit the number of primary participants to people who can consciously agree upon and contribute directly to that which the enterprise
is to accomplish, for whom, and by when." The Fifth Commandment is:
"Employ key people with proven records of success at doing what needs
to be done in a manner consistent with the desired value system of the
enterprise."[31]

Find people who can work together effectively. Find winners who
can accomplish key tasks in ways that are consonant with the value system. In other words, *make great people decisions.*

It Was Always Like This

Let's grant that practitioners and researchers alike agree on the global importance of people decisions to organizations big and small, new and old, up and down the ladder. Maybe this is just a passing fad. Perhaps, several years down the road, some other theory will arise to make this one obsolete? The evidence suggests not. First let's look back into the past.

If you were to ask business historians to name the best manager of the first half of the twentieth century, chances are that the majority would name Alfred P. Sloan, who ran General Motors successfully for some 40 years, despite the pressures of the Great Depression and World War II. Peter Drucker was both an advisor to and an observer of Sloan during that period, and he cited as a key reason for Sloan's success the fact that he "picked every General Motors executive—down to the manufacturing managers, controllers, engineering managers, and master mechanics, at even the small accessory division."

"By today's standards," Drucker concedes, "Sloan's vision and values may seem narrow. They were. He was concerned only with performance in and for GM. Nonetheless, his long-term performance in placing people in the right jobs was flawless."

Bill Gates once commented that Sloan's *My Years with General Motors* was the best book to read if one were going to read only one book about business.[32] Sloan's book, which became an instant bestseller when it was published in 1963, has since been used as a manual for managers, offering personal glimpses into the practice of the "discipline of management" by the man who perfected it.

In a new introduction written for the current edition of *My Years with General Motors*, the late Peter Drucker highlighted the main lessons from what he also considered the single best management book of all time. While underscoring the professional approach to management, Drucker emphasized that "the job of a professional manager is not to like people. It is not to change people. It is to put their strengths to work.

And whether one approves the people or the way they do their work, their performance is the only thing that counts, and indeed the only thing that the professional manager is permitted to pay attention to." Performance, said Drucker, is more than the bottom line: "It is also setting an example. And this requires integrity."

And integrity, of course, resides in the right people decisions.

The World's Most Admired Company

Every year, *Fortune* publishes the ranking of the world's most admired companies. General Electric was number one on their list in the 2006 report . . . and the year before that . . . and for the sixth time in the past decade. And if you think that *Fortune* is unusual in singling out GE, think again. GE also has ranked number one in the *Financial Times'* "most respected" survey for seven of the past eight years, and it topped a recent *Barron's* ranking of most admired companies.

Why is GE so widely admired? There are many answers, of course, but an important one, on which most observers agree, is the fact that GE has been an outstanding breeding ground for great leaders. Not only GE, but many other companies have reaped the benefit of the venerable company's leadership output.

I've already written about Jack Welch, and the near-universal respect he commands among his peers in business. What many people don't realize is that Welch is only a recent manifestation of a very long tradition at GE—a tradition that grew out of a purposeful choice on the part of the company's leaders, more than a century ago, to invest in the right people. Today, few people remember the name of Charles Coffin, a former shoe industry executive before he became GE's president in 1892. Here is what *Fortune* wrote about him:

> Under Charles Coffin, who led the firm from 1892 to 1912, GE set principles of organizational design that would guide large compa-

nies—above all, the idea that the company's most important product was not light bulbs or transformers, but managerial talent.[33]

Most people in my own field of executive search consider a company fortunate if it finds one great CEO, and we consider a company truly blessed if it comes up with two in a row. That opinion seems to be shared by scholars of leadership and organizational effectiveness, as well. "To have a Welch-caliber CEO is impressive," wrote Collins and Porras in *Built to Last*. "To have a century of Welch-caliber CEOs all grown from inside—well, that is one key reason why GE is a visionary company."[34]

Looking Ahead: The Human Resource in the Future

We've looked at people decisions in a variety of settings and concluded that it's hard to find a present-day setting in which they are not critical. What do we see if we attempt to look into the future?

I have no doubt that in years to come, making great people decisions will be even *more* important to organizational performance. Consider the following:

- The fastest-growing companies nowadays, in fields like biotech, life sciences, software, professional services, media, and entertainment, are *human-asset intensive*. In other words, success at these companies (and in these industries) depends less on physical assets, and more on the talents of people, especially including their ability to work together.

- We are living in times of unprecedented change, driven by the explosion of technological development and innovation and the cascading impacts of the genetic, digital, and knowledge revolutions. We are also facing extremely delicate political and cultural issues, in an increasingly complex (and sometimes dangerous) global village. When new skills must be put in place—quickly and effectively—the right people decisions become imperative not just for success, but for survival.

- As Peter Drucker observed in one of his last *Harvard Business Review* articles, many executives today are embarking upon second careers.[35] Let's assume that you're one of these "self-restarters." No matter what your reason—whether you are seeking more flexibility, increased financial reward, or simply independence— it is almost certain that your move into a second career will place new demands on you to make the right people decisions.

- Even for those who stay within the comfortable confines of the corporate world, there is a clear (and healthy) trend today toward cross-functional initiatives, whether for new product development or process redesign. These initiatives require a constant assembly of different teams. As was so forcefully argued by Katzenbach and Smith in *The Wisdom of Teams*,[36] great teams outperform talented individuals. But coming up with a great team, like coming up with a great CEO, is no easy task. According to *The Wisdom of Teams*, some "team basics," including the people choices that go into team composition, are often overlooked.

- In large corporations, many traditional processes are breaking down, and there is an increasing reliance on outside partners via outsourcing and insourcing. This is particularly visible in the innovation processes of technologically oriented companies like IBM and Merck, to name just two. Today, companies know that they have to gain access to the ideas of outsiders. At the same time, they know that their own knowledge workers are increasingly mobile. A shifting capital base, including more active participation by venture capital partners, also pushes for change. As a result, many companies have been moving from a "closed innovation" to an "open innovation" paradigm, as explained by Henry Chesbrough in his seminal book on this topic.[37] And, of course, you have to make the right people decisions when choosing your outside partners.

- Chesbrough (coincidentally, another of our classmates at Stanford) is now a leading researcher and teacher in the relatively new field of "service science." He argues convincingly that innovation has not yet injected itself into the services sector, despite the fact that services account for 80 percent of economic activity across all advanced economies. Think about the implications of dramatically increased innovation in services, from the point of view of the potential impact and criticality of the best knowledge workers. Once again, picking the winners will be the key.

- Finally, a healthy trend that I personally have observed is the *decentralization of people decisions*. In the future, managers (like you) will be increasingly called upon to build great teams. They will be expected to be skilled at finding and hiring great talent. Once upon a time, strategy was shaped by the Strategic Planning group up at headquarters. Then it was pushed down into the ranks, and all managers were expected to be "strategic managers." The HRM function is gradually going the same route. If you want to perform and succeed in your professional life, you simply *have* to get good at this task.

What I Have Learned

After more than 20 years of exposure to some of the most successful individuals and organizations, as well as to some of the best business theorists, I am finally comfortable with the answer to the question that first began to confound me back in my days as a head-barely-above-water student at Stanford's Graduate School of Business.

What leads to success? *Great people decisions* lead to success.

And great people decisions need active management. They are less like a physical infrastructure, and more like money: They achieve their true potential only if you figure out how to deploy them effectively. Mastering great people decisions—building your team, maintaining it, and reshaping it as necessary—is not only the single most decisive skill in determining your own career success. It is also the secret behind great organizational performance. And this is the second reason why *great people decisions* matter to *you*.

■ ■ ■

While great people decisions are essential for personal and organizational success, there are compelling reasons why mastering them is extremely hard—and they are the subject of our next chapter.

CHAPTER THREE

Why Great People Decisions Are So Hard

Here's my best recollection of the worst moment in a meeting that I attended in Cambridge, Massachusetts, sometime in the fall of 1998:

"I can see why people decisions at senior levels are extremely important, and have a huge impact on a company's performance, value, and morale," the *Harvard Business Review* senior editor said, trying to let me down gently. "I grant all that. But I think that these days, most companies know pretty well how to make these decisions. So I'm sorry, but I don't see how we can go forward with your proposal."

I had a lot riding on that meeting. My proposal to write an article for the *Review* about people decisions would be either accepted or rejected on the spot. There would be no appeal. I wouldn't get a second chance. At this point in the meeting, I didn't like what I was hearing.

By 1998, I had accumulated 12 years' worth of experience as an executive search consultant. I had led our firm's global Professional Development Team for some time, which helped me realize how universal the challenge of *great people decisions* really was.

At the same time, my interest in the underlying reasons for organizational effectiveness had been growing steadily, and had become increasingly focused. I had read hundreds of books, studies, and research reports on people decisions. I was genuinely convinced that there were enormous opportunities for improvement in these decisions, and I wanted to help others take advantage of those opportunities—with or without our firm's professional help. Writing about the topic seemed to be the obvious way to go, and I had chosen as my first priority to get an article published in the *Harvard Business Review* (HBR), generally considered the most influential business journal in the United States.

Of course, I knew that this would be an uphill slog. *HBR's* acceptance rate on unsolicited proposals ran at an infinitesimal 2 percent. I had never published anything, anywhere, up to that point. A good friend of mine (who happens to be one of the world's bestselling business authors) had recently shared with me the hurdles he had leaped over the previous 18 months, working with *HBR* editors to shape and polish his piece, which finally had been published.

Back to the meeting: The senior editor who had punctured my balloon began looking for a polite way to wrap up the conversation. Fighting for authorial survival, I came back hard. I said, forcefully, that I strongly disagreed, that my global experience told me that even the *best organizations in the world* made all sorts of mistakes when it came to people decisions.

She wasn't impressed. I started citing examples both from my personal experience and from the public domain. None of these gambits worked. It became painfully clear that I was only treading water, and I was failing to bring the editor around to my point of view. So I changed tactics. I asked her, "What about your own *personal* experience? What about *here*, at HBR?"

It was like one of those moments in a Hollywood film from Way Back When, when the clouds part, and the column of sunlight breaks through, and everyone gets dewy-eyed. I had touched a nerve!

The editor was a brilliant person who, having graduated with high honors from a top MBA program, had accumulated impressive experience in a top management consulting firm before joining *HBR*. Accepting my challenge, she started reviewing her own experience with clients in her former employer, in her own work at *HBR* when looking at the

unvarnished stories of companies, and even *HBR*'s own people decisions. You could almost see her turning the pages, in her mind, and her
shifting expressions suggested that she was remembering many disturbing problems in all of these contexts. She realized that if these fine
places, which at least in theory have access to the best ideas *in the world*
about management, had so much room for improvement in their own
people decisions, then maybe the idea of an article on the topic wasn't
so bad, after all.

But then came the second difficult question, which again almost
got the door slammed on my fingers. "I have to ask you," she said. "Are
you a good writer?"

This one looked like a dagger pointed at my authorial heart. Again,
I decided that a blunt response was the best course. "No, I am not a good
writer," I confessed. "In fact, I'm not a writer at all. I've never written a
book, or even an article, actually. And as you can tell from my accent,
English is not even my first language. So clearly, the renowned editors at
HBR would have to help me with the writing. What I *do* have to offer,
however, is a unique combination of experience, knowledge, and reflection about how to drastically improve people decisions. And, of course,
my passion to help companies get better."

Candor turned out to be the best policy. She said that not only did
she like my proposal, on second thought, but that *HBR* preferred to work
with authors who were open to an editor's input. I was in!

So off I went from the meeting, delighted with the affirmation that
comes with winning a 1-in-50 longshot. But now I had a new problem: I
had no idea about what I was going to write in this unlikely article. It
wasn't that I didn't have *ideas* (in fact, I had far too many of them), but I
lacked a structure for those ideas.

Eventually, I figured out the missing structure. The article, entitled
"Hiring Without Firing," was published in the July/August 1999 issue of
HBR.[1] It achieved instant success, was a bestselling reprint for the next
six years, and was adopted as mandatory reading at several universities
and companies.

Six years after publishing that initial article in *HBR*, I published "Getting the Right People at the Top" in the *MIT Sloan Management Review*.[2] This article was also an overnight success (assuming you don't count the months it took me to write it, of course) and instantly became one of the 10 most popular reprints from that journal.

I'd like to say that this success grew out of my great talents as a writer, but that wouldn't be true. The main reason why these two articles achieved success is because their subject matter was *hugely* important to people in organizations of all shapes and sizes, and there wasn't much out there. (There still isn't, unfortunately.) A lesser reason is that I hit upon a good structure for presenting my ideas. After several false starts, I realized that I had to start with what I called the "traps"—the reasons why getting the best people was, and is, so *hard*.

That's what this chapter is about. If you want to pick winners, you have to stay out of certain traps. We'll look at four of the most important:

1. The odds are against you.

2. Assessing people for complex positions is inherently difficult.

3. Powerful psychological biases impair the quality of the decision-making process.

4. Misplaced incentives and conflicts of interest can easily sabotage these decisions.

A note of caution: I recently came across a book that promised to make me as good an investor as Warren Buffett without requiring any significant study or experience on my part. On the face of it, that's absurd. To be as good as Buffett, you need Buffett's skill, and probably some of his luck. On the other hand, you certainly can learn some general principles, such as *Don't keep all your eggs in one basket, Don't buy what you don't understand*, and *Don't count on outsmarting the market*.

This chapter offers similarly general principles, and also tells you where to go if you want to dig deeper. I hope that as you become aware of the typical traps in people decisions, you will not only avoid disasters—gross failures, embarrassments, and scandals—but also start winning a number of small victories.

The Odds Are Against You

As discussed in the previous chapter and illustrated in Figure 2.3, the distribution of talent has a very large spread. In many cases, there are only a small number of exceptional performers. For this reason, you are *much more likely* to hire an average performer than an exceptional individual. Simply put, the odds are against finding a winner.

But as noted earlier, the difference in expected performance between a typical person and an exceptional one can be absolutely enormous. As a rule, the company that hires mediocre executives performs badly, especially when compared with companies that are able to identify, attract, and integrate exceptional performers. Obviously, then, you have to bend the odds more in your favor.

The Difficulty of Assessments

A second problem is the fact that assessing people for complex positions is inherently difficult. This is true for several reasons, including the significant impact of assessment errors, the unique and changing characteristics of many jobs, the difficulty of assessing intangible traits, and the limited accessibility of many candidates. Let's look at each in turn.

The Impact of Assessment Errors

One reason why assessing people is so difficult is that mistakes get compounded. This is a straightforward probabilistic consequence. But because many people find it confusing, we'll go into it at a little greater length. How can we have a high error rate when we are pretty good, even very good, at assessing? The answer is that *high selectivity is very hard to achieve.*

To understand this point, ask yourself the following question. Assuming that you want to hire only the top 10 percent of candidates for a position, and that you are 90 percent accurate in assessing them, what will your success rate be? Many people might expect it to be 90 percent, but the true answer is just 50 percent. Here's why. If you assess 100 candidates, then 10 of those will be top 10 percent (although you don't know which 10). Of those 10, you will rightly assess nine as "top" because you are 90 percent accurate. So far, so good; but the problem is those other 90 candidates. Your 10 percent assessment error will have you wrongly categorize as "top" another nine candidates who don't belong there. (See Figure 3.1.) So out of the 100 candidates, you will have classified 18 as

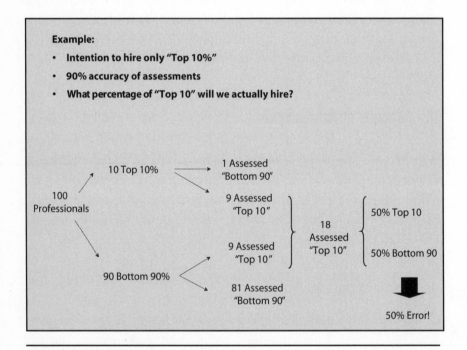

FIGURE 3.1   It's So Hard to Be Selective

"top," when in fact half of them aren't. If you hire all 18, you'll be hiring nine turkeys.

Unique Jobs

When assessing candidates for any position, companies need to predict two things more or less concurrently:

1. What skills and attributes are truly needed?
2. What will each person really deliver?

True, there are some positions for which the skill set is very well defined, and the company has significant experience regarding the background and competency characteristics required for success. This includes certain kinds of manual labor, such as many positions on certain assembly lines (but not *all* assembly lines). It can also include certain jobs within the white-collar ranks. Even for many sophisticated graduate populations working for top companies, some positions are very clearly defined, and deep and sustained analyses have demonstrated what attributes are correlated with successful performance.

A classic example these days would be the creative people with high IQs hired by organizations such as Microsoft. In his book, *How Would You Move Mount Fuji?*, William Poundstone describes the use of the puzzle interview as a way to filter top creative, out-of-the-box thinkers, which seems to be a highly desired trait for many of their hires.[3] And there are many other positions, such as the brand manager of a consumer goods company, which typically require a series of general skills that have been clearly identified by most multinational corporations, and properly guide their assessment efforts.

But many knowledge worker jobs are truly unique. The higher we move up the organizational pyramid, moreover, the more unique these positions become. As Nathan Bennett and Stephen A. Miles have recently argued, the role of the COO is defined primarily in relation to the CEO—a relationship for which no two potential COOs are equally qualified.[4] The COO position (which I'm using only as a good example) seems to be concrete, specific, and easily defined. In real life, it's highly situational; the COO may serve as implementer, hatchet man, change agent, Bad Cop (to the CEO's Good Cop), heir apparent, and so on.

Changing Jobs

To complicate matters, jobs at the top have little stability. Their requirements and priorities can rapidly shift as a result of macroeconomic, political, competitive, or technological changes. Simply put, what's needed today can be quite different from what's needed tomorrow.

In "Hiring Without Firing," I referred to an example that at that time was front-page news around the world: the case of Franco Bernabè, who had recently been hired to run Telecom Italia. This company was a large, recently privatized conglomerate with a poorly performing stock price and a history of management turmoil. At the time, Bernabè appeared to be the perfect choice for the job: Between 1992 and 1998, he had led the transformation of one of the world's largest energy companies, ENI, into a highly respected and profitable publicly traded business, which also had a legacy of extreme senior-level upheaval. Bernabè's skills were considered so appropriate for his new position that Telecom Italia's stock rose 5 percent the day Bernabè's appointment was announced—a multibillion-dollar increase in market value based on Bernabè's reputation alone.

Only two months later, though, Bernabè's job changed drastically. Telecom Italia became the target of a hostile takeover attempt by the Olivetti Corporation. At that point, it became irrelevant that Bernabè excelled (for example) at leading cultural change. To fend off Olivetti, he needed to quickly improve short-term financial results, rapidly assess the value and synergy of core and non-core business combinations, and almost instantly construct intricate investment and business obstacles that might thwart a takeover.

In the end, it wasn't enough—or Bernabè wasn't versatile enough. Olivetti succeeded in its takeover, and Bernabè stepped down just six months into his once-promising tenure.

Intangible Traits

Even if companies know exactly what they are looking for, determining whether a particular candidate can fill the bill is an entirely different matter. The differentiating competencies for top leaders are usually in "soft" areas, which are much harder to evaluate than qualities such as general IQ or knowledge of a particular industry.

One of the first times I realized that successful industry experience is not enough was also in the context of a telecommunications company, this one based in the United States. It was seeking a CEO for its new division in Latin America. The division was not a startup, per se, but a joint venture between two established local companies that had both been purchased by the U.S. business. As often happens, the former CEOs of the two acquired companies were appointed to the board of the joint venture and remained large shareholders. The board agreed that the new CEO would certainly need expertise in strategy formulation. The marketplace was getting crowded; it was now or never for entrants to establish their positions. And because the new venture had no marketing plan to speak of, the new CEO would also need expertise in high-tech sales and distribution. An international search was launched.

Three months later, the board hired an industry veteran who appeared to be tailor-made to run the new division. He had been extremely successful at the helm of a telecommunications company in the same sector, although in a different part of the world. He was an effective strategist (some said brilliant) and a proven marketing expert. He understood the company's technology, products, and customers far better than any of the other nine candidates.

But his run lasted less than a year, and was nothing short of a disaster. It turned out that he lacked the two skills that the job really required:

negotiation expertise, and cross-cultural sensitivity. On the first point—negotiations—this new CEO had to answer to three bosses with different agendas. The U.S. parent company wanted to use the new entity to push its own products and services in a new region. One former CEO–shareholder was more focused on the bottom line; he wanted to maximize profits by increasing prices. And the other former CEO–shareholder wanted to cut prices; volume was the key to success, he said. The new CEO was eager to make everyone happy, which turned him into everyone's enemy.

The bickering was exacerbated by cultural differences in communication styles. The Americans were confrontational. The Latin Americans were deferential, but only in public. Behind the scenes, their anger and frustration brought the company to a standstill. Senior executives, caught in the crossfire of warring bosses, started leaving the company in droves. Key distributors quickly picked up on the friction and abandoned the joint venture, sourcing its products elsewhere. By the time the CEO was fired, a brief six months later, the company was nearly bankrupt.

But there's a happy ending. A new CEO put the company back on track, even thriving, within six months. While he had no experience in the telecommunications industry, the new CEO was a native of the Latin American country where the joint venture was based, and he was known and respected by its principals. He had also worked for 10 years in the United States, which gave him special insight in understanding and dealing with the parent company's executives. But the key to his success was his truly exceptional knack for bridge-building, which quickly unified the new venture under one strategy.

Some of the most common competencies that companies seek for senior positions include not only results orientation, but also the ability to collaborate, develop people, lead teams, and manage change. But just looking at this list, you can imagine that there are many obstacles to measuring these intangible traits, these "soft skills," in any meaningful way.

One way to look at this issue is to start with *self*-assessment. (If we can measure anyone's performance, it should be our own, right?) It turns out that we humans are not very good at this. Even in domains with constant, immediate, and objective feedback (like sports, for example), there's a correlation coefficient of about 0.5 between our self-assessments and our true ability. (If our assessments were fully accurate, that coefficient would be 1.0.) Technically, the way to measure the explanatory power of an assessment is to raise that correlation coefficient to the square power. In this case, raising 0.5 to the square power would give you 0.25, which means that only 25 percent of the variance in performance is explained by our self-assessments, implying quite a large lack of self-awareness.

Now let's move to the realm of complex social skills, which is characterized by occasional, delayed, and ambiguous feedback. Here, the correlation coefficient drops dramatically, with values as low as 0.17 for interpersonal skills and 0.04 (basically zero) for managerial competence.[5]

Now let's imagine trying to assess the soft skills of *other* people. You can see why this is such a tricky business!

Inaccessible Candidates

To complicate matters even further, many candidates have no tolerance for any kind of thorough evaluation. They have little available time, and are likely to be very concerned about the confidentiality of the whole process. As a result, their participation in any assessment process may be very limited.

The problem with candidate availability becomes even more serious for those candidates who are not *looking* for a new job. Since at a given point in time most people are not actually looking for a new job, the problem of candidate accessibility is pervasive, and can severely restrict the value of an external search of candidates.

Even worse, the problem of candidate availability grows exponentially with the seniority of the job. As a rule, students who are about to graduate and are looking for a job have no confidentiality issues. They make themselves available for all sorts of tests, and submit themselves to grueling interviews and in-depth reference checks. At the other end of the spectrum, however, senior executives have very little tolerance for any similar kind of thorough evaluation—whether because of their complex agendas, their current job satisfaction, or their legitimate concern about the confidentiality of the whole process, which could seriously damage their own careers and perhaps even damage the reputation of their current employer.

Psychological Biases and Emotional Traps

A third major factor that complicates people decisions is the fact that finding the right person for any job is hindered by various psychological biases and other forces, operating within both the hiring team and the company at large.

There are fundamental reasons that lurk behind these forces. Our minds and our bodies have been shaped by hundreds of thousands of years of evolution, and are not too different from those we had when living some 10,000 years ago as semi-nomadic clans and hunter-gatherers on the savanna. Evolutionary psychologists tell us that evolution has not kept up, as our society and our lives—including work and organizations—have changed over the last few thousand years, especially in light of the accelerated pace of change in the last century and in current decades. Our hardwired brains helped us survive and reproduce in the past: an extinct form of living. They don't mesh well with our current challenges.

We can't change our fundamental human nature, or our hardwiring, in the short run. But we *can* seek to understand that nature, in order to manage our instincts and stay out of traps.[6]

The impact of emotional biases on seemingly rational decisions has been well documented in several fields, including economics and finance. For example, Daniel Kahneman won the 2002 Nobel Prize in Economics for having "integrated insights from psychological research into economic science, especially concerning human judgment and decision-making under uncertainty." Meanwhile, the rapid development of the field of behavioral finance, brilliantly summarized by Peter Bernstein in his best-selling book, *Against the Gods*, has given us tools to recognize and deal with the biases that tend to affect our financial decisions.[7]

Likewise, a series of emotional biases work against our people decisions. Most of these biases operate within the realm of what one researcher has called our "adaptive unconscious." By definition, they are inaccessible to our conscious minds, and yet they still strongly influence our judgments, feelings, and behaviors.[8] The higher the stakes, that is, the more senior the appointment, the stronger these forces tend to be.

My list of typical biases includes:

- Procrastination
- Overrating capability
- Snap judgments
- Branding
- Evaluating people in absolute terms
- Seeking confirmatory information
- Saving face
- Sticking with the familiar
- Emotional anchoring
- Herding

I'll devote a section to each of these distinct biases. First let's look at an example taken from real life that illustrates a number of them.

An international technology company needed to hire a team to head up a major new service line. The process was led by the CEO, a former partner of a top management consulting firm who had recently joined the company. The CEO recruited each of the key team members directly, either through his personal relationships, or as a result of referrals from acquaintances.

Sticking with the familiar, the CEO hired several management consultants, and these hiring decisions were based on snap judgments. Specifically, the company never conducted any thorough analysis of the competencies needed. Candidates were considered "good" just because of their impeccable educational backgrounds, outstanding employment history, impressive appearance, and superb speaking skills. There was no effort to search for any disconfirmatory evidence, either by interviewing them extensively to check their true accomplishments and behaviors in relevant situations or by conducting in-depth reference checks beyond formalities. The CEO also used the wrong frame of reference: He compared the candidates with other management consultants, rather than with managers who had capabilities relative to the task at hand, which required both an outstanding level of technological know-how as well as remarkable leadership, operational, and collaboration skills.

By the time the board members knew enough to become worried about the nominations, the CEO had already made the appointments. As a result, saving face quickly came into play. Reversing the decisions would require confronting the CEO, whom the board had hired. So not only would the CEO have to admit his mistake, the board would also have to recognize that it, too, might have erred in hiring the CEO. "Herding" (the very human instinct to "hide in the herd" and not stick one's head up) further delayed a decision to stop the nominations, which initially could have been accomplished at a relatively low cost. But the team was hired and the result was a debacle. Gross technical errors coupled with a major overinvestment and unacceptable tensions within the rest of the organization finally forced the company to kill the project, disband the team, and fire the CEO, all at a cost of hundreds of millions of dollars.

Now let's look at some of these biases in greater depth.

Procrastination

Are you spending as much time as you should managing your financial investments? Are you properly planning for your retirement? If you're like most people, you probably are not. Research shows that we tend to procrastinate when faced with these kinds of decisions.

Likewise, we tend to procrastinate about our people decisions. Especially when things seem to be going reasonably well, the tendency is to exaggerate the risks of change and to disregard the opportunity costs of the status quo. Thus, most boards react late, firing a senior executive only when that person is already in deep trouble. Analysis of CEO turnover and performance data has consistently shown that top executives perform much better during the first half of their tenure than they do in the second half.[9] The logical inference is that many companies wait far too long to get rid of an underperforming CEO.

Let me stress this point. The ever-shortening tenure of CEOs has led some observers to conclude that CEO turnover is "out of control." I take the opposite position. Most evidence shows that CEOs tend to stay far too long, and many end up destroying value in their company. Returns to shareholders (adjusted by industries and regions) are significantly lower in the second half of CEO tenure, regardless of whether the CEO was forced to leave or whether it was a more orderly transition. (See Figure 3.2.)

When segmenting by length of CEO tenure, the message becomes even clearer. It seems that CEOs who *systematically* perform poorly are properly prevented from staying on for too long. But it's also true that for CEOs who stay for long periods (more than 10 years), the difference in performance between the first and second halves of their tenure tends to be dramatic, in the negative direction.[10] (See Figure 3.3.) Yes, there's probably some flagging of energy on the part of the CEO, as he or she gets out beyond that tenth year. (Being CEO is an incredibly demanding job!) But that's all the more reason to spot and put a stop to procrastination by board members.

Overrating Capability

Another typical bias involves believing that those whom we hire or promote to top positions are more capable than they actually are. The first

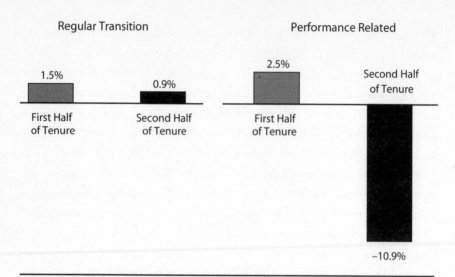

FIGURE 3.2 Decreasing Performance of CEOs—Median Normalized Annual Return to Shareholders

Source: Booz Allen Hamilton, Global Data, Tenures Ending in 1995, 1998, 2000, 2001, 2002, and 2003.

Tenure (years)

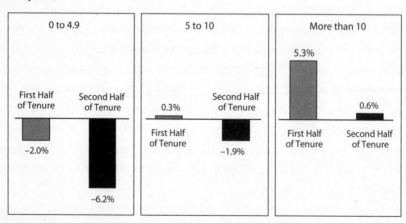

FIGURE 3.3 Decreasing Performance of CEOs—Median Annual Return to Shareholders

Source: Booz Allen Hamilton, Global Data, Tenures Ending in 1995, 1998, 2000, 2001, 2002, and 2003.

reason for this bias is that individual self-assessments are, as mentioned, usually very inaccurate. They are also highly optimistic. More than two decades ago, two graduate students at the University of Pennsylvania (Lauren Alloy and Lyn Abramson) conducted a pioneering experiment that showed that while depressed people are accurate judges of how much skill they have, nondepressed people think they are much more skillful than others judge them to be.

Subsequent studies clearly confirmed these findings. One of the best was published in December 2004 by David Dunning, Chip Heath, and Jerry M. Suls.[11] It integrates decades of research to show how we overrate our performance in quite dramatic ways. The great majority of people tend to rate themselves "above average"—clearly, a mathematical impossibility! In a survey of nearly 1 million high school seniors, for example, 70 percent stated that they had "above-average" leadership skills, while only 2 percent felt their leadership skills were "below average."

This type of self-congratulatory bias doesn't go away with advanced education; in fact, it gets worse! For example, 94 percent of college professors say they do above-average work. The "above-average" effect also abounds in the business world. As mentioned, studies of hundreds of engineers at two high-tech companies found that 32 percent of the engineers in one company and 42 percent in the other—four out of ten—rated their own performance in the top 5 percent of all engineers.

So we bring this inflated sense of our leadership skills to the job-filling challenge. And we listen to or read the self-descriptions of people with similar delusions. No wonder things so often go wrong in the people-finding process!

The bias to overrate capability is usually based on two incorrect assumptions. The first is that people can change more quickly, and to a greater degree, than they actually can (and, of course, that the company can afford to wait while those individuals learn on the job). The second faulty assumption is that a high correlation exists between the *motivation* to perform and the actual *capacity* to do so. The simple truth is that even highly motivated individuals can fail miserably if they don't have the necessary skills, attributes, or experience. But it's all too common for us to promote an individual to a position as a result of his or her strong interest in it, without doing the necessary due diligence as to the individual's competence.

Snap Judgments

In addition, we often make snap judgments. We don't usually calculate the probabilities, and when we do, we aren't very good at it. We are accustomed to categorizing things, including other people, immediately. When assessing others, first impressions play a major role, as do gossip and other second-hand information about candidates. Sometimes, one piece of bad information eliminates an individual who, on balance, may be the best candidate.

To exacerbate matters, as suggested earlier, most managers and executives believe they are *very good* at sizing up and choosing people, despite their lack of preparation, experience, and (in many cases) a track record replete with mistakes. All too often, we rely heavily on unreliable indicators, such as a candidate's charisma, to predict future performance. In other words, our snap judgments tend to be long on snap and short on judgment.

Branding

I once had a conversation with Jack Welch concerning the cases where GE (departing from its home-grown traditions) had gone outside to look for top talent. He explained that when starting a new business in a sector where the company had no previous experience, including the plastics business and a few other cases, GE's leaders had decided to go outside. He emphasized, however, that this approach was fraught with peril. By way of illustration, he cited an interlude when GE hired several people from DuPont simply because they *were* from DuPont, without evaluating them in depth. "I'm sure in at least some of those cases, DuPont was delighted that we were taking them away," Welch recalled ruefully. "We were making a branding mistake."[12] In other words, GE was buying a reputation, rather than an individual who *embodied* that reputation.

Evaluating People in Absolute Terms

Another frequent bias involves evaluating people in absolute terms. In business, in particular, it's very common to both praise and criticize in an exaggerated, even an extreme, way. We tend to refer to our colleagues in absolute terms, without taking into account the circumstances under which they work. So Jim is an "outstanding manager," while Bill is "a loser."

These absolute evaluations are particularly dangerous when making people decisions. How can we assess a candidate's performance without a full understanding of the circumstances in which it was turned in? Great performances (and also poor performances) are often inseparable from context. While GE is an outstanding "CEO factory," not everyone who leaves GE to become a CEO at another company performs successfully. Many of them perform exceedingly well when there is a good match, while others don't when there is a poor fit. Some of the GE alumni who did not perform well in their first leadership position after GE later went on to perform *extremely* well. What changed? They returned to circumstances similar to those in which they had flourished at GE—circumstances that closely matched their natural strengths and experiences.[13]

It seems self-evident that to some extent you need to evaluate a candidate on his or her own terms, in light of his or her context. And yet, I have often observed interviewers who have a prescribed set of questions that they ask, regardless of the particulars of the situation. These questions are the ones that you, as a job applicant, hate to have thrown at you—questions like, "What are your strengths and weaknesses?" or "Where do you want to be five years from now?"

These are bad questions because they tend to turn an experience into an abstraction by cutting it off from its roots. The answers that come back come out of an experiential vacuum. And, in addition to always asking the same questions, poor interviewers would not probe further. Consider the following slightly tweaked version of the first question above:

> Give me an example in which you brought your personal strengths to bear on your current job. What was your specific role? What were the circumstances? Exactly what did you do and why? What were the consequences?

I'll have much more to say about interview questions and interviewing in subsequent chapters. For now, I simply want to make the point that, when it comes to people decisions, very little is absolute; almost everything is relative. Your job as the hiring entity is to figure out how someone has performed *in a particular context*—and figure out whether that experience comes to bear on your own context.

Seeking Confirmatory Information

Several of the above biases will lead us to very rapidly form an initial impression about the individual we are assessing. At this dangerous stage, the problem becomes compounded when we begin to seek confirmatory information for what we believe to be true, while turning our eyes away from any evidence that might contradict our newly embraced conclusions.

In his book *Judgment in Managerial Decision Making*, Max Bazerman reviews the list of personal biases that influence our judgment, thus sabotaging our decisions, investments, and negotiations.[14] When discussing the confirmation trap, he asks the reader to perform the following exercise (which draws upon a previous study by the legendary psychological investigator, Peter C. Wason):

> Imagine that the sequence of three numbers below follows a rule, and your task is to diagnose that rule (Wason, 1960). When you

write down other sequences of three numbers, an instructor will tell you whether or not your sequence follows the rule.

2–4–6

What sequences would you write down? How would you know when you had enough evidence to guess the rule? Wason's study participants tended to offer fairly few sequences, and the sequences tended to be consistent with the rule that they eventually guessed. Common rules included, "numbers that go up by two," or, "the difference between the first two numbers equals the difference between the last two numbers." In fact, Wason's rule was much broader: "any three ascending numbers." This solution requires participants to accumulate disconfirming, rather than confirming, evidence. For example, if you think the rule is "numbers that go up by two," you must try sequences that do not conform to this rule to find the actual rule. Trying the sequences 1–3–5, 10–12–14, 122–124–126, and so on, will only lead you into the confirmation trap.

In order to fight the confirmation trap, you must make a special effort to *falsify your own initial hypothesis*. You have to be prepared to test those intuitions that feel so uncertain, right out of the box.

The confirmation trap is one reason why so many projects that look good on paper fail: People ignore the warning signs. It is also the reason why many hirings fail. It takes enormous discipline to assess candidates in depth, sifting through both positive and negative impressions and pieces of data to arrive at each person's *true* qualifications for a job. It feels unnatural to falsify your initial hypothesis about a job candidate, especially when it takes so long to find a promising one. But it's a great habit to get into.

Saving Face

We're all human; we hate to fail. And when we *do* fail, we do our damnedest to save face. As organizational behavior expert Chris Argyris has pointed out, the smartest people become quite stupid when they feel embarrassed or threatened.[15] The impulse to cover our mistakes, however irrational, becomes dangerously strong. Obviously, this impulse comprises the bad people decisions we make.

The University of California's Paul Ekman is a renowned authority on the subject of emotions-related research and nonverbal communications, celebrated for his groundbreaking research into lying. In *Telling Lies*, based on his interviews and data with children and adults, he summarizes nine different motives for lying:

1. To avoid being punished

2. To obtain a reward not otherwise readily obtainable

3. To protect another person from being punished

4. To protect oneself from the threat of physical harm

5. To win the admiration of others

6. To get out of an awkward social situation

7. To avoid embarrassment

8. To maintain privacy

9. To exercise power over others[16]

Now reread that list in light of the need to *save face* after a bad people decision. With the possible exception of wanting to avoid physical harm, all of these motivations can come into play when we start trying to cover up our people mistakes. And while this may sound retrospective in nature (after all, "covering up" involves past mistakes), it has very strong forward-looking implications. As in the case of the international technology company at the beginning of this section, we don't like to be the first ones to make others aware about our poor people decisions if they haven't noticed. Even worse, we may try to justify a poor people decision we have made in order to save face, when acknowledging the mistake and acting on it could avoid further damage and rapidly start a recovery trend before it's too late.

Sticking with the Familiar

As a rule, we humans like to stick with the familiar. When we hire people to work with us, we talk about finding a "good fit" between the organization and the individual. In many cases, that's code for hiring a person
who represents the comfortable and the familiar, as opposed to seeking
the best combination of competence and complementarity. If you think
logically about it, complementarity necessarily implies diversity, which
may argue *against* a "good fit."

Sticking with the familiar partly explains why most organizations
promote from within for their most senior positions. And when looking
for outside talent, most organizations still seek familiarity. Thus, former
consultants frequently hire other consultants, often from the same
school and firm. Certainly, familiarity can bring stability to any community. But it can also lead to myopia and self-absorption, which can be
particularly dangerous when a change is needed that requires completely
different competencies.

Emotional Anchoring

We all have a tendency to fall prey to a phenomenon called *emotional
anchoring*—that is, judging candidates relative to someone familiar (or
to each other) rather than on their own merits. The most extreme
case might be that of the jilted lover who persists in holding up every
new acquaintance against the impossible ideal of the departed
boyfriend/girlfriend, and finds nobody who can measure up. The emotionally anchored individual fails to see individuals and circumstances
on their own terms.

A related problem is the sequence effect, in which we tend to remember the earliest and most recent experiences in a series most clearly.
As a result, in a sequence of interviews, the first and last candidates are
likely to get the most attention. The ones in the middle of the pack wind
up as "middling," in our minds.

People decisions shouldn't be held hostage to impossible ideals or accidents of sequence. We have to guard against arbitrariness when it comes to making great people decisions.

Herding

Finally, we often fall into the psychological trap of "herding." Picture a herd of deer or antelope. If you're a member of that herd, the safest place is *in the center*. The deer that takes an extreme position, at the edges of the herd, is most likely to get picked off by predators.

When we herd, we *imitate*. We follow the majority rather than acting independently. This can be the result of fear, as indicated above, or of the desire to be a team player, or even of laziness. Whatever the motivation, the phenomenon is amazingly common. Even high-powered executives (who have little to fear, who are paid to lead and be energetic) are sometimes hesitant to express a view about a candidate that differs from that of their colleagues.

Think of our ambivalence toward "whistleblowers," who by definition step outside the herd. And think of the recent cases of entire corporate communities going astray. Clearly, herding played a part from the shop floor to the boardroom.

Filtering Out Biases

We've looked at the 10 psychological biases and emotional traps that tend to impair the decision-making process and sabotage people decisions. Combating these biases is hardly a simple matter, but two strategies can help:

1. Building awareness
2. Having the right advisors, both inside and outside of the organization

Consider the real-life case of a large retailer that (at the time we became engaged with them) had multiple brands in many channels, ranging from supermarkets to department stores. The company was suffering from massive brand confusion, and as a result, loss of market share. It decided to promote its head of the supermarket division to become its CEO, believing that a retailer was needed to fix its problems. Mainly because that individual's experience was limited to a single retail channel (supermarkets), his performance was little short of disaster. He was persuaded to take an early retirement.

Belatedly, the company conducted an in-depth analysis to identify the strategic challenges, managerial priorities, and key competencies needed. Based on those specifications, a subsequent executive search suggested that the best person for the job was Candidate X—an individual who, as it turned out, had no experience whatsoever in the retail sector.

That conclusion bucked several strong forces. Sticking with the familiar argued for promoting an insider, or at least someone fully familiar with the sector, as had been the tradition throughout the entire company's history. In addition, the chairman, who supported the nomination, faced strong opposition from several board members and internal executives. Their tendency toward herding was amplified by extensive media coverage, which repeatedly questioned the wisdom of such an unorthodox nomination.

To make a long story short, this highly controversial choice was eventually ratified. The individual was hired, and he's proven very successful at running a complex, multibusiness corporation, thanks largely to his focused and simple management approach. He has viewed his role as that of managing a group of retail businesses, and has top-quality retailers now leading each of them. After a decade of going backward, the company is flourishing

By doing his homework and using external resources wisely, the board chairman overcame a whole host of biases and traps, and greatly broadened his company's range of options. The result was the recruitment of a competent, broad-gauge generalist, who slipped into his new role like a hand into a favorite glove.

Wrong Incentives and Conflicts of Interest

So far, we've discussed three types of factors that tend to work against your people decisions: statistical odds, difficult assessments, and psychological biases. We will now focus on the final factor sabotaging these decisions, which is the existence of bad incentives and conflicts of interest. These forces can come from the candidates' circumstances, or even from strong political pressures within the organization.

Candidate Circumstances

The first type of malicious incentive that can sabotage people decisions is the whole set of what I call "candidate circumstances."

In my somewhat strict Catholic upbringing, I was taught to believe that our behavior grows out of our values, and our ability to hold fast to those values. What I've come to realize, both through my personal experience and my professional inquiries, is how much our personal circumstances influence our behavior. We humans try to hold to absolutes, but in fact, we are relativists and situationalists. Where we stand depends on where we sit.

Whenever I am working on a search assignment, I really try to understand the individual circumstances at hand, in order to try to correct and filter out the wrong incentives. Typically, a person who is without a job and needs work is likely to conclude *very quickly* that a particular employer or position is perfect for him or her—and, of course, that he or she is uniquely qualified for the job.

Conversely, individuals who are happily employed are much more critical about (and objective toward) any proposed new alternative.

They are also more skeptical about their own qualifications for the proposed new role.

In other words, candidates' circumstances can push them toward either self-serving dishonesty or unfairly self-critical honesty. The former, obviously, is a bigger problem. The high stakes of job hunting make cheating alarmingly frequent. One of the largest studies, reported by David Callahan, indicates that in some cases, 95 *percent* of college-age respondents were willing to lie in order to get a job—and that in fact 41 percent of the students had already done so! (I admit that I was shocked.) Another study, reviewing 2.6 million job applications in 2002 by a U.S. firm that conducts background checks, revealed that 44 percent contained at least some lies. In another large survey, an Internet company that does background checks found that 80 percent of all resumes were padded.[17]

Challenging personal circumstances may make individuals who would otherwise be extremely candid and honest in their actions behave badly. As Malcolm Gladwell describes in *The Tipping Point*, our behavior is to a great extent a function of social context.[18] This sociological insight has been substantiated by numerous experiments over the decades. For example, in the 1920s, two New York–based researchers (Hugh Hartshorne and M.A. Hay) conducted a landmark set of experiments with 11,000 schoolchildren aged 8 to 16, giving them dozens of tests over several months, all designed to measure honesty. What they found, in a nutshell, was that (1) a lot of cheating goes on, (2) older children cheat more, and (3) so do less intelligent ones. So you can expect significant cheating from job candidates, and probably more from the more seasoned ones and from the least qualified.

Another quite disturbing experiment was conducted by two Princeton University psychologists (John Darley and Daniel Batson) using a group of seminarians as their guinea pigs. The researchers contrived a situation in which these seminarians would run into a man "slumped in an alley, head down, eyes closed, coughing and groaning." The question was, who would stop and help? Only 1 in 10 of the seminarians who were in a rush to get to their next appointment stopped, while more than 6 in 10 who weren't in any particular hurry did stop. The same group, with similar backgrounds and overall motivations, broke out very differently based on a single differentiator: *am I running late?*

What these (and many other) studies and experiments seem to indicate is that things like honesty and compassion are not fundamental, absolute, reliable human traits. When we're put under intense pressure, we may behave in ways that are not only socially and morally unacceptable, but run counter to our own deeply held values. Does this unpleasant truth come to bear in job hunting and people decisions? Absolutely.

In fact, there are many ways in which candidates' circumstances can sabotage the people-decision process. The most basic one, which often surprises the people I talk with, is our own limited understanding of ourselves as individuals. As explained in the fascinating *Strangers to Ourselves*, by Timothy Wilson, we humans don't know much about who we are, or what we feel, or what we might feel under new circumstances.[19]

Hasn't it happened to you that you've finally been able to buy what you have always longed for (that car, house, boat, or farm), only to lose some sense of purpose in your life, and feel far less happy? Extrapolating from this to the job-hunt context, most of us aren't very good at looking forward and imagining how our new lives on a new job are likely to look. We may overaccentuate the positive or the negative, but we're unlikely to get it right.

A second problem with candidate circumstances, according to the relevant research, is that while we are risk-averse when we are doing well, we become embracers of high risk when we are in trouble. When we're in desperate economic, emotional, and social circumstances, we don't mind taking on a job that is beyond our capability, not only because we have "nothing to lose" (which is almost never true), but because a big roll of the dice feels like the only way out.

For all of these reasons, we have to make a special effort to understand a candidate's circumstances. We have to use that understanding to root out exaggerated accounts of competence—and equally, to discredit overly self-critical assessments. We need to spot and head off the plungers, high-rollers, and risk-takers who feel they have nothing to lose. They *always* have more to lose, including their reputations. So heading off sabotage is right for both the would-be employer and the would-be employee.

Political Pressures

Unlike our previous incentive problem, the second type of incentive problem lies entirely within the organization and its stakeholders. This final hiring trap—politics—also happens to be the most pervasive and daunting of them all. Politics are so pernicious in people decisions that they deserve to be escalated out of the category of simple "trap," and likened to a pool of quicksand. I can honestly say, having started my third decade in the executive search profession, that the most spectacular hiring mistakes that I have seen have been the result of well-meaning people who just happened to have agendas.

People like to hire their friends. Take the case of a forceful, dominating board chairman who proposed that his college roommate succeed the company's fired CEO. Intimidated, the rest of the board agreed, and waived the standard search and evaluation process. In less than a year, the new CEO had fully demonstrated that he lacked flexibility and strategic vision, and he had to be fired.

Some agendas are more Machiavellian. When joint ventures appoint senior executives, partners engage in all sorts of backstage scheming to get their candidates elected, hoping to have an ally in charge, regardless of his or her particular skill set. I've even seen people advocating for weak candidates to avoid risks of becoming redundant, or even to enhance their own chances of getting ahead in the organization, in the long run. (*That person will surely crash and burn, and I'll be the next alternative.*) In still other cases, candidates get jobs in return for favors rendered. For instance, a candidate might be hired with the anticipation that he will hire friends of his "supporters," or use the services of their companies.

Such appointments, while common, can have a devastating effect not only on the company's performance, but also on its morale. No one likes to work in an organization dominated by cronyism or other kinds of internal politics.

To summarize, we've reviewed the four factors that make it so difficult for companies to make the best people decisions at the top. Figure 3.4 lists these factors.

It's a long list; collectively, these factors help explain why making people decisions is so damnably difficult.

Statistical Odds

Difficult Assessments
- Impact of assessment errors
- Unique jobs
- Changing jobs
- Intangible traits
- Inaccessible candidates

Psychological Biases
- Procrastination
- Overrating capability
- Snap judgments
- Branding
- Evaluating people in absolute terms
- Seeking confirmatory information
- Saving face
- Sticking with the familiar
- Emotional anchoring
- Herding

Wrong Incentives
- Candidate circumstances
- Political pressures

FIGURE 3.4   Why Getting the Best People Is So Hard

Note that these factors are widely ignored by the press, when they report on cases of dramatic CEO failures. That's unfair. Having personally fallen into each of these traps several times, I have nothing but respect for those executives and board members who put themselves on the line, accepting the people-decision process as part of their leadership mandate, and deal successfully with all these difficult and challenging problems. It's almost never easy. Again, Jack Welch got it right: "Hiring great people is brutally hard."[20]

The good news is that forewarned is forearmed. The best protection against all of the traps laid out in this chapter is *awareness*. In that sense, you're already ahead of the game, having read this chapter. Stay out of the traps that I've described, and you will certainly avoid gross failures.

But I want to conclude this chapter on a more upbeat note. When I asked Jim Collins about the single most important mistake he has observed in top leaders' decisions, he thought for a moment, and then responded as follows:

Looking for the dramatic big decision that will catapult a company to greatness in one fell swoop; greatness just doesn't happen that way. When you study the long course of great companies, looking at their development over years, we see that no single decision—no matter how big—accounts for more than a small fraction of the company's total momentum. Greatness gets built by a series of good decisions, executed supremely well, added one upon another over a long period of time.

Certainly, some decisions are bigger than others—Amgen's decision to invest in the bioengineered drug EPO, Southwest Airlines' decision to use only 737 aircraft, Intel's decision to launch the microprocessor, IBM's bet on the 360, and so forth—but even these decisions account for a small fraction of the total outcome. In the long arc of a great company, no single decision makes for even 10 percent of the ultimate greatness of the institution.[21]

■ ■ ■

Building true greatness into a company calls for managers with the discipline to carefully analyze and implement every important decision, including people decisions. Yes, avoiding the traps described in this chapter is an essential step, but it's only the first step. In order to be able to pick winners all the time, you will also need to master each step of the people-decision process—all the way from knowing when a change is needed to helping integrate those great people you've hired.

And that will be the subject of our next six chapters.

CHAPTER FOUR

Knowing When a Change Is Needed

Let's begin addressing this difficult topic—figuring out when a major people change is needed—with two scenarios from the real world. As you'll see, the scenarios have very different outcomes.

Scenario 1: The man sitting across the desk from me looked truly lost, almost bewildered. Mercifully, however, he still had the presence of mind to act. In the midst of a wrenching personal drama, rather than fatalistically accepting the loss of his wealth, his family business, and even his life's meaning, he had decided to seek help. And that's why he was in my office on that particular afternoon.

He was the son of the founder of a very successful food business, and had succeeded his father as CEO. Having specialized in the technical aspects of the operation, he had been instrumental in major decisions involving capital investments and new products. Collectively, those decisions had led to impressive growth and profit records, and helped create the platform that made the company the third largest player in its market.

But in the past few years, the world had changed. Massive concentration in the sector through intensive M&A activity, the sudden appearance of new international players, and changes in distribution channels had weakened the company's competitive position in a surprisingly short period of time. Meanwhile, the company's growth had been financed with short-term loans in the local financial markets—loans whose interest rates were suddenly shooting upward. The company was caught in the pincers of mounting operating losses and spiraling interest payments, which combined to make it impossible to borrow from international lenders. As a result, the company was literally on the brink of bankruptcy.

Unable to find a way out, he shared his dilemma with a smart and thoughtful corporate lawyer. That lawyer eventually referred him to us. "So the question is," he said to me, obviously pained by the question he was about to ask, "can a new CEO save my business?"

It was the right question, and the answer ultimately turned out to be "yes." To our client's credit, he acted quickly and decisively. As soon as we brought an acceptable candidate to him, he turned over his executive responsibilities to that person and stepped aside. And despite the company's dire circumstances, this new CEO managed to steer the enterprise safely to calm waters, and it has been growing and prospering for almost a decade since that time.

Scenario 2: At about the same time, the shareholders in a successful agro-industrial exporter—two brothers—came to see me. They were not only the principal owners of the company, but also its top two executives. Although the business was still reasonably healthy, it was starting to face financial difficulties as a result of its overleveraged capital structure and shaky financial management.

From our side of the table, it was clear that the company dearly needed much stronger management, and we told them so. (In our line of work, we have to be candid.) The brothers thanked us for our opinion, but decided to keep running the company on their own. Within two years, it had gone into a downward spiral of increasingly expensive borrowing, which brought it to bankruptcy and liquidation.

Taken together, these two scenarios illustrate the key points of this chapter. First, it's never easy to reach the decision to make a people change, especially at a senior level. Sometimes, it's hard even to *see* the need. The protagonist in our first story, despite his personal investment in that unfolding business drama, was able to understand that new challenges required different talent, and that a wider pool had to be considered in order to find it. The two brothers in our second scenario didn't see (or didn't admit to seeing) the need for change, and so they marched together to the sad end of their business journey.

Second, it's difficult to implement such a change, even after it's been decided upon. Feelings can be hurt, and reputations damaged.

But "difficult" is no excuse. This is our third lesson: When it becomes clear that a change is needed, someone has to bite the bullet. At that point, the goal should be to *do it right*.

This chapter describes ways to determine whether an executive, a professional, or a senior manager should be replaced. I will briefly review when and why change tends to happen in real life, but I will concentrate most of the discussion on when change *should* happen. So this chapter is less about problem solving and more about problem *finding*. In subsequent chapters, I'll outline strategies for implementing changes properly and fairly.

When Change Usually Happens

Since 1992, the North Carolina–based Center for Creative Leadership (CCL) has sponsored significant research in the field of executive selection, conducting in-depth interviews with hundreds of executives at the top three levels of subject organizations. To that growing storehouse of data, CCL has added insights from the direct observation of top executives as they participate in an impressive multimedia simulation of an executive-selection process. The result is a very rich source of data that helps us understand how selection *actually takes place* in organizations, as opposed to what organizational policies say is *supposed* to be happening.[1]

The CCL database shows that, as you might expect, executive

selection frequently takes place in the context of some kind of organizational discontinuity such as dramatic growth, a turnaround, a major cultural or strategic change, or a restructuring. Even more frequently, a change in the senior executive ranks reflects a developmental decision, such as creating an opportunity for an executive to develop a broader skill set through job rotation. But the most frequent scenario *by far* for an executive change involves neither an organizational discontinuity nor a developmental goal, but rather a determination to sustain the organization. In fact, in more than 60 percent of the cases reported on by CCL, an executive change was aimed mainly at maintaining the status quo.

The CCL data also touch on (1) the impact of the specific hiring circumstance, and (2) the relative success rates of insiders versus outsiders. For example, according to CCL, in the cases of mergers or acquisitions, only 31 percent of the executives appointed were successful. Likewise, only limited chances of success (roughly 50/50) were observed when the organizational goal was to promote cultural or strategic change or to launch a startup. In both of these latter circumstances, external hires in the CCL sample were less successful than internal ones.

CCL's survey also confirmed that when it came to senior-level changes, by far the most frequent decision makers were the person directly up the ladder from the position being filled (in 67% of the cases) and/or the CEO/president/owner (66%). The HR department was a key decision maker in a significantly lower percentage of cases (36%), closely followed by the peers of the superior (33%) and the people in a peer relationship with the incumbent in the position.[2]

A final and very disturbing finding from CCL is that *succession plans play a very limited role in executive selection*, despite the critical importance of people decisions at that level. When analyzing the different selection techniques used in practice, succession plans were the *least*-used source for candidate information—employed in only 18 percent of the cases! By contrast, the most common methods used to gather candidate information were interviews (87%), resumes (73%), and references (69%).[3]

What else do we know about changes in the executive suites? As has been so often highlighted by the press in recent years, executive turnover is frequently precipitated by poor performance. A recent study about the relationship between corporate performance and top executive dismissal confirmed that top executives are indeed fired for poor performance. According to this same study, however, only truly wretched performances trigger top executive dismissals. In other words, corporate performance has to plummet, *dramatically*, to precipitate a senior executive job separation.[4]

And finally, we know that when changes at or near the top happen, they usually set off a cascade of changes at the next several rungs down the ladder. Top-level turnover increases markedly around times of CEO turnover. In particular, the departure of a long-tenured CEO increases the chances of managerial turnover at the next organizational levels.[5]

When and Why Change *Should* Happen

Our firm has conducted several studies of state-of-the-art executive career management. The consulting firm McKinsey & Company has conducted similar studies on a parallel track. Both sources of research confirm that most companies fall far short of best practice when it comes to making people decisions. To me, the results are astounding. More than *three-quarters* of the executives surveyed believe that their organizations:

- Don't recruit highly talented people
- Don't identify high and low performers
- Don't retain top talent and assign the best to fast-track jobs
- Don't hold line managers accountable for people quality
- Don't develop talent effectively

That's worth underscoring: Three out of four respondents said that their own companies came up short in these critical areas! Even worse, more than 90 *percent* of executives reported that their organizations aren't good at removing low performers quickly.[6]

As I noted in Chapter 3, human nature inclines us to procrastinate in our people decisions. Even when things are going badly, we move slowly. And perversely, we become especially risk-averse when things are going well (*if it ain't broke, don't fix it*). All of this adds up to one thing: In good times and bad times alike, we tend to postpone making important people decisions until it is too late.

But this simply isn't good enough. As the world moves faster and faster around us, we can't keep moving slowly, or fail to move at all. We have to be *proactive*. "Leaders relentlessly upgrade their team," Jack Welch observes, "using every encounter as an opportunity to evaluate, coach, and build self-confidence."[7]

Inept managers not only do their own jobs badly; they also destroy the performance (and potential) of the people around them. In their recent book about what they call "evidence-based management," Jeffrey Pfeffer and Robert Sutton reviewed the findings of research on organizational climate over the past half-century. They report that "60 percent to 75 percent of the employees in any organization—no matter when or where the survey was completed, and no matter what occupational group was involved—report that the worst or most stressful aspect of their job is their immediate supervisor."

"Abusive and incompetent management," Pfeffer and Sutton continue, "creates billions of dollars of lost productivity each year." And study after study, they conclude, "demonstrates that bad leaders destroy the health, happiness, loyalty, and productivity of their subordinates."[8]

Again, the focus of this chapter is problem *finding*. Given our very human tendency to procrastinate, how do we build in a bias toward action—toward rooting out problems and acting on them? I believe the first step is to be aware of, and on the lookout for, the kinds of situations that tend to call for change more urgently or more powerfully.

Acts of God, Acts of People

Sometimes, the need to change horses arises out of a dramatic, even horrific, event.

I will always remember the day in May 1995 when José Estenssoro's private jet crashed in the Andes. At the time of his death, Estenssoro was highly respected in the international business community, in large part due to his remarkable restructuring and privatization of YPF, Argentina's largest oil and gas company. His unique leadership had achieved a very impressive initial turnaround (which included cutting staff by 90%), which was followed by a successful international expansion. The story was so remarkable, in fact, that Harvard Business School produced a series of five cases about the transformation of YPF, from its revitalization in Argentina to the successful acquisition and turnaround of a troubled U.S. oil company, on the company's road to becoming a global enterprise.[9]

At the very peak of all this success, Estenssoro's plane went down. The company never regained its momentum, and it was ultimately taken over by Repsol, Spain's largest oil company. The damage wasn't limited to YPF alone: Most analysts believe that the lack of leadership at YPF following Estenssoro's death caused a significant decline in oil exploration and a resulting failure to scout out additional oil and gas reserves in Argentina.

By definition, we can't head off, or even anticipate, acts of God. The best we can do is understand that these events, if and when they hit us, may have a devastating impact on our organization. Does our company have a robust succession plan in place? At the very least, do we have a consensus candidate to step in and take the reins if the "hit-by-a-bus" scenario actually comes to pass? I'll return to these subjects in later chapters.

But acts of God are the rare exception. In business, as in most of life, acts of *people* are what we have to worry about. So, what are the man-made scenarios that are likely to call for people changes, and which we can successfully anticipate and respond to?

Some scenarios, especially those that originate outside the company, are pretty straightforward. People changes have to be made with increasing frequency in response to *macro-level forces*, such as globalization and the rapid evolution of technology. In its February 2006 article on "The Toughest Jobs in Business," *Fortune* pointed out that while yesterday's managerial headaches were mostly generated by challenges like sourcing, making, and marketing goods in a manufacturing-based economy, today's headaches grow out of continually altering business models in an information-based economy. In the past, you needed massive market power in commodity businesses; today, you have to contend with greatly increased customer and investor power in all businesses. In the past, *Fortune* pointed out, you had to know how to negotiate with unions; today, it's all about attracting and retaining top talent.[10]

Where does your company's leadership—including your board—fit into this picture? Are they looking forward, or backward?

In addition, people changes often have to be made in response to *industry-level forces*. Some of these forces are implied in the macro-level changes outlined above, for example, technology shifts within your industry. But they can also be viewed from the opportunity side of the industry ledger. A study by Wasserman, Nohria, and Anand that attempted to measure the impact of leadership on company value also focused on the conditions under which leadership matters the most.[11] They concluded that senior leadership has a much higher impact on company value when (1) the organization has abundant resources (including low financial leverage and high organizational slack), and (2) opportunities in the industry are scarce. If your company meets these two conditions, the potential benefit of making the right people decisions, including people changes, is likely to be very high.

Finally, people changes often have to be made in response to *discontinuities*. In this category I include things like launching new businesses, doing mergers and acquisitions, developing and implementing new strategies, dealing with performance problems, and coping with growth and success.

Let's look at these five discontinuity scenarios in turn, with an eye toward the need for people changes that may be presented by each.

Launching New Businesses

As a rule, companies must grow or die, and one of the critical growth paths for most companies is the development of new businesses. But as the research from CCL clearly indicates, the failure rate of executives in startup situations is very high in the case of both internal promotions and outside hires.

Even the organizations with the best leadership-development skills may decide to hire from outside when entering new businesses. When GE Medical Systems entered the ultrasound business, for example, the company chose to hire a highly qualified number-two prospect from a key player in the market. Why? Because, as Jack Welch explained to me, that individual "built a $1 billion business from nothing over 10 years, whereas before that, we had failed in that business at least three times."[12]

Industry knowledge counts for a lot. An analysis of GE "graduates" who signed on as CEOs of other companies confirms the fact that those individuals were much more effective when they took the reins of a company in a similar industry. So the technical, regulatory, customer, or supplier knowledge unique to an industry is an invaluable asset for performance, and a particularly valuable one when launching a new business.[13] If you don't have this talent inside, you'll have to go outside.

On the other hand, it's not *always* a great idea to go with an outsider when launching a new business, even if all of the desired industry wisdom is not resident inside your existing businesses. Why is this so? Because in order to successfully launch a new business, an executive team needs to be able to deal effectively with political, social, and cultural issues within the parent company, and this is a task at which (only) internal candidates tend to excel. In short: When the launch of a new venture calls for a people change, both types of candidates—internal and external—should be properly considered.

A frequent people-decision mistake that companies make in the context of new ventures is putting someone of limited competence or seniority in charge. This consciously or unconsciously reflects the small initial size of the venture, but it can be a self-fulfilling prophecy. The point, as Jack Welch indicated in the same conversation mentioned earlier, should be to *put the best people where the most potential is.*

Making the right people decisions when entering new businesses is critically important, not only because of the significant challenges and low success rate of startups, but also due to the company's lack of familiarity with the new sector. Among other challenges, monitoring performance is usually harder in an unfamiliar context, and the warning lights may not start flashing until it's too late.

Doing Mergers and Acquisitions

Five years after joining Egon Zehnder International, I found myself dealing with a market that was practically *exploding* with unprecedented demand for managerial skills.

The setting was Argentina in the early 1990s, when a new government sparked a wave of privatizations of state-owned companies in major sectors, including telecommunications, electricity generation and distribution, water distribution, oil and gas, airlines, and several others. Collectively, these industries comprised a major proportion of the country's gross national product and domestic employment.

The leaders of the businesses within these industries were faced with the massive challenge of simultaneously adjusting to the new demands of a deregulated market, increased competition, and fundamentally different shareholder objectives. From the outset, it was clear that achieving a much higher level of productivity and effectiveness in these industries would be critically important.

But it would not be easy. Some of the companies were plagued by incredible levels of ineffectiveness, beginning (but not ending!) with phantom employees. (In more than one case, 10% of the payroll simply vanished when proper ID checks were put in place.) Most of these companies lacked not only the necessary telecommunications infrastructure, but also the data that would be needed to fuel the business once all the fiber-optic cables, routers, and servers were finally in place. I've already cited the case of YPF, the oil and gas enterprise that José Estenssoro helped transform. As a result of the efforts of Estenssoro and others, which included substantial restructuring, spinoffs, and some acquisitions, productivity at YPF multiplied *tenfold*.

A crucial step in combining and transforming those companies was determining the skills that would be critical to succeed in the new environment, identifying those existing managers who could reasonably be expected to develop them, and also agreeing on which positions could be filled only through external recruitment.

Equally important, and perhaps even more vexing, was the merger-related challenge of dealing with the "two bodies for each slot" phenomenon. (For example, when two companies merge, the combined entity needs only one CFO.) Fortunately, the shareholders in those businesses quickly recognized the benefit of a specialized and independent appraisal process in order to decide whom to retain, develop, and replace.

This gave me the opportunity to participate in a number of major management appraisal projects in the context of mergers and acquisitions. Based on those and subsequent experiences, I learned that mergers and acquisitions almost always prompt a host of critical people decisions—and all too often precipitate corporate malpractice. A case study published in the *Harvard Business Review* captured the essence of these challenges.[14] It describes the hypothetical merger between two pharmaceutical companies, which caused predictable anxiety among both groups of employees, up to and including the senior ranks. The CEO of the merged company had to decide who would stay, and who would go—against the backdrop of a sagging stock price and the outmigration of some of his most talented executives.

In cases like this, it's especially important to avoid playing politics or playing favorites. But it's also important to avoid the phenomenon of "horse trading": *I'll take a less qualified candidate from that group because I just took a strong candidate from this group.* All of these are direct paths to poor people decisions.

At the risk of sounding like I'm advancing the interests of my own industry, here's where an objective, specialized, and independent assessment of the key managers can prove invaluable, especially when it comes to deciding who goes and who stays.

One of the first cases of this type in which I participated involved the privatization of a large service utility. Meeting the investment and service targets within a tight timeframe constituted an extremely tough challenge. At the same time, the organization completely lacked a results orientation, and was totally divided internally as a result of a polyglot management team, representing the different partners of the joint venture that was awarded the privatization: local managers from the former state-owned company, other managers from a new local shareholder, and foreign managers of two different nationalities.

The managerial challenge was dramatically compounded by the political games of the various shareholders, who defended their own representatives while bargaining for the key managerial positions. Because of all of these difficulties, the owners of the enterprise decided to conduct an objective and independent appraisal of the senior management team in order to confirm the key people decisions. The result of this appraisal is summarized in Figure 4.1.

The CEO decided to act on these assessments at a juncture when approximately *half* of the most critical positions were filled with a highly suspect manager—either in terms of general competence, or of experience that might be relevant to the position. Obviously, this corporate overhaul was far from easy. But as a result of this CEO's willingness to bite the bullet and do the hard thing in the short term, the company very rapidly achieved remarkable levels of growth and profitability. In fact, for several years it outperformed the other large competitor in the

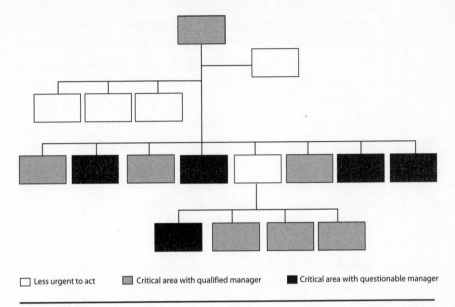

☐ Less urgent to act	▨ Critical area with qualified manager	■ Critical area with questionable manager

FIGURE 4.1   Short-Term Actions for Top Positions

same market, which had none of the complexities of a joint venture with two technical operators and several partners representing three different nationalities.

Developing and Implementing New Strategies

By any meaningful measure, the pace and scope of change in organizations has grown enormously over the past several decades. I've already touched on the impact of powerful global economic and technological forces that push companies to reduce costs, change business processes, improve the quality of products and services, locate new opportunities for growth, and increase productivity. Very often, the scope of change extends even to the core corporate strategy.

A recent book, *Breaking the Code of Change*, presents a very comprehensive review of change in human organizations, including purpose, leadership, focus, and implementation issues. It includes a chapter by Jay

A. Conger, who convincingly argues that—depending on the magnitude of change and the risks and investments that are involved—senior executives are the best-positioned individuals to lead successful organizational change efforts.[15]

That may sound obvious enough. But shortly after starting my executive search experience, I began focusing on the logical extension of this premise: that *different strategies require different managers*. The prevailing myth of the "universal manager" who could manage anything, under all circumstances, was just that: a myth. When you change strategies, you very often have to change horses.

One of the first clients I worked for was a major conglomerate that had all sorts of businesses within its portfolio. In the upper-middle ranks of this sprawling enterprise was a very impressive young manager, who recently had completed a major turnaround in a situation where success seemed almost impossible—so much so that many seasoned executives had refused to take on the job.

The details are relevant to our story. This outstanding manager had taken over a business that was recording losses in excess of *30 percent* of its sales, which was in a highly leveraged financial position, and where—due to the influence of an extremely powerful union—layoffs appeared impossible. Despite these very real obstacles, our young star was able to dramatically cut expenses while still growing sales and restoring the company's profitability. In the end, against all expectations, he was able to sell the business for a modest profit.

So far, so good; based on his success, however, he was promoted to manage one of the stars in the portfolio: a highly competitive consumer goods company in a rapidly growing market. A year after this glorious appointment, the manager was fired; his performance was so poor that he had gone from hero to goat. What happened? You can probably anticipate the answer. His ruthless, iron-fisted managerial style—outstanding for cutting costs and extracting productivity in a very limited market—didn't fit the new context, which required skills in competitive analysis and the ability to listen and rapidly respond to his new market. In other words, the new context required a completely different leadership style.

In 1983, MIT's *Sloan Management Review* published an interesting article by Marc Gerstein and Heather Reisman, entitled "Strategic Selection: Matching Executives to Business Conditions."[16] The authors summarized seven common strategic situations (startup, turnaround, dynamic growth in existing business, new acquisitions, etc.), described the leadership requirements for each of the seven, and outlined a profile of the "ideal candidate" for each situation.

The authors argued (for example) that a startup requires a leader with a clear vision of the business, core technical and marketing expertise, and the ability to build a management team. In contrast, the liquidation or divestiture of a poorly performing business requires completely different skills, such as cutting losses, making retrenchments without demoralizing the remaining troops, and so on. Again, each of these situations requires a different leadership profile.

But there's more: In order to successfully implement a strategy, not only do the right leaders need to be chosen, but those leaders need to be aligned across the different hierarchical levels of an organization. A group of researchers in California conducted a very comprehensive study of the implementation of a strategic initiative in a large U.S. healthcare system, and concluded that *aligning leaders at all levels* was critically important. What does this mean, exactly? The researchers concluded that the medical department's performance, for example, was actually not primarily driven by the effectiveness of the CEO, the medical center leader, or departmental leaders. Instead, it grew out of *effective leadership at multiple levels*. When leadership improved on all of those individual levels, the overall performance of the organization improved significantly.[17]

For the purposes of this discussion, the lesson is that a change in strategy has to ripple across multiple levels in a complex organization. Not only do you have to contemplate changing the highest levels of leadership, you also have to look at changes elsewhere in the organization.

A second, somewhat paradoxical lesson is that *every situation is unique*. While I advocate making people decisions in light of the strategic situation, I *don't* endorse the rigid application of a generic strategy-manager matching model. What might appear to be a sensible match could in fact be counterproductive, or leave money on the table. For example, while it might appear to make sense to match a manager in the "caretaker" phase of his or her career with a product nearing the end of its life cycle, it might actually be smarter to put a young, aggressive, ambitious manager in that slot—the type of leader who might breathe some life back into the sagging product. Strategy is critically important, but *context* is what makes sense out of strategy.

There's one more interesting way in which strategy and staffing can intersect. Neal Schmitt, Walter C. Borman, and several coauthors have discussed a hiring model in which staffing decisions are no longer limited to implementing strategy, but extend to the *development* of strategy.[18] In other words, some organizations select outstanding individuals with deep skill sets and broad vision with an eye toward defining a new direction for the company, up to and including the definition of an entirely new corporate strategy. I'm reminded of Jim Collins's *Good to Great*, in which he articulated his "First Who . . . Then What" principle: "They *first* got the right people on the bus, the wrong people off the bus, and the right people in the right seats—and *then* they figured out where to drive it."[19]

We'll return in later chapters to the challenges of who should get a seat on the bus and who should get off the bus. For now, my point is simply that strategy changes, including prospective changes, usually precipitate people changes.

Dealing with Performance Problems

In at least four out of five situations in which clients have asked me to help them find a new manager, the compelling reason for a change has been either a performance- or relationship-related problem. Of course, relationship problems are always with us. (People will always have interpersonal challenges.) But my own professional experience tells me that performance-related problems are becoming a much more frequent reason for people changes—particularly in public companies, where senior executives face increasing performance pressures (as described earlier) and intensifying scrutiny from analysts and the media.

Recent research has analyzed in detail how CEO performance affects CEO turnover. A first finding is that boards generally focus on deviation from *expected* performance, rather than performance alone, in making the CEO turnover decision. Thus, failing to "make your numbers" is more likely to get you fired than turning in limited results that are in line with your board's (limited) expectations. This is particularly true when there is a large cohort of analysts following your firm.

So, current practice is to make a change when performance is low vis à vis expectations. In such a circumstance, there is also a greater tendency to hire an outsider rather than to promote an insider. One study suggests that boards are more likely to appoint an outsider when (1) forecasted five-year earnings-per-share growth is low, and (2) there is greater uncertainty among analysts about the company's long-term forecast.[20] But is this common practice actually a *good* one?

The best short answer is that this is a smart response to poor performance *on average*, by which I mean to underscore the fact that, in many cases, this strategy can go very wrong. The best analysis of this topic has been conducted by Harvard's Rakesh Khurana and Nitin Nohria.[21] Their study confirms that in cases where the predecessor has been fired, typically as a result of poor company performance, hiring an outsider tends to enhance company performance quite significantly. (In all of these situations, of course, the relevant measurement of performance is industry-adjusted performance.) But in the case of a "natural" succession (when the outgoing CEO has not been fired, and company performance is strong), the best strategy tends to be picking an insider.

The upshot is that you need to be open to changing management when the company is experiencing performance problems. You should be open to the possibility of hiring an outsider. But you should also remember that these are rule-of-thumb conclusions, and that what may work *as a rule* may be the worst remedy for your specific situation.

Keep your eye on the *real* challenge and the real solution. What really accounts for your company's short-term performance problems? Are you adrift and in need of a stronger hand on the rudder? Or have your leaders administered medicine that, while painful in the short run, is exactly what's needed over the longer term? Do things have to get worse, temporarily, before they can get better? Keep in mind the trap described by psychologists as the "fundamental attribution error": When individuals observe an outcome, they are more likely to attribute it to the person involved, rather than to external circumstances. In the same vein, recent research shows that in many cases, shareholders and analysts misattribute poor performance to the CEO, rather than to the real culprit: external circumstances that were beyond any individual's control.

Are you experiencing a bumpy ride in your car? Well, is it the car? If so, get a new car. Is it the road? If so, don't dump the car. Consider a broader range of options.

Coping with Growth and Success

Sometimes people are surprised to find this scenario included on my list of reasons why people changes may be needed. But not everybody can deal successfully with success.

I was recently asked to speak to a gathering of venture capital firms about how to build a successful company. At the time, this group of VCs was investing primarily in biotech companies in Europe and the United States. I gave them a reading that they didn't necessarily want to hear. In this sector, I told them, you often find that successful companies eventually have to unload their (brilliant) founder—not only to maintain their success, but even to survive! Why is this so? Because scientists as a rule put too much faith in the magic of science, and too little faith in the art of management. The vehicle that has brought them their success to date— brilliant science—can't carry them any farther. It's time for a change.

More broadly, this phenomenon pertains not only to biotechs, but to any situation where a technical person has played a key role in the initial development of the company. Eventually, the level of complexity increases so much that the managerial skill sets involved simply have to change, and change significantly. Harvard's Noam Wasserman, who studied the histories of more than 200 Internet companies, describes the very common phenomenon of a founder being compelled to back out of the executive suite at the very moment of his or her greatest success.[22] Is product development completed? It may be time for a change. Have we secured significant financing from outside investors? It may be time for a change.

If the consensus is that change is needed, make sure it's a clean break. Involuntary successions that include a lot of face-saving compromises (e.g., giving the founder effective control over the board) don't leave enough space for the incoming CEO to manage the company. This is why when venture capitalists are involved in critical financing events, you often see pressure for wholesale managerial changes, including not just responsibility, but *authority*. If you're hiring a samurai, don't take away his sword!

Anticipating Future Challenges

All of the examples cited earlier involve significant discontinuities. These tend to be more or less obvious to savvy observers. (The question is not whether we need to act—we can *see* the challenge!—but rather, *how* to act.) A much more challenging situation is one in which no discontinuities are evident, but there may still be a need for change. It may be necessary for the company to anticipate and deal with an entirely new challenge—a looming threat or opportunity.

The leaders of a company (or any human organization, for that matter) actually have two jobs. On the one hand, they need to manage the present. Meanwhile, they need to anticipate the future. Running a successful business in the present requires a clear strategy and a skilled implementation of that strategy. But looking into the future and changing a business calls for different kinds of resources and skills. A recent book by George Day and Paul Schoemaker addresses this challenge.[23] They make the case that most senior managers in the United States and Europe have only a limited capacity for "peripheral vision," which they define as the ability to recognize and act on weak signals from the periphery before it is too late. But the more complex and volatile the business context, they argue, the greater the need for this kind of vision. They point out that in the human eye, 95 percent of retinal cells are devoted to peripheral vision, whereas only 5 percent are devoted to focal (straight-ahead) vision.

Think about nature's ratio, and then think about your own organization. What percentage of your "vision resources" are focused on tomorrow, versus today? If the answer is "not enough," it may be time for a people change.

A couple of years ago, a private equity fund that had invested in a major retail chain in an emerging market came to discuss their situation with us. When the original investment was made, the retail company was on the verge of bankruptcy, due to an economic collapse in the country (external) and a near-fatal dose of mismanagement (internal). A new CEO was hired at that juncture, and the combination of better management practices and a recovery of consumer spending nationwide brought the company back to breakeven in less than a year. All operational objectives were achieved, and the company was able to successfully restructure its debt.

But the private equity fund was not content to rest on its laurels. Instead, it decided to assess the company's leadership against *future* challenges. In doing so, it quickly realized that, in order to bring the company to the next level beyond mere survival, a much higher level of strategic orientation at the top was necessary, not only to develop new product categories and market segments, but also to implement new alliances. In other words, with the initial tough turnaround successfully completed, a completely different profile of leadership was needed. A firefighter is not necessarily a builder.

Fortunately, the company's vastly improved public image enabled it to attract a much higher caliber of candidate for this redefined leadership role, and led to a significant strengthening of its top team. Since then, it has achieved a level of growth and profitability far in excess of its initial survival-related goals.

Confronting and embracing new challenges, even as things are going relatively well and the organization is experiencing success, requires courage and foresight. It's the most difficult circumstance under which to initiate a people change, but it can yield the biggest benefits when the right decision is properly made.

The bottom line is that in a rapidly changing world, organizations must periodically look into the future, decide what that future may look like, and then decide whether the right human resources are in place to deal with that future.

How Do You Know Where You Stand?

Let's imagine that your organization is confronted with disruptive contextual change (environmental or industry-specific), is experiencing one or more of the discontinuities mentioned earlier, or is confronting a new business challenge. What do you do?

The first priority is to *figure out where you stand*. Later chapters in this book will analyze in much more detail *what* to look for when making people decisions, *where* to look for candidates, and *how* to appraise people. Before you can take those steps, however, you have to make sure that you invest enough time and effort in objectively assessing your management.

In circumstances of change and discontinuity, external advice can be particularly valuable. (Your organization may not have seen this circumstance before, but there are probably people out there, for example, in the strategy or executive-search fields, who have seen something similar.) Regardless of whether you choose to use external help, you need to identify the key competencies needed for success—given your understanding of the present and the future—and assess as objectively as possible your current management against these needed competencies.

The first large management appraisal I ever conducted was for a petrochemical company. It had been extremely successful, but its long-standing monopoly was about to be challenged by a new entrant. In other words, a new scenario was being imposed by macro changes and a new strategy was required. Figure 4.2 illustrates a simple picture of the scatter diagram of the top management in the petrochemical company.

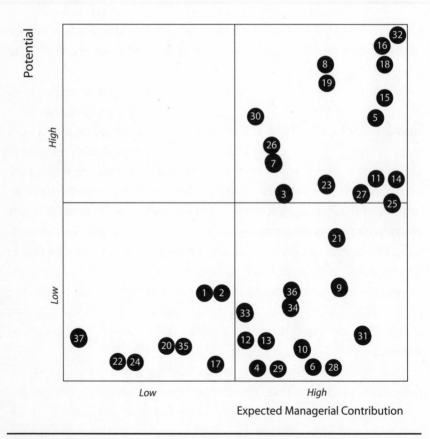

FIGURE 4.2   Strategic Classification—Individual Distribution

The dots represent the relative position of each senior manager in terms of expected managerial contribution and growth potential.

How do you get to such a snapshot? While we will discuss the details about what to look for in the next chapter, the first step is to reach agreement within the organization on the key determinants of the expected managerial contribution, as well as how "potential" will be measured. Simply having this discussion within the organization is salutary; it pushes people toward developing a framework for assessing managers which is something other than a purely subjective assessment. And note how the explicit separation of assessments along two different dimensions—immediate expected managerial contribution and future growth potential—opens a window on both the present and the future. Only *after* these discussions are completed should you undertake the individual assessment phase.

In this particular example, there was a significant spread of both managerial competence and growth potential. We grouped the rated managers in four categories: *strategic resources*, *solid operators*, *question marks*, and *successors*. There were several strategic resources (i.e., people who excelled along both dimensions), a significant number of solid operators who could be counted on to contribute significantly in the coming years, a few question marks, and no successors. The most urgent lesson to emerge from this study was that the company had to work hard to hire and develop successors if it hoped to realize its ambitious growth plans.

There are lots of other ways to peel the same onion, some of which can and should be conducted concurrently with the manager-focused analysis. Look at Figure 4.3, for example, which puts the petrochemical company's functional and corporate units through the same present/future screen. When the company's leaders analyzed this chart (and the data behind it), they quickly determined that Human Resources was not up to the future challenge. The future would demand a level of competence at hiring and developing professionals and managers which far exceeded that of the incumbents. A people change was needed.

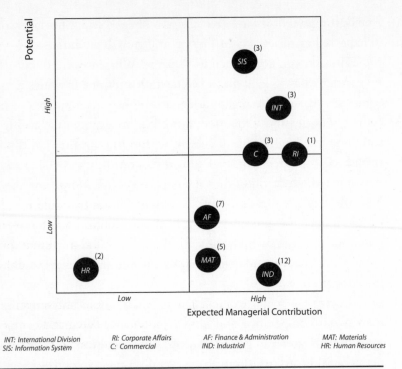

AREAS　INT: International Division　　RI: Corporate Affairs　　AF: Finance & Administration　　MAT: Materials
　　　　SIS: Information System　　　C: Commercial　　　　IND: Industrial　　　　　HR: Human Resources

FIGURE 4.3　Strategic Classification—Average by Functional Area

What Do You Do After You Know?

Let's face it: Even when people changes are justified, it's usually very difficult to implement them. This is especially true when it comes to moving out people whom we ourselves have hired, or with whom we've worked for extended periods.

Once again, your goal should be to define your decision-making process in advance, so that it will be as disciplined and objective as possible. I'm assuming, of course, that you aren't being driven by inappropriate motivations, and that you truly want the best outcome for your organization. Well, if that's true, then your real challenge is to make your processes transparent and predictable—in other words, to reflect your good and honorable intentions. People can buy into outcomes, even un-welcome outcomes, if they believe that the process that led to those out-comes was fair.

A few years ago, I was involved in the appraisal of the management team of a very successful telecommunications company. Despite its ex-cellent performance, reputation, profitability, and financial condition, it was quite evident to many in the company that a new set of challenges was likely to arise in the coming years. These included service deregula-tion and increased competition in the local market, even while this player had to push aggressively to develop its international operations. Internally, the going-forward strategy would require a much more effec-tive integration of the different businesses, as well as a cultural transfor-mation that would allow the sales force to place far more emphasis on services and solutions. Last but not least, talent management would be-come key, given both the need to develop new skills and to retain their most strategic resources in an increasingly deregulated and competitive environment, where several new entrants would almost certainly at-tempt to raid this incumbent for talent.

Anticipating a lot of resistance to change, we decided together with our client to sketch out a decision tree depicting the potential out-comes of a management appraisal exercise, covering the full range: from confirming, retaining, and developing some strategic resources that were properly allocated to their current position, all the way out to immedi-ately replacing questionable managers in critical positions where there were clear alternative candidates and low switching costs. Only after agreeing on the logical process to be followed, once each manager had been assessed, would we start discussing individual cases.

Figure 4.4 shows the decision tree that emerged out of that analysis. To make a long story short, this exhibit (or more accurately, the work that lay behind it!) made it clear where the company had to place its bets. As a result, several changes were implemented, and the company significantly enhanced its performance (despite the new challenges) over the following few years.

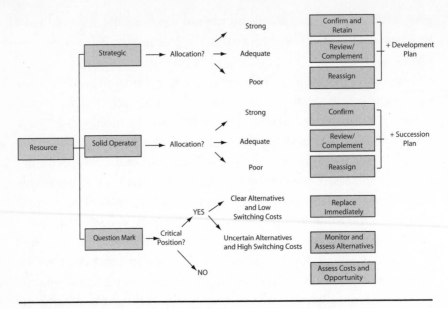

FIGURE 4.4   Management Appraisal Outcome and Actions

Forces that Fight Change

Let's assume that you know exactly where you stand, and (based on that understanding) you know exactly what you need to do, in terms of the people changes that are required to move your organization forward.

Unfortunately, that's still not good enough. It's one thing to know, and quite another to *act* on that knowledge. I've already mentioned the difficulty of implementing change when close subordinates or long-time colleagues are involved in a proposed reorganization. Now let's look in greater depth at the powerful forces that tend to work against change. I'll point to three such forces.

The first is the universal human impulse to favor short-term comfort over a possibly-better-yet-uncertain future. In my own industry, the professional-services sector, our real problem is not to come up with the right strategy. Rather, our challenge is to implement the chosen strategy with discipline. As David Maister (an expert in the management of professional service firms) once observed, the primary reason why we humans don't work at areas in which we know we need to improve is that the rewards are in the future, while the disruption, discomfort, and discipline needed to get there are immediate.[24]

People changes are the same. You and your fellow change agents may absolutely agree on the potential for gains in the medium and long run. But the short term remains uncertain. The cost of searching for and hiring alternative candidates is likely to be high, not to mention the almost guaranteed emotional costs of frustrating some incumbents, painfully separating others from the organization, and breaking longstanding attachments with still others.

In this context, a very predictable chorus is likely to arise: *The need for change isn't that urgent. Why act now?*

A second typical problem involves values and cultural differences. Based on my experience, the typical manager from an Anglo-Saxon tradition is far more likely to implement the people changes called for by an objective assessment than is a typical manager from other traditions, in which personal relationships tend to trump "the rules."

Finally, even the most altruistic people find it extremely hard to optimize their decisions under what appear to be business-as-usual circumstances. They underreact when things are tranquil on the surface, and overreact when a crisis erupts. This phenomenon has been well documented in the world of nongovernmental organizations and philanthropy, where sudden emergencies attract significantly more funds than chronic conditions, even though this often generates highly inefficient distributions of charitable dollars.[25]

Staying Honest

In light of these powerful forces that work against change (sometimes in combination!), you need to make a special effort to "stay honest." In other words, you have to act on what you know to be the truth, even when that's an unpopular path.

Staying honest is hardest when it comes to people changes. "Sometimes the hardest gut calls," writes Jack Welch, "involve picking people."[26] (I take that to include both "picking people to stay" and "picking people to go.") Welch goes on to assert that candor, another aspect of staying honest, is very hard to achieve and even runs up against human nature. Is candor difficult? Sure, says Welch:

> So is waking up at five in the morning for the 6:10 train every day. So is eating lunch at your desk so you won't miss an important meeting at one. But for the sake of your team or your organization, you do a lot of things that aren't easy. The good thing about candor is that it's an unnatural act that is more than worth it.[27]

As I write this today, I've just finished a meeting with Howard Stevenson, a legend in the field of entrepreneurship at Harvard. During our meeting, I asked him to draw on his own experiences (in academia, in entrepreneurial activities, and in numerous public and private organizations) to describe the most common mistakes he had encountered while making people decisions. He didn't hesitate: "You never fire people early enough." In other words, rather than acting honestly, we stall, dissemble, and prevaricate.

Fire people sooner? you may well be asking. What about the well-documented value of loyalty? Isn't it important to hold onto your people, to offer them stability and security, and win *their* loyalty and productivity?

Researcher Frederick Reichheld offers a solution to this seeming dilemma. His study of a large U.S. sample of employees suggests that employees are willing to extend their loyalty only to leaders and organizations that exhibit high integrity.[28] In other words, if you as a boss are "loyal" to an incompetent employee, that makes you appear less honest and therefore costs you more than it gains.

Howard Stevenson himself has written about what he "power of predictability" in earning employee loyalty.[29] He ass___ ... that the manager's primary responsibility is to ensure that the organization does what it sets out to do as efficiently as possible. *Be predictable*, he advises. Be honest in your promises, and deliver on them.

What does this mean, in the day-to-day business of people development? It means having clear rules and sticking to them. Some professional services firms are outstanding at this. At McKinsey & Company, for example, a rigorous up-or-out system is adhered to religiously. Consultants joining the firm know, *for certain*, that they have a very low probability of making it all the way to director—certainly less than 10 percent. On the face of it, this might seem like unpalatable medicine for aggressive, high-caliber people who are accustomed to succeeding at almost everything in life. Why sign up with a place where the washout rate is 90 percent? But in fact, the clarity and consistency of the McKinsey rules, together with the firm's brilliant management of its relationships with its "alumni," combine to make recruiting great people *easier*. When it comes to people, you can be as tough as necessary as long as you're also fair.

For more than two decades, Jim Kouzes and Barry Posner have conducted research into the values that people admire in their leaders.[30] Kouzes and Posner have administered their questionnaire to more than 75,000 people around the globe, updating their findings continuously. When they ask respondents to select the qualities that they "most look for and admire in a leader, someone whose direction they would willingly follow," four characteristics come up consistently:

1. Honest
2. Forward-looking
3. Competent
4. Inspiring

Since 1987, the first time the survey results were published, these four characteristics have come in at the top, in this order. People really do want honesty in their leaders. Will you bruise egos and damage friendships by making people decisions? Almost certainly. Will people respect your decisions, if they believe you've made them honestly? Almost certainly. So acting wisely and promptly when it comes to tough people decisions is a precondition both for organizational performance and for your own personal success.

Implementing Change

In order to properly implement change, you first need to confirm the decision to actually change a manager. As noted, this is almost never easy, not only because of the human dimension and the social ties, but also because of our inclination to deny failure, which tends to escalate our commitments.

This phenomenon has been well documented in other types of exit decisions, such as when companies need to leave a project, a business, or even a whole industry. In all these cases, many executives try to *hang on*, despite clear signs that it is time to bail. The *McKinsey Quarterly* recently published an article that discusses ways of making better business exit decisions.[31] The first step, according to McKinsey, is to assign someone new to assess the project, which I'll argue is the equivalent of conducting an independent management appraisal.

The second step is the use of *contingent road maps* that lay out signposts to guide decision makers through their options at predetermined checkpoints over the life of a project or business, which I'll call the equivalent of the decision tree discussed earlier, once the assessment has been conducted.

But in the end, the final decision needs to be implemented. When

Jim Collins was asked how "good to great" companies decide who should get off the bus, and how they implement those difficult decisions, this was his answer:

> They are rigorous, not ruthless. To be ruthless means hacking and cutting, especially in difficult times, or wantonly firing people without any thoughtful consideration. To be rigorous means consistently applying exacting standards at all times and at all levels, especially in upper management. To be rigorous, not ruthless, means that the best people need not worry about their positions and can concentrate fully on their work.[32]

Rigor without ruthlessness; honesty without brutality: When you realize that it's time for a change, these are excellent watchwords. Figure 4.5 summarizes the key points discussed in this chapter.

Change is usually needed in the case of
- New businesses
- Mergers and acquisitions
- New strategies
- Performance problems
- Growth and success
- Anticipating future challenges

In order to diagnose the need for change you should
- Assess the competence and potential of your key people.
- Clearly draft your decision process.

Once you have diagnosed the need, you should
- Be aware about the forces against change.
- Stay honest.

FIGURE 4.5   When Change Is Needed

■ ■ ■

What comes next? After deciding to change a manager, you need to do your homework and follow a systematic process to determine exactly *what* you should be looking for in your new manager.

That is the subject of our next chapter.

CHAPTER FIVE

What to Look For

Once you have confirmed that a "people change" is needed, a new path opens up in front of you. Your first step on that path is figuring out *what to look for*.

Deciding what you're looking for is obviously a critical step, since everything that follows will be fundamentally bounded by this initial focus. I personally have sat in on a few thousand interviews conducted by our firm's clients, and I've also talked with our clients at length about the type of information they consider when defining a need. To summarize a key takeaway from those many hours of conversations: *This first step is rich with potential, but also fraught with potential challenges.*

The first challenge involves settling on the best predictors of successful performance in a job—the central theme of this chapter. For some potential employers, including many Europeans, a strong educational background, as well as a resume studded with the names of distinguished former employers, are extremely important. For many North Americans, *performance on the job*, captured in terms of achievement and hard results, is much more critical.

Some people put a very high weight on IQ scores, while others look primarily to experience. Still others concentrate on "personality" (drawing on one or more of a vast storehouse of personality theories). Some potential employers take into account emotional intelligence–based competencies; others focus on values. Some try to determine and give extra weight to a candidate's *potential*, as assessed by means of one or more tests.

As noted, I've seen an enormous variety of theories and behaviors. I recall one executive who always asked candidates for senior managerial positions what type of animal they would like to be. (I don't remember what the right and wrong answers were.) A trainer with whom I once discussed interviewing techniques shared with me his list of favorite questions, one of which was, "If you were a vegetable, what kind would you be?" (The correct answer was "broccoli.") One of my colleagues presented more than a dozen highly qualified candidates to a client, who rejected each of the candidates almost immediately, with no explanation. Finally, the client's assistant revealed that her boss would *never* hire someone who was not a Virgo. And indeed, a Virgo was hired for that position.

Figuring out exactly what you're looking for is extremely important, for at least three reasons. First, although each situation is different, there *are* generalizations that we can make about the best predictors of performance in a job. But to draw upon that wisdom successfully, you have to know what you're looking for.

Second, you face all kinds of practical challenges when you're looking for candidates, including the fact that you don't have enough time to scrutinize each potential candidate in depth. One way or another, you need to *prioritize* and *focus*. By focusing on the most valid predictors of performance on the job, you can perform better assessments while investing less time, therefore making your work both more effective and more efficient.

Third, while focusing on the candidate's most valid predictors of job performance you will be avoiding any type of discrimination.

A final reason why knowing exactly what you're looking for is very important is that, most likely, *the ideal candidate doesn't exist*. In the real world, you'll have to make tradeoffs. And in order to do that successfully, you'll have to understand which strengths are critically important and which weaknesses aren't fatal.

Those Difficult Tradeoffs

A few years ago, I was working with a client who decided to change the overall management of a large financial institution. A new scenario, sketched out with the help of a strategy consulting firm, had persuaded this client to completely change the financial institution's strategy.

In the first year, the company swapped out all six of the key reports to the CEO. Two years after that, this CEO (to whom the six new individuals had been reporting) was moved to a nonexecutive position within the same group. The plan was to promote one of the six direct reports to succeed the outgoing CEO. But all six were talented and ambitious executives. How would the company choose? *What was it looking for?*

Figure 5.1 profiles the six internal candidates. It summarizes the

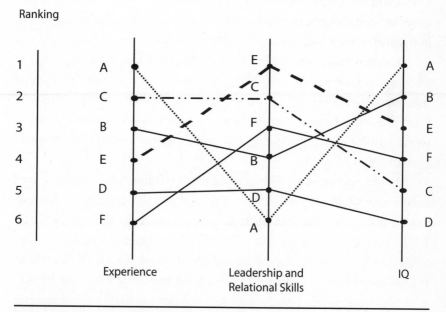

FIGURE 5.1   Choosing the CEO's Successor, Part I
Profiles of Six Internal Candidates

decision makers' ranking of each of the candidates along three different aggregated dimensions. The first dimension was *relevant experience*, including market, business, functional, and situational experience. For example, Candidate A had by far the most exposure to relevant types of situations, while Candidate F had a very limited relevant previous experience. The second dimension was *leadership and relational skills*. Interestingly, Candidate A (the one with the most relevant experience) scored lowest along this second dimension. The third dimension analyzed was *IQ*, as a proxy for verbal and analytical intelligence.

Figure 5.1 underscores the need to make very difficult tradeoffs. Would you go with Candidate A, who is the most intelligent, and has by far the most relevant experience among this group, but has very limited leadership and relational skills? Or would you go with Candidate C, who is the second-best, both in terms of experience and "soft" skills, but is one of the less intelligent in the group? Or would you go with Candidate E, who has the best leadership and relational skills, but is not the smartest in the group, and has less relevant experience than most of the individuals who would become his direct reports?

Later in the chapter, I'll return to this (real-life) example, explain what decision was made and why, and summarize the consequences of that decision. For now, my point is that these kinds of tradeoffs are never easy. They become *much easier*, however, when you know exactly what you're looking for, and therefore can give different weights to the various relevant criteria.

First I will review some general findings about the relevance and significance of different predictors of success in a job, including IQ, experience, personality, emotional intelligence, potential, and values. Then I'll describe the evolution of a tool called the *competency model*, and describe how it relates to the emotional intelligence model. I'll talk about potential and how to look at it, and examine individual competency versus team competency. Finally, I'll provide some practical tips for making your people decisions effective and efficient.

Does IQ Matter?

Let's begin our review of possible predictors of job performance with the venerable *intelligence quotient* (IQ). Simply put, IQ tests (of which there are many) attempt to determine an individual's general intelligence. These tests are *normed* so that the median score always falls at 100, meaning that half of the population scores below 100, and half scores above. They are widely used to predict academic performance, job performance, and even socioeconomic success. But do they work? Do they have what the social scientists call "predictive validity"?

For many years, psychologists Frank L. Schmidt and John E. Hunter have examined the validity of different selection methods. They have synthesized the conclusions from a huge number of studies using 19 different selection procedures for predicting job performance, and have also analyzed some of these procedures in combination.

Schmidt's and Hunter's work confirms that IQ is indeed very important. In fact, they tell us, when you hire employees who have no previous experience in the job, the single most valid predictor of future performance and learning is *general mental ability* (GMA), which can be measured using commercially available IQ tests. Schmidt and Hunter further tell us that when you look at combinations of general mental ability and each of the 18 other selection procedures, the three combinations with the highest combined validity for job performance are:

1. GMA plus a work sample test
2. GMA plus an integrity test
3. GMA plus a structured interview[1]

So the answer is yes, IQ matters.

Does Experience Matter?

Not too long ago, I discussed with Jack Welch the cases of "GE graduates" who had become very successful CEOs at other companies. I asked Welch whether he could make any generalizations about what made those managers successful despite the special challenges faced by all incoming outsiders, who by definition lack any company-specific experience.

In response, Welch discussed examples that confirmed the importance of previous experience. One was Jim McNerney, whom he described as a "strong will in a velvet glove." The team-oriented culture at 3M called for changes that were evolutionary rather than revolutionary, and thus McNerney had the right profile to win the necessary internal support and succeed.

Previous experience, the new context, and the individual's personality interact in subtle but powerful ways. The *Harvard Business Review* recently published an article that examined the cases of 20 former GE executives who had gone on to high positions elsewhere.[2] The authors concluded that while all 20 had been successful at GE, and all were highly qualified in terms of their general management skills, their previous situational, functional, and industry-specific knowledge was critically important in determining their degree of success in the new job. For example, when analyzing the 20 GE graduates in terms of their situational fit (what the authors call "strategic human capital," which refers to expertise gained from experience in situations that require specific strategic skills, such as cutting costs, driving growth, or maneuvering in cyclical markets), they found that 9 of the 20 executives had a good match, while the other 11 were mismatches. Where the strategic need matched the strategic experience of the recycled GE executive, companies enjoyed annualized abnormal returns of more than 14 *percent*, on average. Meanwhile, mismatches generated negative returns of almost 40 percent.

So again, the answer is yes, experience matters a lot.

What about "Personality"?

IQ and experience are "hard" factors, in the sense that they can be more easily verified, and it is somewhat easier to agree on terms and interpretations. Personality is a much softer and broader area. But we all know (or suspect) that it's a key factor. One of the first things I heard from my colleagues when I became an executive search consultant some 20 years ago was that *you get hired on experience and you get fired on personality.*

What is personality, and how much does it matter, and when? Personality refers to the unique organization of characteristics that define an individual and determine his or her pattern of interactions with the environment. These characteristics include thoughts, feelings, and behaviors. Obviously, these are fairly stable characteristics, which means that the individual is likely to be consistent across a variety of situations.

So far, so good; but going further in deconstructing the concept of personality and putting it to work in people choices is not an easy task. In the English language, for example, there are something like 18,000 trait terms—far too many to put on a matrix and work with! What is needed, then, is a model that captures and simplifies the key elements of personality.

A series of tools have been developed to look at personality, and these tools can be grouped in two basic categories. The first includes self-report questionnaires, such as the Big Five, the California Psychological Inventory (CPI), and the Myers-Briggs Type Indicator (MBTI). (The Big Five model, for example, summarizes personality along five dimensions: extraversion, agreeableness, conscientiousness, emotional stability, and openness to experience.) The second category includes projective techniques. Two of the best known of these are the Thematic Appperception Test (TAT) and the Miner Sentence Completion Scale (MSCS).

Companies use personality tests quite frequently when making people decisions, particularly in the case of junior candidates who don't have much relevant experience.[3] (My own guess would be that some tests are used in about half of the hiring processes today.) Even though they're ubiquitous, however, they're not particularly valid. Looking at the Big Five model, for example, "conscientiousness" is important in all occupations, but the test simply isn't very good at capturing that trait in a useful way.[4]

One of the key reasons why personality tests are not particularly useful for making people decisions is because they are not job specific. "Extraversion," one of the Big Five dimensions, is obviously more important in some occupations than in others. Extrapolation from the Big Five results (interpreting them in a specific hiring instance) remains the prospective employer's challenge. If someone tests out to be an obsessive-compulsive type, is that good or bad? Well, if you're hiring a high-level accountant, it's probably good (even very good!). If you're hiring a manager, it's almost certainly bad.

I'm confident that personality theories and related testing techniques will only improve over time, as researchers continue to make huge advances in the neurosciences. Meanwhile, though, personality tests should be used and interpreted with a grain of salt.[5] You need to go well beyond them if you want to make great people choices.

The Power of Emotional Intelligence

In the early years of my executive search career, I spent a lot of time trying to understand the foundations of personal success and outstanding organizational performance. I read everything that I could get my hands on that seemed to be related to this topic. I was very surprised to discover the huge number of books and articles that made assertions about performance but lacked both a comprehensive theory and the research needed to back up that theory.

In 1995, two of my colleagues suggested that I read a book entitled *Emotional Intelligence*, by a researcher named Daniel Goleman.[6] Goleman (as I was soon to discover) had a keen mind that had been well trained. He had received his PhD in clinical psychology and personality development from Harvard, and then embarked upon an outstanding journalistic career, which included two nominations for the Pulitzer Prize and a Career Achievement Award for journalism from the American Psychological Association. He was elected a Fellow of the American Association for the Advancement of Science in recognition of his efforts to communicate the behavioral sciences to the public. As a co-founder of the Collaborative for Academic, Social, and Emotional Learning (CASEL), which helps schools introduce emotional literacy courses, Goleman has had an impact on thousands of schools around the world.

I read *Emotional Intelligence* and was much impressed. Goleman defined emotional intelligence as the intelligent use of one's emotions, or (alternatively) as the ability to manage ourselves and our relationships. I'll provide more details about Goleman's theory in subsequent sections. But of particular interest to me, back in 1995, was Goleman's contention that this quality that he called "emotional intelligence," or emotional competence, could be more important to personal success than IQ. This was *not* because IQ was irrelevant. Rather, particularly at the top levels of organizations, most people have similarly high IQ levels, as a result of having been filtered and sorted throughout their student days. (The cream has had plenty of time to rise to the top.) But people differ significantly in their emotional competency, even at the top, and Goleman argued that this phenomenon has not been given enough attention.

It was a "hard" book that brilliantly treated a "soft" issue, although it focused more on the personal level, rather than the organizational level. I decided that I wanted to meet with Goleman to discuss the implications of his findings for organizations.

In October 1996, I finally caught up with Goleman. (He graciously invited me to his home in Maine.) We talked for several hours about what made organizations perform and managers succeed, and the relevance of emotional intelligence–based competencies to businesses. I found it fascinating, even thrilling. The depth of knowledge that Goleman had accumulated, together with his remarkable objectivity and intellectual honesty, convinced me for the first time that there was indeed an impressive body of serious research demonstrating the value of soft skills for success in life, in society, and at work—as well as a powerful framework for assessing and developing these crucial skills.

We agreed to continue the conversation. All the way home (on a small plane to New York, and then for the duration of the overnight flight to Buenos Aires), I thought about the profound implications of Goleman's work for people in organizations. In fact, rather than catching up on some much-needed sleep, I drew up a list of issues that I wanted to discuss with Goleman at future meetings.

Over the next year, we kept talking. The issues we discussed included topics such as the spread of managerial performance, predictors of successful performance, research on evaluation methods, the relevance of emotional intelligence globally, cross-cultural differences in emotional intelligence, management teams, and organizational and leadership factors that encourage and enhance emotional intelligence in an organization.

As we will see, I came to believe more and more fervently in the power of the emotional intelligence construct.

The Foundation: Competencies

Meanwhile, I also dug deeper into the roots of Goleman's powerful model, to better understand both its origins and its potential applications. Without a doubt, the individual who has had the most significant impact on the tricky field of predicting performance on the job, particularly for senior managerial roles, is the late David McClelland.

One of the leading psychologists of the twentieth century, McClelland in 1973 published a landmark paper entitled, "Testing for Competence Rather Than for 'Intelligence.'"[7] In it, he pointed to the ubiquity of intelligence and aptitude tests in the United States. These tests were employed by all kinds of institutions, and with obvious success. But

McClelland argued that this success was too narrow. He argued that intelligence testing alone failed to account for successful performance, especially in high-level executive positions.

In his seminal paper, McClelland proposed the term *competency* to describe any characteristic that differentiates typical from outstanding performance in a specific job. That characteristic could include motivation, traits, self-image, knowledge, skills, and, yes, IQ. Starting with some very simple assumptions, such as that past behavior is the best indicator of future behavior, McClelland made the case that actual job-related behaviors were the best indicators of potential success.

"If you want to test who will be a good policeman," McClelland wrote, "go find out what a policeman does. Follow him around, make a list of his activities, and sample from that list in screening applicants." But don't rely on supervisors' judgments as who the better policemen are, because "that is not, strictly speaking, job analysis, but analysis of what people think involves better performance."

In his research, McClelland compared two distinct groups: the top 5 to 10 percent, as identified by clear outcome measures, and "typical" performers. Through a complex and iterative process, "competencies" were identified (i.e., behaviors that outstanding performers used more frequently and more consistently than typical performers).

In the years since 1973, McClelland's work has sparked a true revolution in the workplace. Competency-based people decisions have reduced turnover, improved job performance, and deepened the pools of "promotable" staff. Competencies also have been used to support other significant organizational applications, including training, with significant and lasting positive effects.

McClelland's pioneering work in the competency movement was taken up by several of his students. In 1980, for example, Richard Boyatzis (whom we'll return to shortly) published *The Competent Manager*, which pulled together the early findings in the field and added new understandings.[8] Drawing on a sample of 2,000 people across 12 companies,

Boyatzis identified a core set of competencies crucial to successful management. In 1993, Lyle and Signe Spencer published *Competence at Work*, which further accelerated the competency movement.[9]

The Essentials for Managers and Executives

At this point, before returning to my personal odyssey, let me make several observations about competencies. First, each combination of job and organization calls for a distinctive set of competencies for outstanding performance. Second, the list of typical key competencies for managers and senior executives tends to be short. Third, for each specific position, the relevance of each competence and the required level for successful performance tends to be unique.

Over the last several years, we at Egon Zehnder International conducted an extensive analysis of our global experience in executive search and management appraisals in our 62 offices worldwide. Based on that analysis, we identified key executive competencies. First, successful managers need to have a strong "results orientation" (i.e., be focused on improving the results of the business). A weak results orientation means simply wanting to do things well or better; moderate levels translate into meeting and beating goals; above that comes the introduction of improvements; and finally—at the top—comes the determination to *transform* a business.

The second key competency is "team leadership," which permits leaders to focus, align, and build effective groups. People with low levels of this competency focus on setting goals for the team; moderate levels are about building a productive team; high levels are about building a high-performance team.

A third key competency is what we call "collaboration and influencing." Those demonstrating this competency are effective in working with peers, partners, and others who are not in the direct line of their command to positively impact business performance.

And finally, "strategic orientation" enables leaders to think beyond the pressing issues of the day, and beyond their own sphere of responsibility. It enables them to think *Big Picture*.

In addition to these four core key competencies, there is a second group of five second-tier competencies, which may also contribute to success at the top. These include "commercial orientation," demonstrated by the drive to make money; "change leadership," which means leading people in an effort to transform and realign an organization; "developing organizational capability," which is about developing the long-term capabilities of others in the organization; "customer impact"; and "market knowledge."

Figure 5.2 summarizes the frequent competencies of effective leaders.

FIGURE 5.2 Frequent Competencies of Effective Leaders
Source: Egon Zehnder International.

There are, of course, other competencies that can be particularly relevant in specific situations. But these nine (the core four plus the second-tier five) cover most of the waterfront.

Setting the Targets

In addition to identifying the relevant competencies for each job, it is important to determine what *level* of each competency is necessary for each position. While the topic of scale competencies exceeds the scope of this book, you ideally should try to identify a target level for each relevant competency for successful or outstanding performance for each job.

For example, Figures 5.3 and 5.4 depict the circumstances of a life sciences company that was having a difficult time finding the right managers for the key position of project manager within its technical ranks. As Figure 5.3 summarizes, few heads of laboratories could make it to the

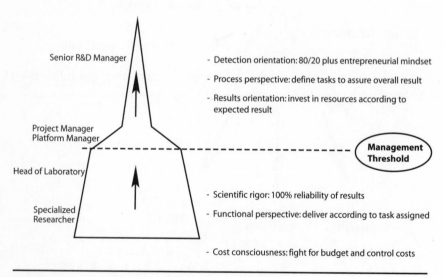

FIGURE 5.3   Understand What You Need, Part I
Example: From Scientist to Manager

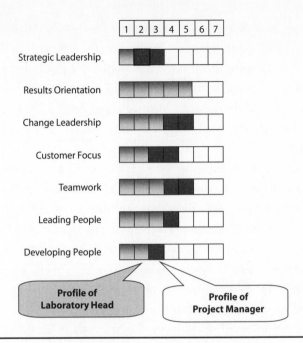

FIGURE 5.4   Understand What You Need, Part II
Example: From Scientist to Manager *(Continued)*

project manager level, let alone become a senior R&D manager. An analysis of the requirements for each of these positions confirmed that the profile of the project manager differed in highly significant ways from that of the laboratory head, particularly in the areas of teamwork, customer focus, change leadership, and strategic orientation. Briefly stated, much higher target levels in each of those competencies were needed for success in the new position.

Learning from My Own Failures

Now let's return to my own explorations of competencies and emotional intelligence.

On the basis of my interactions with Daniel Goleman in the late 1990s, he invited me to join the Consortium for Research on Emotional Intelligence in Organizations (CREIO), which he co-chairs. For several years, I had the pleasure of working with a remarkable group of individuals in this powerful think tank. Most of them held a PhD in organizational psychology, and many of them were former students of the late David McClelland.

As a result of my exposure to both Goleman and CREIO, I began analyzing my own professional experiences to see whether emotional intelligence–based competencies were (as Goleman argued) critical to success. By that point, I had some 11 years of experience, and I personally had interviewed some 11,000 people. Out of that very large sample set, I selected a subset of individuals whom I knew very well, who had been hired by me or by a very close colleague, and whom I had followed consistently before, during, and after their hiring.

This sample included 250 individuals, mostly in Latin America, out of whom 227 (or slightly more than 90%) had been quite successful. It also included 23 individuals who, in my opinion, had failed at their jobs. A "failure" did not necessarily imply that they had been fired; it meant more broadly that they had not met expectations in terms of either hard results or relationships, or both.

For those interested in the details, I summarized this analysis in a chapter in a book (*The Emotionally Intelligent Workplace*) edited by Daniel Goleman and Cary Cherniss.[10] Simply put, I tried to figure out which had been the one or two most salient characteristics of the hired candidates, and determine whether there was any correlation between those characteristics and their success (or failure) on the new job. I did look at three broad categories: IQ, experience, and emotional intelligence. These were relative evaluations, in the sense that I was comparing each of the hired candidates with other candidates for the position in each case.

The results of that analysis completely transformed my perspective.

First, as illustrated in Figure 5.5, the most frequent combination I realized I was usually looking for was *relevant experience* plus *high emotional intelligence (EI)*, which turned up in 40 percent of the cases. These candidates turned out to be extremely successful, with a failure rate of only 3 percent. Stated slightly differently, when I went looking for candidates with outstanding EI and a very relevant experience, 97 percent of the cases had been successful, despite the challenges of appointing a new manager.

As also illustrated in Figure 5.5, the other two typical combinations (either experience plus IQ, or EI plus IQ) each were present in one out of four of my searches. Notably, however, when candidates excelled in terms of IQ and relevant experience, but did not have a high level of EI, they failed 25 percent of the time!

I found this startling, and illuminating. As a result, I did additional analyses on this data, such as that illustrated in Figure 5.6, which displays the profiles of failures versus successful managers, indicating the

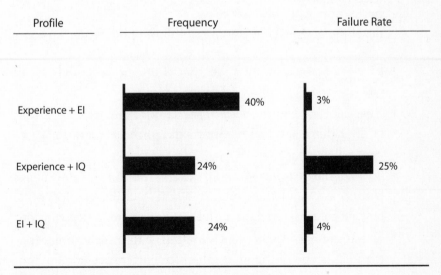

FIGURE 5.5   **Failure Rates for Various Profiles**

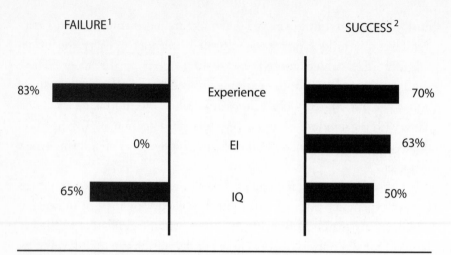

FIGURE 5.6   One of the Two Most Salient Characteristics, Part I
Profiles of Failures vs. Successful Managers
1. 23 cases from Latin America.
2. 227 cases from Latin America.

frequency with which they present each of these three categories as one of their two most salient characteristics.

Some of the obvious conclusions to be drawn from Figure 5.6 are:

- *Experience counts.* A full 70 percent of the successful individuals had a relevant previous experience.

- *Experience alone is not enough to predict success.* In fact, 83 percent of the failures also had relevant experience as one of their two most salient characteristics!

- *IQ is not enough of a predictor for success.* Two-thirds of the failures had IQ as one of their two most salient characteristics, while only 50 percent of the successful managers were in that category.

- EI was present in successful managers with a higher frequency than IQ as one of the most salient characteristics (almost two-thirds vs. 50 percent). It seemed that *for successful managers, EI mattered more than IQ.*

- Finally, while EI was one of the two most salient characteristics of successful managers in two-thirds of the cases, none of the failures in that sample had EI as one of their two most salient characteristics. In other words, *lack of EI is very highly correlated with failure.*

Dealing with Tradeoffs

Fascinated by this evidence, I processed this data in yet another way, looking at the combination of the *two* most salient characteristics of successful managers and failures. This is presented in Figure 5.7, which summarizes the relative frequency with which success and failures respectively present each possible *pair* of combinations within the three categories referred to earlier (experience + EI; experience + IQ; EI + IQ).

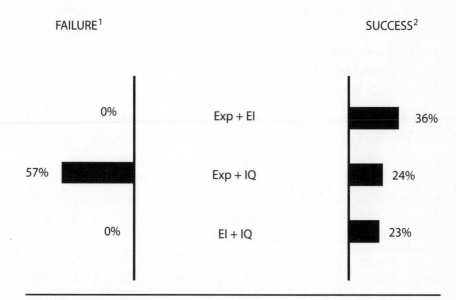

FAILURE[1]   SUCCESS[2]

0%	Exp + EI	36%
57%	Exp + IQ	24%
0%	EI + IQ	23%

FIGURE 5.7   Combination of the Two Most Salient Characteristics Profiles of Failures vs. Successful Managers
1. 23 cases from Latin America.
2. 227 cases from Latin America.

For example, 36 percent of the successful managers analyzed had a very relevant experience *and* very strong EI.

The conclusions to be drawn from the analysis of Figure 5.7 include:

- If only two categories can be achieved for a generic search, then *the most powerful combination to predict success should be relevant experience and high EI.*

- *IQ can be complemented by EI in a favorable way when experience is not possible.* In other words, the combinations of EI + IQ and experience + IQ were equally present in successful managers.

- Perhaps the most important finding from this analysis is that *when EI is not present, the traditional combination of relevant experience and high IQ seems to be much more of a predictor for failure than for success* (57% of the failures were very strong on this traditional combination, while fewer than one-fourth of the successes had that combination for their two most salient characteristics).

Again, this investigation and the findings described earlier had a truly profound effect on me. In fact, reaching these unexpected conclusions completely changed my people decisions from that point on.

Let's now go back to the difficult tradeoff presented at the beginning of this chapter, which indicated the six profiles of the internal candidates to be promoted to the new CEO position in a financial institution. The situation is restated in Figure 5.8.

If experience only had been taken into account, the ranking for potential promotion would have been first A, second C, and third B. If IQ only had been taken into account, the ranking for potential promotion would also have A as a first choice, B as a second, and E as a third. Combining experience and IQ, A seems to be the obvious choice, while B would probably be the second best. Considering the three broad cate-

Ranking

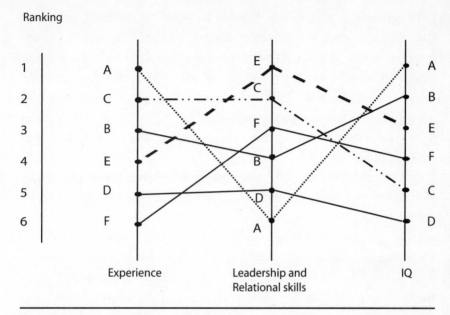

FIGURE 5.8   Choosing the CEO's Successor, Part II
Profiles of Six Internal Candidates

gories, some of the choices for the decision of internal promotion would have been:

- *Manager* A, the "traditional" choice: top in experience and in IQ
- *Manager* C, the "experience" choice: very strong in terms of experience and EI, but not one of the smartest in the room (fifth in terms of IQ)
- *Manager* B, a "safe" choice: highly intelligent, acceptable experience, average EI
- *Manager* E, the "EI" choice: top leadership and relational skills, above average intelligence, limited experience

The decision was to promote Manager E, the "EI" choice. While Manager A was more experienced and clever, his extremely low EI would have generated a sure failure. While Manager C was more experienced than E, experience is a dynamic competency and Manager E was expected to move up the scale with time. Manager E, however, was evaluated structurally stronger than C in the other two less dynamic competencies (EI and IQ). Finally, Manager B, while representing an average across the categories similar to E, and being in fact stronger than E both in terms of experience and intelligence, was below average in terms of EI.

I would obviously not have been so sure about my recommendation in this case had I not analyzed and reflected upon my own previous failures!

In fact, Manager E became the CEO of this company. He was so successful that he actually doubled the value of this financial institution in just two years—a fact that could be objectively measured, since the company was sold at the end of that period. As a fringe benefit, the new CEO's very strong leadership and relational skills made it easier for the other five managers (who were previously competing for the CEO position) to accept his promotion. It was indeed an emotionally smart decision!

Success and Failure in Different Cultures

Surprised by what the analysis of my own experience was telling me, I shared my findings with Daniel Goleman. Typically, his response was to express curiosity about what might come out of a similar analysis of other highly distinctive cultures, specifically Germany and Japan. With this encouragement, I asked my colleagues Horst Broecker in Germany and Ken Whitney in Tokyo to conduct similar analyses, sharing with them my methodology but not my results.

The results from these three highly different cultures (Latin America, Germany, and Japan) were absolutely fascinating. Figure 5.9 displays the profiles of failures versus successful managers for the three

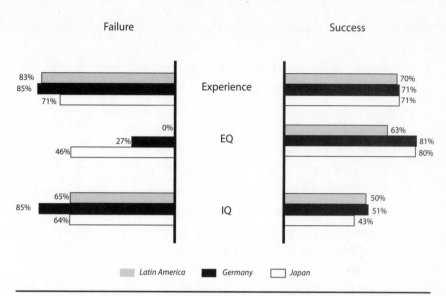

FIGURE 5.9 One of the Two Most Salient Characteristics, Part II
Profiles of Failures vs. Successful Managers, Three Different Cultures
Sample of 515 managers from 3 different cultures.
Source: Egon Zehnder International.

different cultures analyzed, indicating the relative frequency with which both successes and failures exhibited each of the three broad categories referred to as one of the most salient characteristics. For example, 71 percent of the successful managers recruited in Germany had a very relevant previous experience as one of their two most salient characteristics.

As you can see in Figure 5.9, the success profiles were almost identical across these three highly different cultures, which I took to be a significant validation of the conclusions from Latin America alone. (The minor differences in the left side of the figure, which present overall the same basic shape, are probably due to the small sample size of the failure cases.) In other words, each of the conclusions listed earlier as bullet points held true. Finally, when looking at the combination of the two most salient characteristics, once again, all of the earlier conclusions applied to each of these three highly different cultures.

I summarize my conclusions about success and failure in different cultures, and the relevance of EI, as follows:

- There has been a vast amount of research in the United States demonstrating how EI competencies are key for success, particularly in senior managerial and executive positions.[11]

- These conclusions are extremely powerful in Latin America. A similar analysis conducted by my colleagues in Germany and Japan reached exactly the same conclusions. The relevance of EI competencies for senior management positions is fully valid on a global basis. Specifically, three main conclusions arise with indisputable strength in all cultures analyzed:

  1. *EI counts more than IQ for success, and the lack of EI is very highly correlated with failure in senior managerial positions.*

  2. If only two broad categories can be achieved in a search for a top manager, then *experience plus EI is in general the most powerful combination for achieving success.*

  3. *The traditional combination of relevant experience plus IQ (with limited EI) is much more likely to produce a failure than a winner.*

Let me add one final note of interpretation, which finds its origins in Goleman's first book on the subject of emotional intelligence. Each of the managers in these samples had a high IQ. None was dull; otherwise, they wouldn't have made it through their undergraduate (and in many cases, graduate) training, let alone be thriving in the challenging levels of middle management. In other words, they were all bright (even extremely bright), but if they didn't have the benefit of a high EI, they had no guarantees of success.

Again, this realization gave me pause.

Why Does Emotional Intelligence Matter?

For some people, the concept of emotional intelligence is a one-size-fits-all panacea. Others dismiss the whole idea as a fad. As I see it, neither view is right. So let me summarize what I think emotional intelligence is all about.

One important point is that emotional intelligence, unlike IQ, is not an index. Instead, it is an *inventory* of competencies. What's the difference? The index of IQ produces the average of a series of highly related capabilities, associated with the analytical/verbal form of traditional intelligence. Emotional intelligence, by contrast, is a collection of a series of different competencies.

What key points grow out of the concept of an emotional intelligence inventory?

- *You need a basic level—a threshold level—in some competencies.*
- *You also need some competencies in each of the four main clusters of competencies* (self-awareness, self-management, social awareness, and relationship management; more on these later).
- *There is a certain critical mass of competencies needed for high performance,* although you don't necessarily need to excel at all of them.
- *Your competency profile should match the demands for the job.* As mentioned before, one of the main problems with most "personality tests" is that they are not job specific. Each job requires different levels of different competencies.

There are many ways in which EI has been defined, and therefore many clusters of competencies and many ways of measuring them. The most useful is the model developed by Daniel Goleman and Richard Boyatzis, which includes four clusters: (1) *self-awareness* (where the respective competencies are emotional self-awareness, accurate self-assessment, and self-confidence); (2) *self-management* (emotional self-control, transparency, adaptability, achievement orientation, initiative, and optimism); (3) *social awareness* (empathy, organizational awareness, and service orientation); and (4) *relationship management or social skills* (developing others, inspirational leadership, influence, change catalyst, conflict management, and teamwork and collaboration).

How are emotional intelligence competencies measured? The most useful tool—the *Emotional Competence Inventory*—was developed by Goleman and Boyatzis. At the risk of oversimplification, the best way to measure these competencies is not through self-assessment, but by means of observations, and particularly 360° assessments.

Why is all of this important for people decisions? Because *emotional intelligence–based competencies are essential for any job and are key for outstanding performance.* As discussed in Chapter 2, performance in complex jobs has a huge spread. If you can assess emotional intelligence–based competencies, you can better predict outstanding performance and therefore generate large economic value.

The Bottom Line on Emotional Intelligence

But that sort of statement won't surprise well-informed leaders and managers anymore. Today, many organizations (even those that don't talk out loud about "emotional intelligence") are well aware that soft competencies are key to success at the top. As a result, many organizations now have a clearly articulated inventory of competencies, and attempt to hire and promote people based on relevant emotional intelligence–based competencies (even though, again, they may not say that's what they're doing). Within limits that are discussed later, they also use EI-based techniques for executive development purposes.

As a result, better people decisions are being made. Daniel Goleman and his colleagues have had an enormous impact. Looking to the next decade, it seems clear to me that this impact will only increase. Our standard of living absolutely depends on *excellence at the top*, which in large part grows out of these competencies. Therefore, they will be used more and more for people decisions, in all sorts of organizations.

Additionally, the concept of emotional intelligence will be called upon to restore and defend the reputation of capitalism and free enterprise. This may sound like a stretch, at first. But if you scratch away at the Enrons, WorldComs, and Adelphias, eventually you find that the root cause of their troubles was not a deficit of either IQ or experience, but a lack of transparency and self-control. What better way to restore faith in business and its leaders than to build emotional intelligence into our organizations?

Finally, an increasingly globalized world is a more *volatile* world. This will require a far higher level of emotional intelligence–based competencies, in terms of adaptability, empathy, intercultural sensitivity, and leadership. For all of these reasons and more, the emotional intelligence model will be increasingly relevant in the years to come.

The Development Dilemma

As an executive search consultant, most of my time over the past two decades has been spent on helping organizations improve their performance by making great people decisions, either with internal or external candidates. In other words, most of my work has not been about *developing* people, but about bringing on board (or moving up through the ranks) the best available people.

At the same time, though, I spent about a decade leading the professional development effort in our own organization globally, and thereby helping my colleagues grow and progress. So I have a first-hand exposure to the challenge of professional development, as well as a personal commitment to getting it right.

But "getting it right" is easier said than done. Today, organizations in the United States alone spend something like $60 *billion a year* on training programs, a major proportion of which goes to management development. But it's far from clear that this money is well spent. The few attempts that have been made to systematically examine the effect of management development have generated confusing results. In most cases, the few quantifiable and positive effects of training and development efforts seem to vanish within a few months after the programs end.

In particular, there's not a lot of compelling evidence that higher-level skills (so vital for success in senior positions!) can be developed in any meaningful way. Perhaps as a result of this, many organizations and managers don't have an explicit developmental emphasis. Instead, they emphasize *selection*, on the implicit assumption that managers either do or don't have the right stuff. In this model, experience basically polishes the manager's key attributes, which are more or less fixed in place—the result of either a good or bad genetic legacy.

As discussed in the first chapter of this book, genetics certainly play a big role. Maybe half of what we are, and can be, is genetically conditioned. (Note I avoided the word *predetermined*.) IQ, for example, is largely a function of the smarts you were born with (with big doses of education and acculturation thrown in, of course). But the other half is determined by development, and, at least in the professional side of our lives, organizations control the degree of that development.

Here's the good news: Emotional intelligence *can* be developed. Richard Boyatzis has not only conducted some of the best research on self-directed learning by adults, but has also pioneered the implementation in an MBA program focused on developing these competencies.[12] In 1996, he published a paper summarizing his work in designing developmental programs for emotional intelligence–based competencies.[13] His conclusion: People *can* increase their competencies, especially those directly related to managerial effectiveness. But, he adds, this will *not* happen in traditional developmental programs.

In *Primal Leadership*, co-written with Daniel Goleman and Annie McKee, Boyatzis presents his theory of self-directed learning, which includes five essential steps toward change.[14] The first step is to *want* to change, and therefore define your ideal self—who you want to be. The second is to discover your "real self." Given the limits of our self-awareness, this requires feedback from others. The third step is to create, again with the help of others, a realistic learning agenda to build on your strengths while compensating for weaknesses.

The fourth step is to experiment with the new behaviors, thoughts, and feelings, practicing them until you master the new competencies. This is an essential point, and it constitutes a major difference between traditional learning and the development of emotional intelligence–based competencies. Yes, these competencies can be learned, but they require much hard work over an extended period, so that new habits can be developed.

The fifth and final condition, which applies to each of the previous steps, is to develop trusting relationships that can help, support, and encourage each step in the process.

In short, the "development dilemma" referred to earlier shouldn't center on whether development is or is not possible. We *can* develop the competencies most important to leadership. The real dilemma is that *development takes time*. It requires a significant personal effort, and has to be properly supported by the organization.

How to Look at Potential

This in turn suggests that one of the things that you should be looking for when making people decisions is potential. You want to place your developmental bets where they have the greatest chance of paying off.

Potential is sometimes defined, narrowly, as the readiness of an individual for a defined role—in other words, whether someone is prepared to move from a current position to one with a different challenge, or one where the size and scope of his or her responsibility is significantly larger.

Here, I'm invoking a broader definition. When I refer to *potential*, I'm asking whether an individual has the ability to grow significantly in the future, and therefore take on larger challenges.

As I see it, potential consists of three main components. First, of course, you need *ambition*. Are you hungry? What are you aspiring to, over the long term? David McClelland pointed to three great motivators: the need for achievement, the need for affiliation, and the need for power.[15] Well, how motivated are you? Are you willing to make major sacrifices to satisfy one or more of those needs?

Second, you need *the ability to learn from experience*. Morgan McCall and others make this case eloquently.[16] Do you seek out opportunities to learn? Do you take risks, seek and use feedback, learn from your mistakes, stay open to criticism, and so on?

Last but not least, the research from our firm's own databases, which includes the assessments of thousands of executives over several years, suggests that some *specific competencies* are a strong indicator of high potential. Do you have high levels of the future-oriented competencies (including strategic orientation, change leadership, and results orientation) that are strongly correlated with high executive potential?

What about Values?

Sometimes, when I get to the end of this list of three indicators of potential, someone raises the issue of values. When you're looking at someone's potential, shouldn't you be looking at that person's values, and whether those values can be developed?

My two-part answer to that two-part question is "yes, and no." The best executives I have seen in action go out of their way to try to test for honesty and integrity in their candidates. They never, *ever*, make concessions regarding values in a candidate. In *Winning*, Jack Welch describes integrity as the first acid test you need to conduct before you even think about hiring someone.[17]

Jim Collins recently addressed the question of what characterizes the people who help a company move from good to great. Here's the first of several criteria he listed:

> *The right people share the core values of an organization.* People often ask, "How do we get people to share our core values?" The answer is: you don't. The key is to find people who already have a predisposition to your core values and to create a culture that so rigorously reinforces those values that the viruses self-eject. A company can teach skills, but not character. Nucor Steel, for instance, hired people from farming towns, rather than steel towns, with the idea that: "We can teach people how to make steel, but we cannot teach them to have a farmer work ethic."[18]

This brings me to the second half of my answer—the "no" part. I've already cited my friend Lyle Spencer's comment: "You can teach a turkey to climb a tree, but it's easier to hire a squirrel." You're better off finding someone who's already on board with your values, and who can focus on moving forward rather than catching up.

What about Teams?

As you are trying to define what you're looking for, it's important to focus on the *team*, and not just the individual. This has several implications. First, it's very important not to overestimate the potential effect of an individual hiring. In May 2004, Groysberg, Nanda, and Nohria published the results of research tracking the careers of more than 1,000 "star" stock analysts.[19] In many cases, the star's performance in the new place was disappointing. Why? Because when the star leaves for Job #2, he can't take with him many (or any) of the resources that contributed to his achievements in Job #1. Performance in highly interdependent jobs grows not only out of individual skills, but also out of resources and capabilities, systems and processes, leadership, internal networks, and training—all of which might be summed up in the word "teams."

It's also important not to overestimate the value of a star-laden team. Many years ago, Meredith Belbin reported on the results of research conducted at Henley, the oldest management college in Europe. The research focused on a management exercise that involved watching eight teams of executives play a game. In one of these experiments, the researchers assembled a team (the "Apollo team") entirely composed of extremely bright people, which they then entered in the larger competition. Since winning the game clearly called for keen and analytical minds, the researchers hypothesized that a team of extremely bright people should win.[20]

But as Belbin later recounted, the first time they conducted this experiment, the all-star Apollo team actually finished last! This outcome appeared to be the natural consequence of a poor team process. The Apollo team members, once assembled, spent a large part of their time trying to persuade their teammates to adopt their own particular point of view—with nobody able to convert anybody else. In fact, in 25 runs of the experiment that included an Apollo team, only three times did the Apollos come in first. Their average ranking was sixth out of eight.

Other researchers have confirmed the "curvilinear" aspect of adding stars to a team (i.e., that more is not necessarily better). In one recent paper, entitled "Too Many Cooks Spoil the Broth," the authors demonstrate that although adding high-performing individuals initially increases group effectiveness, it quickly becomes a process of diminishing returns.[21]

The bottom line is that the power of teams can't be overestimated. Effective teams easily outperform individual stars. But for teams to be effective, they need the benefit of great design and smart processes. For example, fostering diversity is a proven way to enhance team effectiveness. Jack Welch once observed to me that our natural tendency is to pick people simply to "have more hands" for a particular task—in other words, to accomplish the task *my way*. But leveraging an individual is not the main point of a team. People need to complement their own ideas and skills, which in turn means that they have to have highly developed collaborative skills.

In some cases, you may want to hire a (small) team, rather than an individual. Earlier in this chapter, I referred to a *Harvard Business Review* study of 20 GE graduates who went on to become CEOs of other companies.[22] The authors concluded that one of the key sources of value to companies is what they called "relationship human capital." In other words, a manager's effectiveness stems in large part from established relationships with other team members or colleagues. Managers who *moved with selected colleagues* from Job #1 to Job #2 consistently performed better at Job #2, because they brought with them their network of effective relationships and social capital.

The final reason why it is very important to define what you are looking for with a team perspective in mind is that, in many cases, you simply can't find Superman, Batman, and Spiderman (or their female counterparts!) all in the same individual. Looking at the team can help you solve important leadership and managerial challenges that you can't solve just with one key individual, no matter how great that individual.

Putting It All Together

We have covered a lot of ground in this chapter. Figure 5.10 pulls together much of what we've talked about in a reasonably simple framework:

- First, when making a people decision, *never compromise on values*.
- Second, IQ is indeed important, since some of the basic cognitive competencies measured by IQ tests (such as memory and deductive reasoning) are prerequisites for performing at a (barely) acceptable level in most jobs.

- Third, EI-based competencies are absolutely essential for success in the contemporary world of work, and are particularly essential for success in senior managerial and leadership positions.

- Finally, when hiring at the lower levels of the organizational pyramid, always look at *potential*, in addition to near-term job readiness. By hiring individuals with high potential, you most likely will be strengthening the organization for the long term.

For very senior positions, *experience* assumes more importance. Executives typically don't have enough time to learn in highly challenging and visible positions—and the organization can't wait for them to get up to speed.

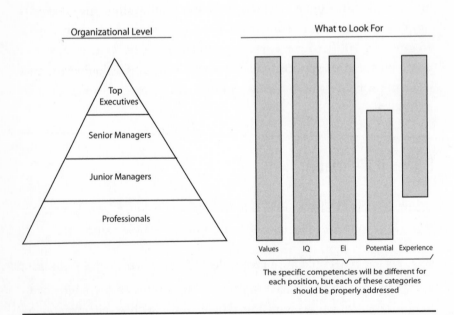

FIGURE 5.10   **What to Look For in a Candidate, Part I**

How to Get to the Answer

Bear with me for one more set of practically oriented recommendations.

Up to now, we've talked about relatively broad criteria regarding what to look for. When you go out to fill a job, of course, you need to get to a much higher level of detail. Since every situation is unique, you need to invest significant effort in understanding what is required for success in each specific job.

If you work for a large organization, chances are that studies have been made about key competencies and target levels for each specific position, especially at the lower levels. If you don't have the benefit of this type of analysis, you either have to go to experts for advice, or conduct your own analysis. I believe that the right experts can add significant value, but let me try to summarize here some recommendations for developing a sound process for figuring out what to look for.

First, establish the *priorities* for the position by answering a series of questions along the following lines:

- Two years from now, how are we going to tell whether the new manager has been successful?
- What do we expect him or her to do, and how will he or she do it in our organization?
- What initial objectives can we agree on?
- If we were to implement a short- and medium-term incentive system for this position, what key variables would matter most?

After generating this list of priorities, you should define the position's *critical incidents*. By this I mean the commonly occurring situations that the new executive will confront and must be able to master in order to be considered a strong performer. It takes time to develop such a list, but you will find that it's well worth that investment.

For example, a consumer-goods company that was hiring a new marketing manager came up with three critical incidents:

1. The new manager was certain to face sudden and unexpected price cuts by competitors, and would have to know how to react swiftly.

2. He or she would have to reposition for one product, despite the fact that its current positioning was much admired internally.

3. He or she would have to recruit, develop, and retain high-potential product managers despite increased competition for those resources.

By explicitly identifying these critical incidents, the company was able to narrow the focus of the search.

The Need to Prioritize

As you work through the problem-definition phase, a list of competencies for the job will emerge. At this point, you should avoid coming up with a list that is so exhaustive (and exhausting!) that you can't possibly find the right candidate. Avoid the trap of thinking that any single candidate will have every quality on your long list. Instead, keep in mind the competencies that are in short supply among your existing team, and look hardest for those competencies among your candidates.

One of the most successful hiring processes that I have witnessed illustrates the importance of this approach. In the 1990s, a French executive was hired to turn around a European conglomerate that was hemorrhaging money. The company had nine large business units that lacked competitive strategies. The new CEO decided to replace every business unit head *quickly*. In each case, he pinpointed the requirements of the open job, and then looked for those competencies within the organization. When they were present in one person, he promoted that person to the top job. In other cases, he moved people with some of the necessary competencies to a lieutenant's position, and hired an outsider with the "rest of the pieces" for the top job.

With each hire, the CEO appointed unexpected individuals. None were stars in their industries (many were relative unknowns), yet each brought the precise skills that were needed. The strategy paid off; over the subsequent decade, the conglomerate created enormous shareholder value.

The Need to Be Clear

As you are assembling your lists of competencies, you should make a special effort to *define them as clearly as possible.*

Competencies are useless unless they are described in behavioral terms. Consider the term *team player*, which is often listed as a competency on job descriptions. But ask three people what "team player" means, and you will get three different answers. Or consider *strategic vision*, another trait frequently put forward as a competency. To one person, the term means the ability to conduct in-depth analyses of the forces at work in an industry. To another, it means the ability to inspire and guide people in a new direction.

The solution lies in clarity. Take the case of a large industrial manufacturer that was looking for a general manager. The search team agreed that the new executive had to be a *marketer*. Some teams stop there. Fortunately, this team went further, using the job description to translate "marketer" in the following way:

> The candidate must be able to recognize an international business opportunity and create an environment that gets all the needed business units committed to the effort. He or she must be able to close the deal if needed, but to step away and recognize when to turn it over to a more qualified person closer to the deal.

Again, defining competencies in behavioral terms forces clarity.

It's All about Discipline

Above all, you have to be *disciplined* at this stage. You need to confirm the key competencies needed in each situation, and you need to establish the relative weight of each of the competencies against which both internal and external candidates will be assessed.

Let me illustrate this point with the case of a major global dairy company that a few years ago was looking for a new CEO. The position had very specific needs in terms of market knowledge, customer focus, and functional competence. It also called for key leadership competencies, including results orientation, strategic orientation, and team leadership.

Before starting the search process, the board met several times to discuss in depth the company's strategic direction.[23] This process enabled the board to identify a strategy with seven specific component parts.

The board then discussed these components with an executive search firm, to determine what overall competencies would be required for an effective implementation of the agreed-upon strategy. These competencies were weighted to reflect their relative importance, with 40 percent of the weighting going to organizational leadership, and another four competencies getting a 15 percent weighting each. Significantly, the board took what would otherwise have been broad competencies ("organizational leadership") and brought them down to specific behaviors (the CEO had to be able to relate well to the more than 10,000 local dairy farmers who collectively owned the company).

A small task force, consisting of members from both the client and the search firm, then determined the *specific leadership capabilities* that were most relevant to moving the organization forward in the near and medium term. This allowed the recruiters to ask the candidates very specific screening questions: For example, had they reshaped the culture of a substantial organization around a new vision? Had they led an organization through a period of substantial growth, including the integration of acquisitions?

Knowing what to look for is important because
- Some characteristics are better predictors of success.
- You need to focus your efforts.
- You will avoid discrimination.
- You will be faced with difficult tradeoffs among real candidates.

All of the following characteristics are important
- IQ (although most candidates for senior positions already have high levels)
- Relevant experience, particularly for senior positions
- Emotional intelligence–based competencies, particularly for senior positions
- Potential, particularly for junior to middle-management levels
- Values, in all cases

A highly disciplined process must be followed
- Confirming the managerial priorities
- Identifying the key competencies required
- Clearly defining them in behavioral terms
- Agreeing on the required levels and relative weight for each key competence

---

FIGURE 5.11 What to Look For in a Candidate, Part II

I should say that this search began with relatively low expectations, in part because of an array of business challenges and political obstacles that were plaguing the business at the time. But a highly disciplined search process, made possible by an absolutely clear sense of what the organization was looking for, turned a potential disaster into a highly positive learning experience for the company and its leaders.

Figure 5.11 summarizes the key points covered in this chapter.

■ ■ ■

Once you have properly defined what to look for, the next step is to figure out where to look for candidates, both inside and out. This is the subject of our next chapter.

CHAPTER SIX

Where to Look:
Inside and Out

I will never forget the first assignment I worked on after becoming an executive search consultant.

I had recently completed my "Grand Tour" of interviews with key people in our firm, Egon Zehnder International (EZI), who were about to become my colleagues. One thing that had become crystal clear, in the course of those interviews, was that if I hoped to be successful in my career, I would need to *consistently help our clients hire successfully.*

Maybe that sounds self-evident for an executive search firm. Actually, it wasn't. What they were telling me, in so many words, was that I was *not* going to be judged primarily on the basis of my productivity, or based on my financial contribution to the firm. Instead, I would be judged primarily on the value added to our clients. If I helped them hire highly successful candidates who went on to make a very significant contribution to their organizations, stay with them, and eventually take on larger responsibilities, my own success would be assured.

After getting some initial training in our Madrid office, I moved back to Buenos Aires, where EZI's practice was just getting off the ground. I was only 30 years old. I had left my native country five years earlier, and by this point, I had almost no business connections. The office was new, so there was no research department. We had no databases, and of course in those days there were no online databases, search engines, or other Internet-based resources.

So that was the backdrop for my first assignment, which was to locate a marketing and sales manager for Quilmes. This was the core beer brand of Quinsa, the highly successful beverage company I described in Chapter 2.

At that point in time, the company was *not* so successful. In fact, it was barely breaking even, which had occasioned a lot of soul-searching. One result of this self-scrutiny was that Quinsa's leaders had decided that the division needed to become far better at marketing and selling its products. This called for more effective segmenting and targeting of key markets, new product development, improved advertising, and much better sales force management. All of this meant in turn that the new manager would need to build a much more professional team.

I remember sitting at my desk, once the assignment had been confirmed, wrestling with two problems:

1. Figuring out where to look for candidates
2. Figuring out when to *stop* looking

Of course, I was fully motivated to do the best possible job. But I felt extremely insecure, because I was painfully aware there was a whole universe out there about which I knew absolutely nothing. How could I know that the candidates whom I would identify would be the best ones in terms of competence for the job, and that there were none better? How could I know whether, if competent, their motivation and compensation expectations were right for our client? What was the best way to look for them: investigating companies, using directories, sourcing with relevant people who might have seen them in action? How many would I have to look at to make sure that those I presented to our client were the absolute best?

These are the kinds of questions that I want to explore in this chapter. (I'll return to the outcome of the Quinsa search later.) And by the way: These questions apply to the most consequential decisions in our life, as illustrated in the sidebar, "A Sideways Glance: How to Find Your Mate."[1]

A Sideways Glance: How to Find Your Mate

Sometimes the best way to tackle a difficult challenge is to look at it obliquely. So before looking directly at the challenge of where to look for limited talent, let's look at the seemingly unrelated issue of how to find your mate. Are there any lessons we can take out of the personal realm into the business realm?

I have always enjoyed the story of Charles Darwin's search for a spouse. One sleepless night, he was sitting at his desk, wondering whether he should get married. In his disciplined way, he started writing down the pros and cons of getting married—the pros in one column, and the cons in the other. He worked at this intermittently, over the course of several days. Gradually, the pros column outgrew the cons column, and the gap continued to widen. So Darwin decided to get married. (In the terminology of Chapter 4, he had figured out that a change was needed.)

But *whom* could he marry? He had been in love with Fanny Owen, but his long trip on the *H.M.S. Beagle* had eliminated that possibility. What should he do? Should he ask his colleagues for introductions? Ask his sisters? Visit his cousins, and impose on them for suitable introductions?

Finally, his thoughts turned to his cousin Emma. She had always been a great backer of him in all of his adventures, and he realized that—although he had never considered her as a potential wife—she was the perfect fit. And so, without generating any alternatives, Darwin married his cousin Emma. As it turned out, they had a very happy marriage and a wonderful family, and Emma proved an invaluable source of support for her husband's outstanding scientific contributions.

Now consider the case of the renowned astronomer Johannes Kepler, whose first wife died of cholera in Prague in 1611. The marriage had been an arranged one, and was not particularly happy. After the requisite period of mourning, Kepler decided to systematically investigate the possibility of a second marriage. He scrutinized 11 eligible women for a period of *two years*, at the end of which his friends persuaded him to choose Candidate #4, who was a woman of high status who commanded a tempting dowry. But Candidate #4 had her pride, and she rejected Kepler for having kept her waiting too long.

(Continued)

A Sideways Glance: How to Find Your Mate *(Continued)*

This was good news disguised as bad: Kepler was now free to settle on his preferred alternative, who promptly accepted him. Together, the happy couple raised seven children, while Kepler laid the foundations for Newton's Universal Law of Gravitation.

Darwin and Kepler illustrate *search strategies*, whereby one chooses an alternative among many candidates who appear in random order, drawn from a population that is largely unknown ahead of time. The question of how hard to work to expand the universe of possible options, rather than getting more information about the known candidates, becomes central. So does the need to focus on real criteria for success, rather than pure emotion, or the pressures exerted by well-meaning acquaintances. So does the need to *act quickly*. If you don't, Candidate #4 may reject your offer, which may or may not be a good thing!

In recent years, researchers have focused on ways to think about problems like this. Statisticians have explored the number of options you need to investigate to maximize your chances of finding "the best." Economists have developed sophisticated models of job searches. And, of course, biologists have investigated the way in which members of different species carry out their search for a mate.

In business, as in marriage, the question becomes, How *do* you find your "mate"? How do you identify the best potential candidates—effectively and efficiently?

Generating candidates is critically important, because it sets the outside limits on people decisions. You can't choose an alternative you are unaware of, and you can't choose an alternative better than the best of those who are put before you.

In a perfect world, an organization would choose a candidate from a large pool of highly qualified individuals. In the real world, many selection committees have at best one candidate who is qualified. (Some have none!) Indeed, research from the Center for Creative Leadership has shown that nearly a quarter of the time (one in four cases!) the executive selected for the position was the only candidate considered.[2]

Generating candidates will become even more critical in the future, given demographic realities. Demand will continue to grow, even as the number of executives in the right age range continues to decline sharply. For example, the number of 35- to 44-year-olds in the United States peaked in year 2000, and will have declined by 15 percent by 2015. Meanwhile, assuming an average 3 percent yearly growth rate, the U.S. economy will have grown by 56 percent. In other words, the supply of executives relative to the size of the economy in 2015 will be *half* of what it was in 2000!

And that is just the quantitative side of the challenge. On the qualitative side, we will need far more sophisticated executives—individuals with global perspective, technological literacy, entrepreneurial traits, and the ability to work in increasingly complex organizations. Meanwhile, large companies increasingly will be competing with small and medium-sized ones, which in many cases provide opportunities for having impact and creating wealth that few large firms can match.[3]

But we don't have to look a decade or more out to see evidence of these problems. As indicated in Chapter 2, they're already with us. Recently, I ran across some numbers in a *Harper's* "Index" that indicated that 40 percent of CEO vacancies in the United States are currently being filled from outside the company, at an average cost of about $2 million, in the wake of which there was a one-in-two chance that the CEO would quit or be fired within 18 months!

Insiders or Outsiders?

An obvious first question is, Should you look inside the organization, or outside? Most organizations believe they are better off looking inside first, and going outside only after exhausting all the internal possibilities.

Most of them are wrong.

At EZI, we always argue in favor of a broader search.[4] Based on our experience across more than four decades, when an executive search extends to both internal and external candidates, a full 95 *percent* are filled through outside hires rather than internal promotions. Yes, it's true that this figure is somewhat skewed, since when clients call us to conduct a far-ranging search, they usually believe that their internal alternatives are limited. But the fact that the vast majority of broad searches ultimately settle on external candidates argues strongly that generating the broadest pool of qualified candidates adds value.

When is it better to go for outsiders versus insiders? As mentioned, a study by Rakesh Khurana and Nitin Nohria speaks directly to this question. Looking at CEO turnover in 200 organizations over a 15-year period, they argue that the type of candidate a firm hires (internal or external) has clear consequences for subsequent organizational performance, independent of other organizational changes. Promoting an insider, according to Khurana and Nohria, doesn't have a significant impact on a company's performance, regardless of whether that promotion was the result of a natural succession or a forced turnover.

Outsiders, by contrast, add great value when the predecessor was fired and change is needed. They tend to *destroy* significant value, however, in the case of a "natural succession" (i.e., when the predecessor simply retired and there is no perceived need for major changes). The performance impact of the new outsider CEOs is very strong in both cases, representing an average increase or decrease in industry-adjusted annual operating returns of some five percentage points. For many companies, this change would mean either doubling their profitability (when the performance impact was positive) or completely wiping away their profits. The conclusions from that study are represented in Figure 6.1.[5]

To improve a company's performance, in other words, an outsider should be brought in following a forced departure. Khurana and Nohria cite Lou Gerstner at IBM as a prime example. "Outsiders have the skills and capabilities to make good on the change mandate," as they put it, "while lacking the 'baggage' that tends to cripple insiders." But beware of moon-dropping an outsider into a successful setting, which—the researchers concluded—precipitates an average 6 percent drop in performance.[6]

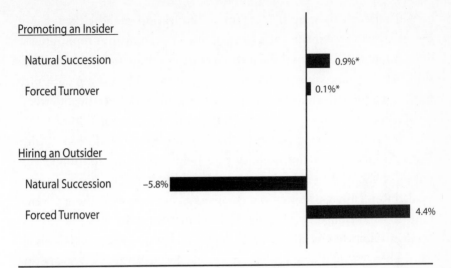

Promoting an Insider

Natural Succession — 0.9%*

Forced Turnover — 0.1%*

Hiring an Outsider

Natural Succession — −5.8%

Forced Turnover — 4.4%

FIGURE 6.1 Performance Impact of CEO Turnover
Change in Industry-Adjusted Operating Returns, Percentage Points
*Changes for insiders were not statistically significant.
Source: "The Performance Impact of New CEOs," *MIT Sloan Management Review*, Winter 2001.

The Problem with Averages

So the answer is simple, right? You should promote an internal candidate following a natural succession, and go outside when the previous incumbent was fired, right?

Not exactly; Khurana's and Nohria's study reports the *average* conclusion. But as I was taught in Statistics 101, if you're unlucky enough, you can manage to drown in a pond that is only 20 inches deep, *on average.*

When Robert A. Iger was promoted from president to CEO of the Walt Disney Company on March 13, 2005, replacing the embattled Michael Eisner, many observers questioned the decision to promote the Number 2 person when the Number 1 person was all but forced from office. Most experts agreed that to succeed, Iger would have to define and deliver on his own vision—in other words, act like an outsider.[7]

That's exactly what he did. First, in a clear signal, he sacked one of Eisner's top lieutenants.[8] Then he reassigned the company's top strategist and announced plans to disband the company's strategic planning division. At the same time, he pledged to push decision-making authority back down into the individual business units, thereby reversing the trend toward centralization that had taken hold in Eisner's reign.

Iger also began rebuilding the all-important relationships with Pixar Animation Studios, a move that helped bring several influential critics of the company back into the fold. (In the same spirit, he persuaded Roy Disney to rejoin the company's board, and serve as a consultant to the company.) He fired the Eisner-installed leaders of the Muppets Holding Company, again signaling that a new day had dawned.

Then the *real* changes began. In January 2006, the company announced that it was acquiring Pixar for US$7.4 billion. This led to Pixar's John Lasseter being named Chief Creative Officer of both the Disney/Pixar animation studios and Walt Disney Imagineering (the division that designs theme-park attractions). It also made Pixar's former owner, Steve Jobs, Disney's top shareholder, and gave him a seat on Disney's board of directors. By means of this one acquisition, in other words, Iger had thrown his net over both a world-class creative talent and a technological genius.

The jury is still out on Iger and the new Disney, of course. But my point is that despite Iger's insider status, he has been acting as an outsider. So, despite the conclusions based on averages, it's clear that some insiders can add great value, even if the predecessor has been shoved aside and major change is called for. Likewise, the right outsider sometimes can add great value to a company, even if the predecessor left with his or her head high and no major change seems to be needed. The trick is to find the best potential candidate for each situation, *considering both insiders and outsiders.*

Looking beyond the average-based conclusions of Khurana and Nohria, yet still drawing on their unique data, we can look at the *range* of performance consequences of CEO turnover. This is represented in Figure 6.2, where a probabilistic range has been constructed by considering

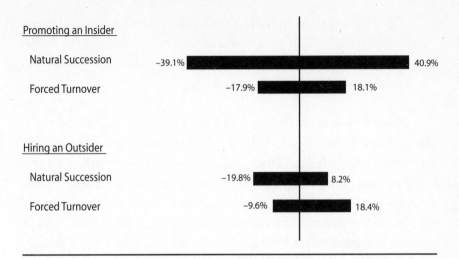

FIGURE 6.2   Range of Performance Impact of CEO Turnover
Change in Industry-Adjusted Operating Returns, Percentage Points
Source: Rakesh Khurana and Nitin Nohria, "The Performance Consequences of CEO Turnover" (March 15, 2000). http://ssm.com/abstract-219129. Author analysis.

a low value of two standard deviations below the average, and a high of two standard deviations above.

Figure 6.2 suggests several key conclusions:

- When things were going well, the promotion of insiders led to a huge spread in terms of performance impact, with some outstanding successes and some formidable failures. So you should be particularly careful, when things are going well, to look at the *future*, and make sure that the person you are promoting has the necessary capabilities.

- While the range of performance impact was also very large in the case of hiring outsiders, with the potential both to add and to destroy significant value, the spread of these ranges was lower. This suggests to me that these outsiders were more carefully scrutinized.

- Looking at these spreads, it's clear that there's no hard-and-fast rule about insiders versus outsiders. In some companies and situations, the best insider is better than any outsider; in others, the right outsider is the best choice.

Nevertheless, two generalizations can be made. First, large companies that are highly skilled at developing internal people, such as GE, will quite likely have the best candidates within, thereby achieving the highest potential values in Figure 6.2. But even these companies, when they venture into completely new businesses, should consider going outside, for all the reasons discussed in Chapter 5. And being large doesn't necessarily translate into having the right talent. When Larry Bossidy left GE to take over Allied Signal, he discovered that—at least in the early part of his tenure—hiring internally was extremely difficult. Only after he had built up a base of talent could he start looking inside first.

The second generalization comes in part from research conducted by the Center for Creative Leadership on executive selections. Their conclusion has been that *it is always better to consider both internal and external candidates for a search.* Specifically, they found that the candidate pools of companies whose internal selection proved successful contained more external candidates than did the candidate pools of companies whose internal selection did not succeed. The findings were similar for companies who selected successful external candidates: Their candidate pools contained more internal candidates than those of companies who selected an unsuccessful external candidate.

In summary, particularly for critical people decisions, you need a well-balanced pool of candidates so that the best one can be identified and selected, regardless of whether he or she is internal or external.[9]

The Innovation Parallel

I've thought a lot about why companies underinvest so significantly in the generation of potential candidates, when the consequences of making the wrong decision can be so devastating and the rewards for making the right decision so huge.

The first part of the answer, I think, is that when things are going well, we humans are naturally risk-averse. Given the difficulty of assessing candidates, we prefer to stay with the "devil we know." On the other hand, when things are going badly, we often lack the emotional strength (or the time!) to continue looking for alternatives. We look to *close fast*, settling for whatever candidates we may have at hand. But by so doing, we increase our failure rates and give up enormous upside potential.

The field of innovation offers a very relevant analogy. The world's top 1,000 corporate spenders on research and development (R&D) invested something like $400 billion on R&D in 2004. Innovation spending has been growing 6.5 percent per year since 1999 (or a whopping 11 percent annually, if measured from 2002).[10]

These may sound like big numbers, even "large enough" numbers. Nevertheless, many analysts believe that companies are still significantly underspending when it comes to innovation. For example, Charles I. Jones of Stanford University and John C. Williams of the Federal Reserve Bank of San Francisco have argued that the *right* level of R&D spending by U.S. companies to ensure consistent levels of growth is more than *four* times the current level.[11]

Once again, as in the case of generating candidates for key posts, we can understand intellectually that we should be doing more and still not do anything about that deficit. Companies that are thriving, based on past investments in innovation, often decide to harvest some of that prior investment. Companies that are starved for new products often fail to come up with the funds to invest in their future.

There's another interesting overlap between innovation and people choices: the inside/outside choice. It doesn't matter how much you spend on innovation if you don't put your money in the right places, and sometimes the right places are outside the company. In his best-selling book, *Open Innovation*, my Stanford classmate Henry Chesbrough makes a strong case for the notion that going outside is a key to boosting return on your innovation dollars.[12]

While there has been only limited research about the profitability impact of going outside for innovation opportunities, some emerging evidence suggests strongly that more open innovation practices lead to better performance. A recent study on innovation performance in U.K. manufacturing firms, for example, underscored the potential profitability of going outside to generate candidates for innovation investments.[13]

Going outside to generate candidates for leadership positions holds the same potential. The challenge lies in generating candidates, benchmarking internal and external candidates, and knowing when to stop looking.

The Need to Benchmark

As we saw in Chapter 2, the "performance spread" between a good and bad manager grows exponentially with the complexity of the job. So the difference between a typical manager and an outstanding performer, especially in high-level positions, should never be underestimated. By logical extension, a company's efforts to fill senior positions should also increase exponentially with the seniority and complexity of the job.

One aspect of those efforts is *benchmarking*. Who's the best out there, and how do our candidates stack up against that outstanding individual?

Let's look at a real-life example. When a U.S. computer hardware company set out to hire a country manager in Asia, it first identified all CEOs, COOs, and other C-level positions in relevant target companies in the region, including similar hardware vendors, relevant software and service providers, suppliers, and even firms from distantly related sectors, such as the telecommunications industry. Preliminary reference checking on every single name (conducted by a search firm) helped reduce that initial long list by about 90 percent. In addition, a second list of Asians with relevant backgrounds working in other regions, mainly in America and Europe, was systematically investigated. A third list of former executives of all the target companies was also generated. Finally, a fourth list included executives from other sectors, such as consumer and durable goods, who had outstanding credentials on the key competencies needed for the position, and seemed to represent a good cultural fit with the company and the country.

The hiring team, which included the regional VP for Asia together with the corporate HR director, then boiled down the aggregated lists of more than 100 potential candidates to a dozen names. Those 12 individuals were then interviewed, and compared to the "best-in-show" managers that the benchmarking exercise had identified.

As a second example, the global dairy company described in Chapter 5 also did a thorough job of benchmarking the candidates. In that case, it was clear—once the competencies and desired target levels were confirmed—that a significant external search effort was needed, identifying potential candidates on a global basis. The hiring team did this with the help of an executive search firm, which identified and assessed candidates all around the world. The external collaboration provided unique access to, and insight into, dozens of potential candidates from several different countries, while still fully preserving the confidentiality of the process.

The team used a simple yet effective benchmarking process, which weighted the five competencies identified as relevant, and then assessed each individual against each competency on a scale of 1 to 10. (Given that the search firm in question often calibrated candidates globally, the chance of "unequal ratings" across countries was minimized.) The total weighted score was then calculated, and complemented by qualitative descriptions of key strengths and issues for each candidate, external and internal.

Good benchmarking of candidates requires a clear profile of the best potential external candidates, but it also requires an objective, in-depth look at internal alternatives. Consider the case of an international software company that still employed its founders. The company used an executive search firm to find an external CEO, a senior executive from a major technology firm, who promptly recruited several other executives from that same firm. But the new team of people could not adapt to the existing culture, and eventually, all of them were fired.

A subsequent search identified one of the internal senior managers (who had previously been overlooked) as a strong candidate. A comparison assessment of that individual with the top two external people revealed clearly that the internal person was the strongest for the job, in part because it was clear that maintaining the company's culture (and stability) were prime considerations.

When to Stop Looking

Now let's return to my first assignment in Buenos Aires, which had me looking for a new marketing and sales manager for Quilmes, Quinsa's leading beer brand.

How many candidates did I have to generate before I could feel sure that I would be presenting the best possible individuals to the client? I decided to find and investigate some 100 candidates, as I did for most of the assignments that I worked on during my first years as an executive search consultant. (Don't ask me where that number came from. I guess I thought that 10 was too low, and 1,000 an impossibility.)

Decision-making experts always advise that you not box yourself in with limited alternatives.[14] Academics studying CEO searches have concluded that as a rule, boards should define their candidate pool much more broadly.[15] So more is better. But again: How do you know when to stop looking?

One answer to this question originally came from statisticians working on the "dowry problem," in which a sultan wishes to test the wisdom of his chief advisor, who happens to be seeking a wife. The sultan arranges to have 100 women from the kingdom brought in front of the advisor successively. The advisor has to choose the woman with the highest dowry. He can, of course, ask each woman about her dowry.

Whenever he sees a woman, he has to make a choice of either marrying her or passing, but *he cannot go back to any woman he has seen before*. If he chooses the woman with the highest dowry, he gets to marry her and retain his position as chief advisor of the sultan. If he fails, he will be killed.

Statisticians have demonstrated that in such a situation, the best strategy is the "37 Percent Rule." The advisor should look at the first 37 women, letting each one pass, but remembering the highest dowry from that set, which we shall call "H." Then, starting with the 38th woman, he should select the first one with a dowry greater than H. This 37 Percent Rule is the best that the advisor can follow to maximize the probability of keeping his head.

But the 37 Percent Rule has obvious limitations. First, in order to make your final choice, you would need to interview at least 38 women (37 + 1) on a base of 100, and most likely, many more. And what if your base is 1,000 candidates, rather than 100? Do you have time to investigate (a minimum of) 371 candidates?

Some researchers have looked into this problem under the rubric of "fast and frugal decision making," trying to come up with ways to achieve better results with a much smaller sample. One group, working on the principle of "less is more," found that much simpler rules—such as "try a dozen," which means analyzing only 12 candidates before starting to compare the succeeding candidates with the former maximum—are not only much more economical (in terms of the number of candidates analyzed), but also more powerful.[16] No, this rule would not maximize the probability of finding the absolute best candidate, but it would be efficient, and it would result in the *highest expected candidate value*, while at the same time reducing the chances of ending up with a poor candidate. Notably, "trying a dozen" works not only for a population of 100 candidates, but even for populations of several thousands.

While this finding can seem intriguing, it is not so surprising when looking at statistics of extreme values. If you take a random sample from a normal distribution, the expected value of the maximum will grow with the sample size. Once your sample size is large enough, however, the expected value of the maximum won't grow significantly with larger samples. If you consider a standardized normal distribution (which has a mean of 0 and a standard deviation equal to 1), and you take a sample of size 1, by definition the expected value will be 0. With increased sample sizes, one can calculate the expected value of the *maximum* of the sample. If we were to take a very large sample, the maximum would quite likely be a number of 2 or slightly higher (a number of 2 by definition would be 2 standard deviations above the mean, which in a normal distribution would happen with low probability).

Figure 6.3 shows the expected value of the maximum of such distri-

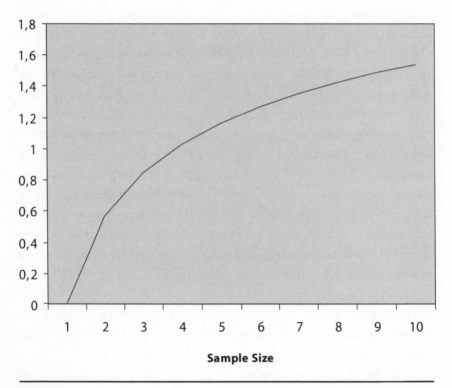

FIGURE 6.3   Expected Value of the Maximum of a Standardized Normal Distribution

bution according to the sample size. As you can see from this figure, a sample of size 10 would already produce an expected value close to 1.6, not that far away from a practical maximum of 2. This gives you a hint about why "trying a dozen" can work even when you are sampling candidates from a very large population.

But What about *Their* Choices?

Maybe you're concluding that looking at 12 candidates before setting your aspiration level is enough. Unfortunately, it's not that simple, because we are dealing with mutual choices. In other words, *the person you pick also needs to pick you.*

If only one in five candidates is likely to be interested in the job you are offering, the "try a dozen" rule implies looking at 60 candidates, rather than 12, in order to set your aspiration level. On the mating front, this challenge of mutual choice has been analyzed by the ABC Research Group.[17] As it turns out, the optimal strategy actually requires that you check some 20 individuals before setting your aspiration level.

There is a caveat, however. Staying on the mating front, you need to estimate your own attractiveness by using two kinds of feedback from members of the opposite sex: offers and refusals. In other words, when someone you consider very attractive proposes to you, you can raise your level of aspiration. At the same time, when someone whom you consider less than ideal refuses your offer, you should lower your level of aspiration. After a period of "adolescence" of some 20 interactions, which you use to gain feedback on the attractiveness of your offer, you should be in a position to choose and attract one of the best potential mates without getting exhausted in the process!

Translated back into hiring terms, this means that you don't need to look for 100 candidates, but rather, something closer to 20, *if* you search intelligently *and* you learn from the market feedback.

Finding Internal Candidates

Think back to our two marriageable scientists: Kepler and Darwin. Kepler's successful second marriage was a result of his systematic investigation of 11 external choices—a two-year effort, with lots of bumps along the way. Meanwhile, Darwin simply picked an "internal candidate" (Cousin Emma) and was also very happy with his choice, which also had the great benefit of being very efficient. Based on this small sample set, you might conclude that the best candidate may be found in-house. And in many cases, you'd be right. Even while you're conducting a benchmarking to help you compare your alternatives, you should definitely invest significant time and effort in identifying potential internal candidates.

Unfortunately, most companies either don't have proper succession plans or don't use them when the crunch comes. As mentioned, according to the Center for Creative Leadership, succession plans are the *least* frequent source of candidate information in executive selection, used in only 18 percent of the cases.[18]

What do you do the other 82 percent of the time? One answer is peer reviews, which were used in 52 percent of these cases. In fact, peer references can be extremely useful. When former GE CEO Reginald Jones asked key executives who should replace him should he get killed in an airplane accident, the most frequent answer was Jack Welch—not a bad choice!

Psychologist Allen Kraut has been studying the career paths of middle-management executives at a Fortune 100 firm. Based on peer nominations from managers in an executive training program, of those identified in the top 30 percent of their group as having high executive potential, 14 percent rose to become corporate officers, compared with 2 percent out of the bottom 70 percent. In other words, says Kraut, "people ranked by their peers in the top 30 percent were 7 times more likely to advance to top corporate offices."[19]

What else can you do, if you have no proper succession plans in place? In the longer term, you can (and probably *should*) conduct a formal assessment of internal candidates, either focusing on likely potential candidates for a specific position, or with a broader focus if you are growing significantly. Finally, if your organization is large enough, you should seriously consider building up an inventory of competencies of your employees worldwide.

Over the last few years, we have helped one of our clients (a leading global supplier of heavy machinery) build an inventory of competencies, supported by an on-line HR tool that they developed to monitor and track competencies on all employees worldwide. One of their objectives, they told us candidly, was to reduce the amount of outside searching they needed to do by identifying strong internal candidates who were trapped in organizational silos. (By the way, we strongly endorsed that effort!)

Their software runs worldwide on a single server. All of the company's HR professionals in some 50 countries have access to it, and use it heavily. It is their central record of today's talent, and it is also used to track changes over time. All appraisals, either special management appraisals or yearly managerial assessments, including assessments of competencies, are entered into it. So if you, as an HR professional, are seeking a person for a particular role, you can search according to multiple criteria: education, experience at the company, special training, and personal characteristics and competencies. For this company, screening candidates using highly sophisticated competency scales has significantly reduced the need to go outside due to internal ignorance or departmental selfishness, while at the same time dramatically improving the success rate of internal promotions.

How People Find Jobs

As Alfred Marshall once observed, analyzing a market from only one side is like trying to cut with half a pair of scissors. While employers are looking for people, people are looking for jobs. Their behaviors certainly have to be considered, as we attempt to match people to jobs.

Mark Granovetter's classic study from the early 1970s of how 282 men in Newton, Massachusetts found their jobs was one of the first to document these behaviors in practice.[20] Granovetter analyzed a sample of professional, technical, and managerial workers who were looking for a job, and specifically focused on the strategies they used. The first group included what he called "formal means," like advertisements, public and private employment agencies (including executive search services), interviews and placements sponsored by universities or professional associations, and placement committees in certain professions. (While they didn't exist at that time, Internet advertisements and web-based services would also fall into this category.) The defining characteristics of Granovetter's formal means were that the job seeker used the services of some impersonal intermediary between himself and prospective employers.

The second basic strategy of job-hunting involved "personal contacts." In other words, there was someone known personally to the job-seeker—an individual with whom he originally became acquainted in some context unrelated to the job search—who either told him about the job or recommended him to someone inside the organization who then contacted him.

The third basic way in which people pursued jobs was through "direct application," meaning that they wrote directly to an organization without using a formal or personal intermediary, and without having heard about a *specific* opening from a personal contact. (Direct application through a company's web site would also fall into this last category.)

Granovetter found that *personal contacts were the predominant method of finding out about jobs*, used by almost 56 percent of the respondents. Job-seekers preferred this approach, believing that they got and gave better information using this strategy. Based on observations from my professional experience, most employers also prefer to work through personal contacts.

In addition to being the preferred method, Granovetter reported, *personal contacts were the most effective way to find a new job.* Those using personal contacts were the most likely to say that they were "very satisfied" with their job, and jobs found through personal contacts also tended to be the most highly paid. Work found through personal contacts also was most frequently associated with a newly created position, which is typically much more attractive, since it tends to involve tailoring the job to the needs, preferences, and abilities of the first incumbent. Likewise, "stayers" were more likely to have been recruited through personal contacts than "movers."

In summary, Granovetter (and later generations of researchers) found overwhelming evidence that the use of personal contacts resulted in better placements than any other strategy used by job-seekers.

The Strength of Weak Ties

What motivated Granovetter to conduct this study? In part, it was his informal observation that even when he knew a great deal about a person's background (his or her family, IQ, educational attainment, and occupation), he still couldn't predict that person's income particularly well. The enormous variations in income that he observed led him to a brilliant hypothesis: that having the right contact in the right place at the right time might be linked to subsequent income levels. Ultimately, his research substantiated this hypothesis.

A second fascinating finding by Granovetter was that your probability of making a major occupational change is roughly proportional to the percentage of your personal contacts who are in occupations different in a major way from your own. Infrequent contact, surprisingly, turned out to be a plus—a notion captured in a wonderful expression: "the strength of weak ties." Acquaintances from fraternal organizations, sports, recreational or hobby groups, neighborhood, college, or summer vacations could be key contacts when it came to major career changes.

The best "weak ties" shared two key attributes:

1. They were occupational, rather than social, contacts.
2. Those contacts resided in "information chains" that were very short (meaning that they either knew the job-hunter himself or herself, or they knew someone who knew that job-hunter).

Successful job-hunters, for their part, tended to share three characteristics. Those not actively searching for a job got better jobs than those who were searching actively. More surprisingly, almost half got jobs without a previous incumbent leaving. And finally, most drew heavily on past contacts and career patterns.

Speculating as to why employers and employees prefer to make use of personal contacts, Granovetter observed that personal ties yielded more *intensive* information, as opposed to more *extensive* information. Investing in extensive information is appropriate when you're shopping for standardized goods, such as a new car. But getting better intensive information is critically important when you're assessing a candidate for a job.

Finding External Candidates

Moving forward from 1974, when Granovetter's study was first published, and changing our perspective from employee to employer, we find that while some things have changed a lot, others have changed very little.[21]

The Power of the Internet

One big change over the past two decades has been the explosion of electronic recruiting, with the proliferation of electronic resumes and career web sites for online recruitment. In addition, you can post openings on a variety of Internet job boards, including general boards, industry-specific boards, government sites, diversity sites, and school job boards.

A great deal has been written about finding talent on the Internet and about making the most of your company web sites, particularly in terms of their *functionality* (what tools are provided for the user), and *engagement* (ways to attract users to the site, in light of the overall proliferation of information). I won't summarize that material here. But one basic rule is to look for ways to bring functionality and engagement together. For example, some companies' web sites offer tools for helping visitors reconstruct their resumes, which of course can then be matched with job openings at that company or downloaded and submitted to other companies. In the cold world of web commerce, *being helpful* to people can be a real differentiator.

Building an engaging web site is clearly more art than science, but it may be a precondition for success in finding applicants in the very near future (if it isn't already).[22] That said, the web has its clear limitations. In February 2000, I attended an executive program at Harvard for leaders of professional service firms. That program was also attended by the President for the Americas of another major executive search firm. This person boasted noisily about the huge investment that his firm was making in Internet search, which he described as the wave of the future. In front of our classmates, he told me that my firm's days were numbered—that we were dinosaurs.

I confess that when I got a handle on the staggering investments that this other firm was making in the Internet, I got worried. So shortly after that, we conducted a major strategic review to figure out whether we should develop an Internet-based business. We reached two conclusions. First, we would continue to invest heavily in technology, and we would use the Internet to enhance our work. Second, we would work hard to avoid the special traps that the Internet posed.

For example, while technology enables you to turn up all kinds of information about candidates, often in a searchable form, the quality of that information is always bounded by the knowledge and honesty of the person who put it on the Web in the first place. In many cases, the job applicant posts the information himself or herself. Well, how self-aware is that person? How honest is that person?

In June 2002, I attended a follow-up program at Harvard, and once again encountered that same representative from our competitor. He confided that they had lost more than $100 million on their Internet investments—a staggering sum. Shortly afterwards, he left that firm.

The Power and Limitations of Advertising

Consider the following ad:

> Men Wanted for Hazardous Journey. Small
> wages, bitter cold, long months of complete
> darkness, constant danger, safe return doubtful.
> Honor and recognition in case of success.

The copy was written by the famed polar explorer Sir Ernest Shackleton. When it appeared in London newspapers in 1900, it provoked an enormous response. As the late Ted Levitt pointed out, the ad successfully targeted people for whom honor and recognition were key motivators:

> Its power lay not only in the novel idea of appealing to the human desire for honor and recognition, though the risks were grave and the work terrible, but also in its deadly frankness and remarkably simple execution.[23]

Almost since I was born, I've been immersed in the world of advertising, and fascinated by it. My grandfather founded one of the first advertising agencies in Argentina, and my father carried on the business. While still in elementary school, I would go with him to the office, and—as a fly on the wall—watch all kinds of creative people exercise their craft.

So I've always been impressed by the power of advertising. But when it comes to trying to find people for a job, advertising has serious limitations.

First, there is the coverage and attention issue. Shackleton had it relatively easy, back in 1900. Not so today—all day, every day, we are bombarded with information through an endless variety of media. Unless you as an advertiser make a *huge* investment, it will be very hard to get the attention of the best candidates.

Second, advertising is an impersonal contact, which requires the other party to act. Even if people notice your ad, they still have to take the initiative to contact you. If the call to arms isn't as powerful as Shackleton's (and few are!), people fail to act. They procrastinate. They get distracted.

Third is the quality issue. Most satisfied people aren't looking for a new job, and therefore aren't looking at help-wanted ads. So these ads tend to be seen by those who are either unemployed or dissatisfied with their current work. As a result, the pool of respondents is typically very large, but of very limited quality. I'm sure Shackleton faced this problem!

Fourth, and most damning, is the seniority bias. Although advertising can be useful for junior positions, it becomes highly limited when it comes to more senior positions. Companies don't want to make others aware of their openings (read "weaknesses"). Currently employed senior people don't want to run the risk of exposing themselves by responding to a blind ad.

A few years ago, I was involved in the hiring of a group of eight senior managers who would report directly to the President of the Central Bank of Argentina. I'm not exaggerating when I say that we faced a dire situation. Hyperinflation was running rampant. The country's entire economy had to be restructured. To head off a meltdown of the financial markets, the Central Bank had to dramatically expand its ability to ride herd on the nation's major banks.

These new banking jobs, in other words, would involve an enormous amount of responsibility and visibility. In theory, at least, they should have appealed to a large number of able professionals. But the public sector at that time had a very poor reputation as an employer, and no one (especially seasoned bankers) wanted to work for the government. What could we do?

For all the reasons stated above, and others, our firm *never* advertises open positions. But because regulations required the Central Bank to advertise its openings, we agreed that they would advertise extensively—not only in all major local newspapers, but also in top international publications, including the *Wall Street Journal*, the *Financial Times*, and *The Economist*. The results were that although hundreds of would-be candidates responded to the ads, we could find only *one* fully qualified candidate out of that whole lot. As it turned out, we already knew this individual and probably would have contacted him directly.

In short, advertise if you must, but don't put all your eggs in that basket—especially when it comes to filling senior positions.

Starting from Scratch

Remember my first search—for a marketing and sales manager for the Quilmes beer brand—back in Buenos Aires, more than 20 years ago? The search that I began without the benefit of contacts, databases, or the Internet? What did I do?

First I drew up a list of all beverage companies (highly relevant), food companies (pretty relevant), consumer-goods companies (less relevant). In each of those companies, I identified the likely potential candidates. Even in a small market like Argentina, this produced a list of some 60 potential candidates.

I also thought that there might be good potential candidates elsewhere, including people in advertising agencies, or "alumni" of some of those consumer-goods companies. So I started *sourcing* (our firm's buzzword for asking people about other people). Given my newness in the market, I had to start by sourcing for sources. I talked to management consultants who specialized in strategy and marketing, advertising people who had seen some of the most important and successful marketing campaigns, and executives in consumer-goods companies.

Two interesting things happened. First, I found some strong candidates who were not in *any* of the obvious places. Second, I developed lots of *qualitative* information from the sources about each of those target candidates, letting me form an idea about the qualifications and even the potential motivations of those targets, even before meeting them. As a result, I was able to come up with a list of more than 100 investigated candidates, including lots of qualitative comments about them that were starting to converge and validate each other.

Because I was just starting and wanted to make sure that I was systematic and exhaustive, I interviewed several dozens of those potential candidates. I found, to my satisfaction, that my in-person conclusions were very similar to those reached by my best sources. Again, I saw *convergence*.

At the end of the day, I brought three truly outstanding candidates to our client, presenting them with a welcome dilemma! The candidate finally hired was an individual named Richard Oxenford, who, by the way, would never have responded to an ad, because he wasn't looking for a job. Nor would he have emerged through a round-up-the-usual-suspects kind of search, because he had retired from another beverage company a few years earlier to work on his own.

To make a long story short, Oxenford was incredibly successful in his new job. He was promoted from his initial position at Quilmes to being a member of the Board of Management and manager of all the international operations of the parent company (Quinsa). He was so successful, in fact, that he made remarkable contributions not only to Quinsa, but also to global giant Pepsi, which had a close relationship with Quinsa.

With that story in mind, let's look a little more deeply into the phenomenon of sourcing.

...wer of Sourcing in a Small World

Sourcing is powerful because we live in a small world. While you may not know me personally, you may know someone who knows me. And if you're reading this book and interested in these topics, the chances are *very* good that you know someone who knows someone who knows me.

This is literally true. In 1967, social psychologist Stanley Milgram asked several people in Nebraska to try to contact an individual they didn't know: a stockbroker from Sharon, Massachusetts. The Nebraskans were instructed to send a letter to somebody whom they knew on a first-name basis, and who might know the stockbroker. If the recipients knew the stockbroker, they could send it to him directly. If they didn't, they were asked to forward it to someone they *did* know who might be closer to the target. How many steps would it take for the letter to get from the Nebraskans to the stockbroker?

You might think the answer would be in the dozens. The result, on average, was *six*. This led to the notion of the "six degrees of separation," well described in the book *Six Degrees* by Duncan J. Watts.[24]

We are connected with one another through very short chains. Assume that you have 100 friends, each of whom also has 100 friends. At one degree of separation, you would connect to 100 people. Within two degrees, you would reach 100 times 100, or 10,000 people. By three degrees you are up to 1 million, by four 100 million, by five about 10 billion people, and by six you are connected to the population of the entire planet.

You might argue that this calculation is skewed due to "clustering"; in other words, some of your friends are also your friends' friends, and so there is some redundancy. But systematic research has shown that, indeed, almost anyone in the world can be connected to almost anyone else just by six links, or fewer.

One study focused on actors, which in the U.S. comprised roughly half a million people, who had acted in more than 200,000 feature films. In this population, as it turned out, connecting any two people through co-stars who had acted together at least once required fewer than four links.[25]

Likewise, similar studies have been made on the roughly 8,000 directors who sit on the boards of the U.S. Fortune 1,000 companies. While 80 percent of these directors belong to only one board, *every individual* in the entire network of directors was actually connected to the others through a short chain of co-directors—not most of them, but *all* of them.

The point is that short chains make sourcing an extremely powerful way to effectively reach the most qualified potential candidates, while amassing valuable qualitative information. At the same time, they also make for an extremely *efficient* search.

Let's assume that you would consider a "real" candidate to be someone who (1) is in the top 10 percent of the pool, in terms of qualifications, and (2) might be persuaded to change jobs. As shown in Figure 6.4, if you approach potential candidates randomly, by definition you would have a 10 percent probability of finding a qualified candidate. If you assume, generously, that 1 in 5 (20%) could be interested in exploring a new job, the probability of finding a real candidate through a random contact growing out of "cold" research (i.e., with no inside information) is only 2 percent. In other words, if you relied on cold research, you'd need to make more than 110 contacts in order to achieve a 90 percent probability of finding at least one real candidate.

In my experience, however, a good source would produce much better candidates in terms of qualification, and also be able to indicate those who might consider a new job, even if they are still not actively seeking to make a change. If you combine conservative estimates about the expected qualification and motivation information from a good

	P (qualified)	P (interested)	P (real candidate)	Contacts Needed*
Cold Research	10%	20%	2%	>110
Sourcing	30%	50%	15%	14

FIGURE 6.4   The Efficiency of Sourcing
*Contacts needed to achieve a 90% probability of finding at least one real candidate.

source, you find (as in Figure 6.4) that you need fewer than 15 contacts in order to achieve a very high probability of finding at least one candidate, both in terms of qualification and motivation.

Sourcing is indeed efficient. In this example, it would make you *800 percent* more productive.

Getting Good at Sourcing

Who can help you source? The obvious outside contacts include suppliers, customers, agencies, trade association executives, trade journalists, and others. But in the end, sourcing is a fine art, one that is mastered only through practice and that requires creativity and strong communication and relational skills to get the most out of your sources.

While I was working on the Central Bank of Argentina search, where it proved so difficult to attract highly qualified people, I decided that managers at top auditing firms working for the financial sector would have the right qualifications. But how could I find people who might be attracted to the Central Bank job?

I knew that most of these firms had an "up-or-out" policy: Each year, a portion of their qualified professionals would not be promoted, sometimes for reasons (such as not being good at selling their services to clients) that didn't matter for the job I was trying to fill. I therefore decided to approach the managing partners of those firms directly and openly. I asked them if we could explore the possibility of hiring, as a group, colleagues who might soon be on their way out anyway.

The plan worked beautifully! The auditing firms were eager to help the Central Bank, because they cared about the stability of the country's financial system. Many of the firms welcomed the search, and soon a group of managers was hired from one of the best auditing firms in the country. Recruiting the whole group of managers to the Central Bank *at the same time* made things easier, because the professionals knew they would be working with colleagues whom they trusted.

Meanwhile, the Central Bank benefited enormously from the relationships the auditors already had with one another. The group was up and running literally within days, and they led the Central Bank through its reform with flying colors. The Argentine financial system became so strong that, shortly after that, my nation safely navigated the "Tequila Crisis" (the Mexican devaluation panic that caused investor stampedes in several countries) without any scars.

It Takes Two Phone Calls

Another of my early assignments was to look for a founding dean for a new university. The selection committee posed a key question to one of the candidates: "How are you going to approach the process of finding the professors?"

I still remember the candidate's response: "It will take me two phone calls: the first one to ask people I know whom I should call, and the second, to the person they recommend."

That person was hired and became so successful that, in just five years, that university achieved the reputation of being the best in the country in its major subjects, competing against others that had been around for more than a century. A key reason was the dean's ability to put together the very best team very rapidly, through effective sourcing.

The general strategy for sourcing is *not to think about candidates, but to think about people who may know the best candidates*. People waste too much time calling too many irrelevant candidates. It makes much more sense to drum up people who are likely to know of several high-quality candidates right off the bat.

Take the case of the CEO of a growing high-tech company in New York in the late 1990s, who was trying to hire a new head of sales. He shared with me his frustration at having run an ad in the *Wall Street Journal*, and then having scanned hundreds of resumes for almost three months, conducting about 20 interviews along the way. He didn't find a *single person* who filled the bill.

He finally ended up where he should have started: contacting knowledgeable people in his industry who could rattle off five or six candidates at a time. He spoke to a former CEO at one of his suppliers, for instance, who was now working at a consulting firm that served the industry; that source supplied four viable candidates. He had lunch with a business school professor who advised several large companies like his own on distribution matters; that source yielded another five candidates. Not only did these sources understand the CEO's company and the job he was trying to fill, but they had years of contacts. The CEO ended up hiring the one person who appeared on both sources' lists, who turned out to be very successful.

When to Do It Yourself

When conducting an executive search, should you look for candidates yourself? Or should you get help from professionals in the field?

There are many people decisions for which you *don't* need help—for example, when the pool of candidates for a job is limited and well known, and the specific need is very straightforward. In this regard, I frequently mention the case of the Washington-based think tank that was looking for an analyst of global economic trends. In that case, the organization had two very talented internal candidates for the job, and its board members were personally acquainted with a dozen or so external candidates, all of whom were scholars or members of other think tanks. In addition, the chairman had a very clear view of what was needed. To the surprise of almost no one, one of the internal candidates was quickly and successfully promoted.

Outside help also makes less sense when a company regularly conducts the same type of search, fully understanding the requirements of a job and the competencies of the person who will represent the best fit.

This is often the case when it comes to highly technical positions, for which specialized know-how and expertise are key. Those "hard" competencies are typically easier to evaluate than "soft" managerial and leadership abilities and, as a result, this circumstance doesn't usually argue for bringing in the outside experts.

At lower levels in the organization, the consequences of an error are less serious, and mistakes can be corrected more easily. And in light of the high frequency of hiring at lower levels, it may be much more cost-effective to build dedicated internal resources rather than constantly going outside for help.

When to Get Professional Help

There *are* situations that present a compelling case for calling in external advisors, including professional search firms. The first is when a company is hiring for very high-level positions that will have great impact on the bottom line. As I explained earlier, when it comes to complex positions, a top performer will be *orders of magnitude* better than an average performer. A senior position entails far more power, and comprises a much broader range of resources and decisions, so the impact of that executive will be much higher in absolute terms. In these situations, if an executive search firm finds a candidate who generates only 1 percent greater profits than the alternative candidate would have generated, the search will pay for itself many times over.

Outside help also makes sense in the case of new jobs created, for example, by diversifications, new markets, joint ventures, or technical breakthroughs. In such situations, organizations may not be familiar with the key competencies required for the open position, and most likely will have only a limited knowledge about potential candidates and how to evaluate them.

Professional firms can also add value when a company wants to cast its net widely in its search for a new executive. This is frequently the case when international searches are conducted, or when, in smaller

Knowing where to look is important because
- Generating candidates sets the upper limit for people decisions.
- Research shows that more candidates should be considered.
- Demographic and economic trends are reducing the relative supply of qualified candidates.

Some of the challenges include
- Where to look: inside and out.
- How many to consider and when to stop.
- Dealing with the problem of mutual choices.

Where to look: inside and out
- Typically, outsiders are recommended when entering new fields or dealing with new problems or major change.
- However, the best practice is to always consider a wide pool that includes both insiders and outsiders.

Knowing when to stop
- The key is to obtain a benchmark of the best potential candidates.
- Targeting the right population, considering some 20 candidates should produce at least one highly qualified alternative.

How to look for candidates
- Large companies should continually invest in succession plans and inventories of talent and key competencies.
- In addition, special internal and external efforts should be made for specific needs, particularly at the top.
- Despite the proliferation of advertising options and the promise of the Internet, direct contacts continue to be extremely powerful.
- Clever sourcing is both an extremely effective and efficient way to identify highly qualified real candidates.
- In many cases, you can generate most candidates on your own.
- Professional help can be useful for senior positions, new jobs, when you need to cast a wide net, or for confidentiality reasons.

FIGURE 6.5   Where to Look: Inside and Out

economies, one is forced to look beyond a specific industry in order to get the right caliber of candidates.

Finally, and reinforcing all of the above benefits, a search firm can conduct external searches in a highly confidential way. The guarantee of confidentiality means that conversations can start that would not otherwise get started, and can continue in productive directions. As Rakesh Khurana has argued, in senior positions executive search firms can buffer high-status actors who otherwise would not engage in an external search. Since both parties have a strong interest in ensuring confidentiality, an intermediary can add great value, minimizing risks for both parties and increasing the probability of a successful outcome.[26]

Figure 6.5 summarizes the key points covered in this chapter.

■ ■ ■

Once you have generated enough potential candidates, you next have to assess them thoroughly to make sure that, for your specific needs, they are as good as they look. This is the subject of our next chapter.

CHAPTER SEVEN

How to Appraise People

It was June 1994, and, despite it being summer by the calendar, it was snowing in the Swiss Alps.

Eight years after joining Egon Zehnder International (EZI), I was meeting with Dan Meiland, who was then our firm's CEO. (He later became our second chairman, succeeding our founder.) We were high up in the Engadine Valley, in Pontresina, on the eve of one of our firm conferences, which would be attended by all of our colleagues worldwide.

Dan surprised me by asking me to head up our firm's global professional development activities. My reaction was one of both enthusiasm and anxiety. I wondered aloud if I was perhaps too young for the job; Dan politely responded that I wasn't all that young anymore, and that I had the necessary credibility to take the job on.

In a sense, Dan's offer was part of a natural progression. In the months before that Pontresina meeting, I had been working very hard with a colleague, Damien O'Brien, on an unprecedented diagnostic effort for EZI. We were trying to understand how well we were fulfilling our mission of adding value for our clients, and also seeking to identify major improvement opportunities. We analyzed the quality of our executive search work in every office worldwide, conducting interviews with many clients all around the world. In addition, we retained a skilled management consultant who specialized in professional service firms.

Damien and I reached several conclusions. First, as a rule, our clients appreciated our candor and commitment, the quality of the candidates we were presenting to them, and our understanding of their specific needs. While we were doing well at the *aggregate* level, however, some offices and some consultants clearly were adding much more value to our clients than others, when assessed by hard measures such as closing rate (percentage of executive search assignments closed with an effective hiring), closing speed, and the hired candidate's ultimate success on the new job.

So immediately after our firm conference in Pontresina, with me wearing a new hat, we launched a massive effort to dig further into our own best practices from all over the world. We complemented that internal effort with a systematic external analysis of every single piece of research published on topics related to our professional work. I remember personally buying more than 100 books in a period of a few months (and reading most of them!) while our research departments in different parts of the world dug up academic papers on relevant topics. We also explored a number of training programs for assessing candidates, since we had identified that as an area in which we wanted to improve on a global basis.

The results of all of that searching and digging were mixed. We learned that a great deal had been published about how to improve people decisions through better assessments. At the same time, I became convinced that most academics and practitioners were largely missing the point in this critical arena. In this chapter, I'll summarize both the published best practices and my own convictions about how to appraise people most effectively.

The Largest Opportunity

Before getting into the *what* and the *how*, let's look again at *why* investing time, effort, and money in better assessments is your largest opportunity for making great people decisions.

In Chapter 2, I described how to quantify the return on people decisions, referring to models that can be used to calculate the expected value of investments in finding, assessing, and recruiting the best potential candidates. If you are interested in the details, Appendix A explains how to calculate that value, based on the example of a medium-sized company. In that example, using very conservative assumptions, a company with an expected profit after taxes of $50 million can increase the expected value of the yearly profits by 34 percent ($17 million).

The relevant point for this chapter is that, by far, *the largest opportunity for capturing that value lies in conducting better appraisals.* Continuing with that same example, a sensitivity analysis shows that an improvement in the quality of the assessments is more than three times more valuable than increasing the number of candidates generated, and more than six times more valuable than reducing the cost of the hired candidate. (See Figure 7.1.)

It quickly becomes clear that the typical cost of a search becomes negligible when compared with the expected return. Specifically, a 10

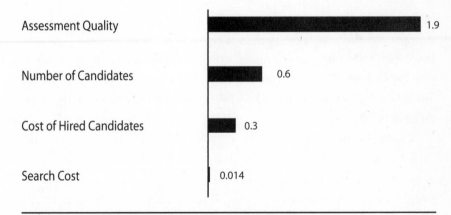

FIGURE 7.1   Sensitivity Analysis of Search Effort
Change in Yearly Profits Assuming a 10% Improvement in Each Parameter (million $)
Assumptions and model: See Appendix A.

percent improvement in the quality of candidate assessments would have an expected return of almost $2 million of additional profits *per year*. If you maintain this higher assessment quality over the years, this would in turn represent some $40 million of increased company value.

Appraisals in Practice

As mentioned in Chapter 4, the selection tools most often used for professionals and managers include interviews, resumes, and references.[1] While many other techniques are called upon, they are either inherently suspect (e.g., astrology and graphology), not practical for complex jobs (such as assessment centers), or not job-specific enough and therefore of limited use for complex positions (such as personality tests).

So what actually works? Which of these methods actually predict performance on the new job?

As far back as the 1920s, impressive research has been conducted on evaluation methods. In addition, over the last three decades, a series of studies demonstrated that information about validity from different studies could be put together to enlarge the sample sizes and reach stronger conclusions. This is known as "validity generalization" (sometimes referred to as "meta-analysis"). Validity generalization has made it possible to reach important conclusions about the relative value of various evaluation methods, including reference checks, various types of interviews, and so on.

In Appendix B, you'll find a list of some 50 references, which include a few useful introductory readings, a large number of introductory books both on interviewing and reference checking, and a summary of more advanced references. In the following pages, though, I'll briefly summarize what I take to be the essence of all that research.

First, an assessment method has to meet two basic conditions: It must be acceptable to the candidate, and it must predict performance on the job. The best tradeoff between candidate acceptability and assessment validity (ability to predict performance on the job) is usually met through a combination of effective interviews and reference checks.

In addition, some analysis of a resume is always conducted. Some companies complement the resume's information with richer biographical data ("bio-data," as it is known in assessment jargon), including more information about the candidate's personal background and life experiences.

Bio-data started to be developed after its successful applications in identifying military officer talent during World War II, but it has been in decline in recent decades. While it was found to be a solid predictor of job performance for entry-level positions, compared with most other assessment techniques it is a very poor predictor of *managerial* performance. The higher you go in the organization, the less predictive power bio-data appears to have.

Reference checks are typically used in practice to *eliminate* candidates, helping to identify a relatively small subset of candidates who should not be considered further for a job. Most specialists agree that although reference checks aren't particularly useful in predicting candidate job success, they may be the only way to turn up information that would point toward an unsatisfactory job performance.

Finally, interviews have been studied for more than 80 years, and have slowly gained favor. Several studies have focused on how the interview can be improved, specifically through the use of the *situational* interview and the *behavioral* interview. We will discuss the details later; the important point for now is that both of these methods have consistently demonstrated high validity in evaluation programs covering a wide variety of jobs. In addition, meta-analytic studies have shown that, for more complex positions, *interviews are more powerful than any other assessment technique.*[2]

Before discussing the details about how interviews and reference checks should be conducted, let's dig a bit deeper into some of the big challenges we face when we set out to assess people. These include lies, fraud, and snap judgments.

On Lies, Fraud, and Scandal

A colleague of mine in Buenos Aires recently shared with me the case of a CEO who falsely claimed to have an MBA. A quick review of his resume showed that he had inflated the importance of his two previous positions. This was happening even in the relatively small world of Buenos Aires, where lies like this are almost bound to surface!

As I mentioned in Chapter 3, we live in a time in which almost all college students admit that they're willing to tell a lie to get a job. Not surprisingly, then, the vast majority of resumes are misleading. I once met a candidate who claimed to have both an engineering degree from my own alma mater and an MBA from Stanford, but he had neither. I contacted the person who had sent this imposter to me and shared my discoveries. He was as amazed as I was, telling me that he had gotten to know that person in church, and he seemed like such a wonderful man.

People can go a long way on false credentials. For example, the *Mail on Sunday*, a U.K. newspaper, told the story of an executive who had worked for the BBC, Philips, Datamonitor, Andersen Consulting, and Arthur D. Little, among others. According to that paper, she had claimed degrees she had never earned, and cited jobs she had never held, in a career of deception that spanned three decades and multiple jail terms. She had been made a partner at an executive search firm, and even joined some company boards. "Astonishingly," the *Mail on Sunday* reported, "the woman who had served two prison sentences for fraud found herself on the company's audit committee, responsible for ensuring nothing was awry in the firm's accounts."[3]

A recent article by James Mintz, president of an investigative firm headquartered in New York, reviews other famous cases of resume fraud at the very top. The techniques he cites include false educational records, inflated experience, name changes, the creation of phantom companies to fill employment gaps, and references that can be traced back to the resume writer himself.[4]

My point is, simply, that even in tightly knit communities, and even in the age of Google, fraud and deception abound and the resume is where much of that deception takes root.

Snap Judgments at Lightning Speed

So the candidate comes to us, in many cases, with dubious credentials. Then, in the interview context, we compound the problem by making snap judgments, and then look for evidence to support those judgments.[5]

In his book, *Blink*, Malcolm Gladwell illustrates both the benefits and risks of our fast, intuitive, even unconscious choices. One of his illustrations of this phenomenon is Warren G. Harding, who, on very sketchy credentials, rose from small-town newspaper editor to become President of the United States.

According to Gladwell, Harding was not particularly intelligent, had some highly questionable habits, was vague and ambivalent in matters of policy, and had no single significant achievement in his whole career.[6] He became President of the United States because he *looked* like a President of the United States. Not surprisingly, the "real" Harding came up short. He presided over a scandal-ridden administration, died of a stroke two years into his first term, and is generally considered one of the worst presidents in American history.

A second illustration of the dangers of snap decisions involves speed-dating, which has become highly popular in recent years. In a speed-dating event, several men and women spend a short time talking to each other (typically about six minutes) before deciding whether they want to meet again. Then they move on to meet their next "date," thus making some 10 new acquaintances per hour. In other words, they get to meet several people in a very short time period, without wasting time on undesirable options.

But consider the analysis of speed-dating conducted by two Columbia University professors, who arranged speed-dating evenings with a scientific overlay.[7] Participants filled out a short questionnaire, which asked them to indicate what they were looking for in a potential partner. They were asked to state their search criteria at four different times: just before the speed-dating event, immediately after it, a month later, and then six months after the event.

The researchers found that participants were so much influenced by the person they were attracted to that they *immediately changed their search criteria*. Consistently, they were interested in specific things before the event, and then, in the heat of the moment, became interested in different things. Then, six months after the event, they reverted to their original criteria.

This finding is fully consistent with my own experience of individuals who, having just interviewed a candidate whom they liked very much, adjust their hiring criteria to fit that individual. But both sets of hiring criteria can't be right!

We humans make snap judgments all the time, and at amazing speeds. Recent discoveries from neuroscience indicate that social judgments, in particular, come quickly. This is true for two reasons. First, a newly discovered class of neurons, called the *spindle cell*, is the fastest-acting brain cell of all, and is dominant in the part of the brain that directs our (snap) social decisions. Second, the neural circuits that make these decisions are always in the "ready" position. As Daniel Goleman describes in his latest book:

> Even while the rest of the brain is quiescent, four neural areas remain active, like idling neural motors, poised for quick response. Tellingly, three of these four ready-to-roll areas are involved in making judgments about people.[8]

It turns out that we make judgments about *people* much faster than we do about *things*. Amazingly, in your first encounter with someone, the relevant areas in your brain are making your initial judgment (pro or con) in just *one-twentieth of a second*.

So one thing, at least, is clear: We need to tackle our people assessments with a special "mindfulness," and a conscious effort to avoid the snap judgment.

The Bad Interview

The interview is the most frequent technique used to appraise people. Nevertheless, most interviews are ineffective at best. Research indicates that in a typical interview, which, after all, is intended to elicit information about the candidate, the interviewer tends to do most of the talking.[9]

This tends to happen when the interviewer attempts to sell the organization and the job to the candidate. But obviously, this is getting the cart before the horse. At this stage, the goal is to gather enough information from the candidate to figure out whether he or she can perform successfully in the new job. Later, after you're convinced that you have the right candidate in front of you, you can work on selling the job.

The typical interview is usually highly unstructured, without appropriate homework having been done about the competencies to be measured and the questions to be asked. As a result, it has a very limited validity, in the order of 0.3, which means that less than 10 percent of the variance in performance on the new job can be explained by this assessment. As I will explain below, however, adding the proper structure can more than *double* the validity of the right interview. It can make the interview the best assessment technique, particularly for complex senior positions.

From Experience to Competencies

As noted in earlier chapters, it's usually impossible to make valid appraisals just by assessing *experience*, since it's so difficult to find similar jobs in terms of goals, challenges, resources, and circumstances. With unique jobs, where intangible traits frequently make the difference between average and outstanding performance, you need to do the homework described in Chapter 5: identifying the relevant *competencies* and describing them in behavioral terms. This process is described in Figure 7.2.

Past behaviors are the best basis for predicting future behavior. So if you could find an individual who has achieved the level of performance you want in a job identical to the one for which you are making the assessment, your problem would be quite simple. But that's not easy. In addition, it assumes that this perfect candidate would be motivated to uproot himself or herself only to undertake the same thing all over again somewhere new. And if *everyone* followed this approach, then no one would ever be promoted to larger or different jobs.

So in the real world, you first need to confirm what you're looking for (as described in Chapter 5), and come up with the list of the key competencies required for the new job. Then you need to assess the performance displayed by the candidates in different jobs. You need to ex-

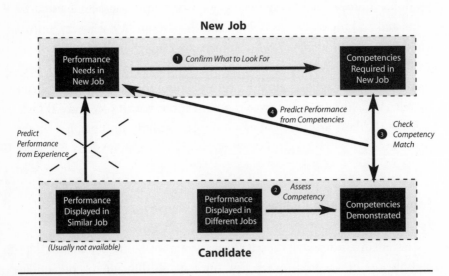

FIGURE 7.2   Predicting Performance from Competencies

amine the competencies demonstrated in those different circumstances, check the competency match with those required in the new position, and predict performance from that competency match.

Assessing performance from competencies is often mishandled. Sometimes, the problem arises when the assessor uses a cookie-cutter approach, relying on generic competencies that either have not been validated or would not be relevant to the specific job. Sometimes the assessor bungles the candidate-competencies side of the equation. But when the right job is done by the right assessor, the prediction of future performance can achieve the highest validity levels of any selection technique.

David McClelland published a 1998 article (finished by his colleagues after his death) demonstrating the value of a competency approach for predicting performance and retention. Following his approach of determining the competencies that differentiate outstanding from typical performers on particular jobs, he identified the competencies that made for outstanding performance in a specific type of job, which included (in that case): achievement orientation, analytical thinking, conceptual thinking, developing others, flexibility, impact and influence, information seeking, initiative, interpersonal understanding, organization awareness, self-confidence, and team leadership.

This approach not only differentiated between typical and outstanding employees, but also predicted who would perform better subsequently in a company, as measured by (1) bonuses received, and (2) lack of turnover.[10]

Another interesting study (by Richard Boyatzis) involved the leaders of a multinational consulting firm. Boyatzis showed that the frequency with which those leaders demonstrate a variety of competencies strongly predicts financial performance in the seven quarters following the competency assessment. Boyatzis analyzed not only which competencies were necessary for outstanding performance, but also *how much* of the competency was sufficient for outstanding performance.

Note that this study focused on the leaders of a consulting firm, where you would assume that technical knowledge and traditional intelligence would be the keys to success. In fact, cognitive competencies failed to explain much of the difference, whereas, once again, emotional intelligence–based competencies had a huge impact. For example, Boyatzis pointed to a set of competencies that he called a "self-regulation cluster," such as the leader's willingness to take a risky stand, and his or her self-control, adaptability, conscientiousness, and values.

Borrowing from complexity theory, Boyatzis also included a "tipping point" analysis. Leaders who were below the tipping point in terms of self-regulation had a level of account revenue of about $900,000, while those who were above the tipping point had an average account revenue of almost $3 million.

But this was not all. Leaders above the tipping point in terms of self-regulation also had an account gross margin of 62 percent, as compared with only 42 percent for those below the tipping point.[11] Integrating revenues and margins, leaders with the right competencies were 500 percent as profitable as those who fell below the tipping point.

This is a wonderful example of "less is more." If you identify the competencies that predict outstanding performance in a job, and focus only on them, you will achieve much better assessments and much more powerful people decisions, and do less work in the process.

In short, research confirms that identifying the relevant competencies for a job, and assessing them through effective interviews, is an extremely valid and powerful way to predict outstanding performance.

The Effective Interview

There are two basic types of interview: unstructured and structured. The unstructured interview involves a process whereby different questions, typically unplanned, may be asked of different candidates. Structured interviews, by contrast, grow out of a sophisticated analysis of the relevant competencies to be assessed, as well as careful thought about the questions to be asked. Since research has shown that properly structured interviews can be the best assessment tool, particularly for senior and complex positions, I'll focus on them here.[12]

There are two distinct approaches to the structured interview. One involves "behavioral" questions, that is, questions aimed at understanding what the candidate has done in a real situation, which may illustrate that he or she has the right competencies required for the new job. A second approach is the "situational" question, in which candidates are asked about the kinds of actions they would take in various hypothetical job-related situations. Although both have their merits, I favor the behavioral approach.

Both approaches require significant preparation, including a detailed plan for each meeting with the candidates, specifying each competency to be investigated as well as the questions intended to measure each one. For an example of such a plan, see Figure 7.3.[13] As illustrated in the figure, your questions should be focused on behaviors, and should be followed up with significant probing to understand what was the candidate's exact role, and what were the consequences of his or her actions.

Imparting Interviewing Skills

The subject of interviewing skills reminds me of a stressful situation from my past. I was working on the development of a training program on interviewing for our firm, and I was the project's first guinea pig. While I interviewed a "candidate" (actually, a graduate student who was willing to help us out), three trainers sitting behind him scrutinized me on a continuous basis, giving me visual cues about what to do. Simultaneously, I had to process their instructions, actively listen to the candidate, build rapport, ask good relevant questions, probe incisively, while also taking good notes. And the whole process was being videotaped!

The session lasted only half an hour, but to me, it seemed like an eternity. How tough that was! Despite having had nine years of

Structured interviews are the result of careful planning and disciplined implementation. In fact, we have found that for a two-hour interview to yield meaningful information, it could take at least that much time to get ready for it. The most important part of preparation is creating a list of questions that will identify whether the candidate has the competencies required for the position. It means asking the candidate about his experiences and behavior, and yet most interviewers usually just let the candidate tell his story. In a search for a marketing director for a fast-moving consumer goods company, we identified five competencies relevant to the position, as well as a series of technical qualifications. Below are examples of some of the questions—focused on facts and behaviors, not opinions or generalities—which we used to measure each:

COMPETENCY	SOME QUESTIONS ASKED
Results oriented	**?** Have you been involved in a business or product launch? What were the specific steps you took to contribute to the success of the launch? **?** Describe the most successful marketing communications project you've led. How did you measure results?
Team-centered leadership	**?** Describe a time you led a team to be more effective. What did you do? How did the team and the organization benefit from your actions? **?** Describe a time you were asked to lead a particularly challenging team project. How did you overcome the obstacles you faced?
Strategic thinker	**?** What are the top three strategic issues that your current company faces? **?** Describe a situation in which you personally have been involved in addressing one of these issues. What actions did you take?
Change agent	**?** Describe a time when you received organizational resistance to an idea or project that you were responsible for implementing. How did you handle it? What resulted from it? Would you handle it any differently now? **?** Given our organizational culture and the changes we need, can you think of specific examples from your experience that would demonstrate that you would perform effectively in, and enjoy, this position?
Ability to respond to deadline pressure	**?** Describe a time you made an extraordinary effort to meet a deadline. What were the results?

FIGURE 7.3   Beyond Conversation: The Hard Work of a Structured Interview

executive search experience by then, I felt I had been awkward and ineffective.

The four of us then spent significant time debriefing, checking to see whether my conclusions were in line with their experience. The good news was that, with the help of my three coaches, I had been able to get pretty good information during that half hour.

For me, that grueling experience confirmed the findings of relevant research: that experience alone is not enough to improve the interviewer's skills. After all, I had conducted thousands of interviews before that one, but that one made me better. To generalize, training and experience together can be a powerful combination, and the most powerful technique for interview training is role-playing.

Research has shown that training programs that extend over a few days—with role-playing exercises, feedback, and videotaping—can significantly improve questioning techniques, interviewing structure, and active listening skills. The best training programs provide participants with models of correct interviewing behaviors, let them interview real candidates, and give feedback that is immediate and specific. Meta-analysis of 120 interview studies with a total sample size close to 20,000 has shown that training helps develop interviewing skills not only for structured interviews, but even for unstructured interviews.[14]

The experience in our firm has clearly confirmed the value of this training. Two years into our training program, I found that our "stars" (colleagues who had strongly incorporated the program's learnings into their working habits) had a 20 percent higher closing rate, and were 40 percent faster in closing overall.

Decoding Microexpressions

All of these traditional training programs aim at improving the process, and focus on developing conscious skills for interviewing. They also include some strategies for becoming aware of, and correcting, our *unconscious* biases and errors.

Recent developments seem to show that, in addition, we may be able to train ourselves to detect a candidate's "microexpressions"—small and subtle emotional signals that flit across the face in less than a third of a second, and which happen so fast that they mostly remain outside our conscious awareness.

In his book, *Social Intelligence*, Daniel Goleman tells the story of a man who had come to an embassy for a visa. While the interviewer asked why the man wanted the visa, a shadow seemed to flash across the man's face, just for an instant. The interviewer interrupted the session, consulted an Interpol databank, and found that the man was wanted by the police in several countries. According to Goleman, the interviewer's detection of that subtle and short-lived expression shows a highly advanced gift for primal empathy.

But there's more: The interviewer was not simply a "natural," but someone who had been trained in primal empathy using the methods of Paul Ekman. Ekman, an authority on reading emotions from facial expressions, has devised a way to teach people how to improve primal empathy despite its unconscious, almost instantaneous nature.

Goleman tells how when he first met Paul Ekman in the 1980s, Ekman had just spent a year gazing into a mirror, learning to voluntarily control each of the close to two hundred muscles of the face, at times even applying a mild electrical shock to isolate some hard-to-detect facial muscles. As a result, Ekman was able to map precisely how different sets of these muscles move to exhibit, in microexpressions, each of the major emotions and their variations.

Because they are spontaneous and unconscious, these micro expressions offer a clue as to how a person actually feels at that moment, even if he or she is trying to hide it. Ekman has devised a CD, called the *Micro Expression Training Tool*, which he claims can vastly improve our ability to detect these previously unconscious clues.[15]

Unless you are screening for security-related or counterterrorism positions, you probably don't need Ekman's particular form of training. But the microexpression example reminds us that there may be more going on than immediately meets the eye, and that raising your awareness of the "weak signal" can be extremely helpful.

The Future of Assessment?

Advances in the neurosciences are likely to transform our ability to assess people in ways that look both powerful and scary. Lawrence A. Farwell has invented the technique of "Brain Fingerprinting," a computer-based technology used to identify the perpetrator of a crime by measuring brain-wave responses to crime-relevant words or pictures presented on a computer screen. Farwell fits a suspect with a sensor-filled headband. He then flashes a series of pictures on a screen, and monitors the subject's involuntary reactions to them. When there's something familiar about an image, it triggers an electrical response that begins between 300 and 800 milliseconds after the stimulus.

This technique, which sounds like something out of science fiction, actually meets the U.S. Supreme Court's reliability and validity standards, and has already racked up some amazing success stories. For example, the Iowa Supreme Court reversed a murder conviction after 24 years, when a Brain Fingerprinting test supported the convicted man's longstanding claim of innocence. Shortly thereafter, the key prosecution witness recanted his testimony, admitting that he had falsely accused the jailed man to avoid being prosecuted for the murder himself.

In another notorious case, the technique enabled police to catch a serial killer. The individual in question had been a suspect in an unsolved murder case for 15 years. A Brain Fingerprinting test showed that the record stored in his brain matched critical details of the crime scene that only the perpetrator would know. Faced with an almost certain conviction and a probable death sentence, the killer pled guilty in exchange for life in prison, and also confessed to the previously unsolved murders of three other women.

According to Farwell, in more than 170 scientific studies of Brain Fingerprinting, which included tests on known criminals, FBI agents, and military medical experts, the technique was found to be 100 percent accurate in determining whether subjects did or did not recognize the probe stimuli.

You could sketch out a scenario whereby, based on this type of technology, a revolution in assessment could be effected. Frankly, though, I doubt that we will be able to see anything like a Brain Fingerprinting test used in candidate assessments any time soon. In addition to privacy and ethical issues, there is the obvious issue of candidate acceptability. (If they won't cooperate, it can't work.) But I mention it here to underscore, again, the subtleties that are at play in the assessment process.

A Better Approach: HOT SHOT

To summarize the research I've cited so far, assuming that we have previously determined the relevant competencies, we can improve the quality of assessments by using well-structured, behaviorally based interviews. When it comes to senior and complex positions, these tend to be the best assessment techniques, and you can get much better at them through a combination of intensive practice and proper training.

That's the good news. The bad news is that, some 10 years ago, after conducting my first comprehensive review of all the relevant research that was out there, I came to the reluctant conclusion that most academics were mostly missing the point. They were falling into the trap of producing statistically significant but managerially irrelevant findings. They had a good view of the trees, but they were missing the forest.

Yes, properly structured interviews can help you achieve a higher validity than that of any other typical technique. Nevertheless, the highest that you can hope to achieve is on the order of 0.7. A validity of 0.7 implies that slightly less than 50 percent of the variance in performance would be explained by the assessment. What about the other unexplained half? Should you really appoint someone to an important job based on tools of such relatively poor predictive power?

In addition, most of the massive research conducted to date has focused on low-level positions. If the spread of managerial performance is greater for high-level positions, and if these positions are more complex (as we've seen in previous chapters), then the validity of these techniques must be even lower at those senior levels.

There are still other important factors missing from much of the academic work on assessments. For example, most pay little attention to the *individual* conducting the assessment (as opposed to the technique involved); most overlook or downplay reference checks; and most ignore the basic question of how many assessments to conduct.

To capture my own conclusions about the conditions and expected benefits of a robust assessment, I came up with what I called the HOT SHOT model, presented in Figure 7.4. The left part of the equation presents the *conditions* for a robust assessment, which include **H**igh-caliber selectors, **O**rganizational strength, and (only as a third factor) the right **T**echniques used for assessing. The factors on the left side of the equation are multiplicative, meaning that all these conditions must be strong to achieve a robust assessment.

The right side of the equation presents the expected *benefits* of a good assessment. If you have high-caliber people working with the right techniques in a coordinated fashion within your organization, you will achieve a **S**uperior assessment, which will allow you to hire candidates with much **H**igher performance on the job, who will stay longer in your organization. At the same time, you will be projecting a very strong image about your **O**rganization in the marketplace. Finally, you will work far more efficiently, avoiding irrelevant, invalid, or redundant assessments, thereby protecting the **T**ime of your management team.

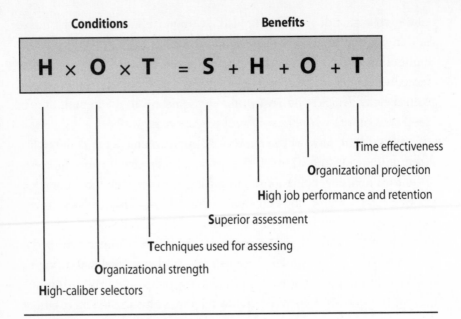

FIGURE 7.4   The HOT SHOT Model for a Robust Assessment

Think of HOT SHOT as an assessment checklist. Are all of these factors at work in your organization? Is your organization getting all the stated benefits? If not, what has to change?

Invaluable References

A few months after our firm conference in Pontresina, near the end of 1994, we held a meeting of our firm's global Professional Development Team in Amsterdam. Participants included myself, several colleagues from all over the world, and our CEO, Dan Meiland. By that time, we had conducted significant external and internal research, and were analyzing in detail what made for the outstanding performance of several of our offices. Indeed, there was a small group of offices that had compiled amazing track records and built stellar reputations for themselves.

Dan had strong opinions regarding what he saw as the single most important reason behind that amazing performance. In his view, the consultants in those offices would *never* present a candidate they had not vetted with *several* individuals well known to our consultants, who had seen the candidate in action and could give us extremely rich, objective, insightful, and reliable references. Furthermore, those offices had a tradition of systematically gathering and sharing those invaluable references among their consultants.

Dan spoke with absolute conviction on this subject of references. His implicit point, as I heard it, was that *we should always remain humble.* We should remember that no matter how experienced we became at interviewing, in the end there would always be prospective candidates who would be able to fool us and our clients—and that this was a risk we could not take.

I took Dan's point, but I asked him how realistic it was to expect to obtain those unbiased and rich references from known sources in very large markets. (Some of our highest-performing offices were in small-to-medium-sized markets.) He responded that by having our consultants specialize either by *sector* or by *function*, in the end even the largest markets could be turned into a small world, and we could always have people known to one or more of us who had worked closely with any potential candidate at a senior level.

At one point in our discussion, Dan walked to a flipchart, which had a list that summarized the various factors contributing to the greatness of those stellar offices. Using a black marker, he drew one, two, or three stars next to each factor. "Proper reference checks" was the only factor that got three stars from Dan.

Today, more than a decade after that meeting, I still believe that was the most useful lesson I've ever gotten in how to achieve a valid and reliable assessment. Since that time, our firm has invested large sums to develop our intellectual capital, to identify the competencies for success at senior levels, to develop a unique set of scaled competencies that have added great power to our assessments, and to train our consultants. Those large investments notwithstanding, we still believe that *proper reference checks are an essential condition for success in any assessment.*

Of course, great leaders outside our industry also follow this principle. When I asked Jack Welch how he *really* found out about a person in those few cases where he looked outside, his answer was that he had GE people contact individuals in the same industry (but not the same company) to develop a composite picture of the prospect. He told me that he *never* trusted the references given by the candidate, but that the opinions of industry peers were invaluable.

The Right Reference Check

The right reference check serves three purposes: First, references can be used at an early stage to verify the candidate's basic credentials. Checking educational background with the listed universities, confirming employment dates and titles with the cited companies, and perhaps even involving companies that specialize in background checks all can go a long way toward weeding out frauds and imposters. This might seem self-evident, but an astounding number of companies fail to meet even this threshold requirement.

Weeding out the outright fakes is entry-level reference checking. The second level involves finding people who can confirm that your candidate's self-reported achievements are real, and that the candidate is just as competent as he or she claims to be. Through this second type of reference, it is important to check basic emotional intelligence–based competencies, which although softer and therefore harder to assess are critical for success.

Finally, a third type of reference helps you hone in on competence and potential, with the goals of confirming the hiring decision, ensuring success in the position, and gathering information to support the integration process of the hired candidate.

But how do you actually approach these references? There are two basic best practices. First, you need to *decide whom to call.* This depends on the type of competencies you are trying to assess. A former boss would tend to be very good for assessing things like results orientation, strategic orientation, or commercial orientation. A peer would be well positioned to assess collaboration and influencing skills. Former direct reports could comment on the candidate's competence in the areas of team leadership, as well as his or her ability to develop others. In any case, *don't limit yourself to the references initially provided by the candidate.* Instead, agree with him or her on additional references for *your* purposes. As you develop this list, try to understand the relationship between the reference and the candidate, including potential conflicts (such as suppliers recommending their best clients).

The second best practice for handling references is to approach them in much the same way that you'd conduct a structured, behaviorally based interview with a candidate. In other words, start by planning your questions about the relevant competencies you want to check. When calling the references, first confirm their relationship with the candidate, then explain to them the type of situation for which you are considering the candidate, and confirm whether the reference has observed the candidate in a similar situation. In that case, check what he or she has done, the way in which results have been achieved, and any evidences about his or her level of competence. Take advantage of the opportunity to gather any other relevant facts that may help you achieve a more reliable assessment, confirm or reject the hiring decision, and prepare for a more effective integration.

In some cases, professionals can add significant value at this stage. Again, make sure that your consultants have had significant continuity and specialization in relevant markets, functions, and sectors. Where possible, confirm that they have an internal culture of gathering and sharing information about sources, references, and candidates. To be of use to you, the knowledge that they possess must flow freely among the professionals in the firm.

Selecting Selectors

Would you rather hear a mediocre pianist play on a superb instrument, or a superb pianist play on a mediocre instrument? I'm sure that you, like me, would take the latter every time.

The same holds true in assessments: It's the professional, more than it's the technique. Assessing people is extremely difficult. If this were not the case, there would be no divorces, the legal profession would atrophy, and I would be without a job.

While there is only limited research on this topic, as mentioned in Chapter 1, a useful book called *The Employment Interview Handbook* includes a chapter that looks at the question of whether some interviewers are better than others.[16] Five out of the six studies concluded that the answer was "yes." In some of those studies, the best interviewers had predictive validities *10 times better* than the worst interviewers. In a large study conducted in 1966, looking at 62 different interviewers who each evaluated a mean of 25 employees, the range of individual interviewers' validities went from *a low of –0.10 to a high of +.65.*[17]

That range deserves some additional scrutiny. A validity of –0.10 implies that the interviewer in question wasn't registering merely a low validity, but a *negative* one. One way of reading this is that you should probably do the opposite of what this particular interviewer recommends!

One of the leading authorities on selection interviews is Rice University's Robert Dipboye, who has conducted the single best study of differences in the validities across interviewers, drawing on a huge sample size. He concludes that some interviewers achieve much higher levels of validity than others, and that those who achieve higher levels of validity tend to be less biased against women and ethnic minorities in their evaluations.[18]

The upshot is that in a world of accelerated change in organizational forms and managerial capabilities, in which new competencies are constantly required, and where some of the most relevant competencies are very difficult to assess, *you need to select the right selectors.*

What do these high-caliber assessors look like? First, given the complexity of the task, it makes sense to select intelligent interviewers who are also familiar with the range of experiences and competencies relevant to the position. This typically implies using senior assessors for senior candidates. Other attributes also correlate with high assessment validity at the individual level, including the ability to decode nonverbal behavior, self-monitoring, listening skills, and the ability to plan and act in parallel.

One of the most important attributes of the best interviewers, somewhat surprisingly, is their *motivation* to conduct a sound appraisal. This was discovered by researchers more than half a century ago. According to that study, individuals who are good judges of people possess appropriate judgmental norms as well as general and social intelligence; however, "probably the most important area of all is that of motivation: if the judge is motivated to make accurate judgments about his subject and if he feels himself free to be objective, then he has a good chance of achieving his aim."[19]

How Many Appraisals?

When I think back to my first search, conducted some 20 years ago, this rings true. I had almost nothing going for me *except* motivation—and, of course, a good client. Of course, I did my part, investigating and interviewing a huge number of candidates, and checking references in great detail. But what really made the difference was the fact that three highly qualified individuals on the client side conducted sequential, independent, and thorough assessments.

The first client interviewer was the retiring CEO of Quilmes, Frank Benson, who was a seasoned veteran of countless corporate skirmishes.

He knew the reality of Quilmes, and its current challenges, inside out. The second interviewer was David Ganly, the incoming CEO of Quilmes, who was transitioning in as we were conducting the search. While new to the company, he was extremely knowledgeable about the key marketing and sales issues in a fast-moving consumer goods company, and had a deep understanding of local consumers. The final filter was the CEO of the holding company Quinsa, Norberto Morita, an outstanding judge of people.

What happened in that case illustrates another extremely powerful best practice for improving the accuracy of assessments: having a few highly qualified assessors interview *sequentially* and *independently* the finalist candidates. I call this strategy the "sequential filters model," illustrated in Figure 7.5.

The rationale for this strategy builds on a point introduced in Chapter 3, when I analyzed the impact of assessment errors. As you may remember from that analysis, if we want to hire only "top 10 percent candidates," even if our assessments have a very high level of accuracy (on the order of 90%) we would still have a 50 percent error rate in our hiring decisions (as illustrated in Figure 7.5) as the result of just one filter. But if you add a second independent filter to those candidates initially assessed as "top," you can reduce your 50 percent error to only 10 percent.

How does this work? Assume that you have 100 candidates before this second filter, of which 50 percent are really top-notch. Your 90 percent accuracy would make you assess as "top" 45 of the right ones, while your 10 percent error would make you assess as "top" another 5 from the

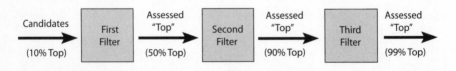

FIGURE 7.5   Sequential Filters Model

wrong category. Out of the 50 candidates who would have passed this second filter, 45 (or 90%) would already be top. Following this same logic, if you work out the numbers, you will find that adding a third sequential filter reduces your final assessment error to just 1 percent.

Too Many Cooks Spoil the Broth

Perhaps you're tempted to take this logic to its extreme, by adding even more appraisals to the process, and pushing the assessment error closer to zero. Don't! This would have significant *negative* consequences, for two reasons. First, you would eliminate too many qualified candidates. Second, you would need to generate a huge number of initial candidates, in order to get even one through all the successive filters! This is illustrated in Figure 7.6, which presents the consequences of three sequential independent filters with different accuracy levels of the assessors.

In the example we just discussed, with three filters and an accuracy level of 90 percent, the probability of assessing as "top" a bottom candidate would only be 1 percent, which is certainly great news. Meanwhile, though, you'd be wrongly eliminating 27 percent of the top candidates! In order to be able to find one top candidate, in fact, you'd need to generate 14 and to conduct a total of 17 assessments—hard work! Adding

Accuracy of Assessors	False Positive[1]	False Negative[2]	Number of Candidates Needed	Number of Assessments Required
90%	1%	27%	14	17
70%	42%	66%	17	25

FIGURE 7.6 Example of Three Sequential Independent Filters with Different Accuracy Levels of the Assessors
1. Probability of assessing as "top" a bottom candidate.
2. Probability of assessing as "bottom" a top candidate.

more filters would not add much in terms of accuracy, given the already low false-positive error, but it would generate a huge proportion of false negatives, and a huge burden of extra work.

Keep in mind that many interviewers just search for a reason to reject a candidate.[20] Keep in mind, too, that systematically rejecting highly qualified candidates isn't just unnecessarily time consuming. It may also cost you credibility in the marketplace, which can only hurt in the long run.

Figure 7.6 also illustrates the importance not only of having a limited number of assessors, but also of having *all of them be highly qualified* (the H factor in the HOT SHOT equation). In the second row of that figure, I summarize the conclusions of three sequential independent filters with a lower accuracy level—on the order of 70 percent for each assessor. In this case, even with three filters, you would still hire a turkey 42 percent of the time, while you would be rejecting *two-thirds* of the truly qualified candidates. And you'd need to work very hard to achieve this miserable result, generating 17 candidates just to hire one (with a 42% chance of error) and conducting a total of 25 assessments!

This analysis dramatically demonstrates the need to have only highly qualified assessors, and a limited number of them, in order to obtain the full benefit of the SHOT side: Superior assessments, High performing candidates, a strong Organizational projection, and an effective utilization of your Time.

Team Interviews

A final approach to consider is the team interview, or panel interview, in which several people interview the candidate at once.

Team interviews should be thought of as a useful tool in the later stages of the sequential model above, since it doesn't make sense to involve multiple interviewers until the candidate has survived at least some initial screening. Research suggests that team interviews are slightly more valid than individual interviews, in part because interviewers can challenge each other regarding the basis for the assessments. Team interviews also appear to be more effective for higher-level positions, more complex jobs, and also jobs that involve interacting with multiple constituencies. They also can have the benefit of reducing the duplication and exhaustion of back-to-back interviews, and using high-level selectors' time wisely.

In order to be more effective, however, team interviews must be disciplined. The interviewers must be highly qualified, knowledgeable about the competencies they want to assess, and disciplined in their process of questioning and probing.

The Decision Team

While multiple constituencies may be involved in defining the *need*, when it comes to making the final hiring decision, the best result typically emerges from a small, competent team that is free of conflict. Letting just one person decide may not allow room for questioning assumptions, fighting biases, and discussing difficult tradeoffs among candidates. Having too many participants decide risks increasing the false-negative effect (eliminating valid candidates), demotivating candidates through a longer process, and reducing the competence and relevance of the decision-making team.

When a CEO needs to be appointed, a small, highly qualified team (e.g., three board members) should lead the whole process, from defining the need to integrating the new executive. At lower levels, a similarly sized team may include the direct boss, the boss's boss, and the most senior HR executive (assuming he or she is senior to the position). *Make no compromises if an unqualified executive volunteers to be in the hiring team*, even if that individual is a high-level person, up to and including a board member. The stakes are simply too high.

The case of the dairy company introduced in earlier chapters illustrates some of the best practices for making the final decisions. The Appointments and Remuneration Committee conducted their own final assessments, checking both competence and cultural fit. This committee included the chairman, and comprised four highly qualified members of a 13-member board. The process was both rigorous and comprehensive, going over the evidence in candidates' previous histories that demonstrated the required level of each competency critical to success.

Because this small team of competent and motivated participants clearly knew what it was looking for, it could easily reach a decision and hire the best candidate that came before them.

Decision-Stage Best Practices

When the final decision approaches, strict discipline becomes absolutely crucial. In all too many cases, expediency intervenes, discipline breaks down, and terrible people mistakes are made.

"Discipline" means reviewing, once again, the performance expectations that were defined in writing at earlier stages of the process. It also means reviewing the evidence pertaining to each key competency, as well as the candidate's potential for growth. This involves listing and reviewing each candidate's key actions, achievements, and behaviors that are related to each major expectation.

Finally, discipline means making a *behavioral prediction*, particularly if there are some minor gaps in some competencies, or if several candidates could meet expectations, but in different ways. Which bet do you want to make?

Where minor gaps in competencies exist, your behavioral prediction may include cross-correlating the candidate's potential with existing or planned organizational supports, to see whether and how the candidate could likely be successful despite those gaps.

For very large organizations that hire very frequently for similar positions, as well as for some specialized professional services firms, some more advanced decision-making processes and models have been developed. For example, our firm uses an advanced competency-scales model for senior executives, and we rigorously define properly validated target levels required for each position. In some cases, multiple regression models have been developed, which weight each key competency using different types of decision rules (sequential or nonsequential, compensatory or noncompensatory). Finally, some people have experimented with a technique called "bootstrapping," whereby a model for decision-making is built based on an expert's intuitive predictions, with the surprising effect that, when that model is used, it outperforms the expert. It appears that the model gets the best out of the expert, while reducing random noise from fatigue, boredom, stress, or anxiety.

Dealing with Intuition

A final goal for your appointment decision is to *achieve a proper balance between rationality and intuition*. This is a balance that will change over time.

As you start making your first people decisions, it will be very hard for you to distinguish facts from stereotypes or emotions. Relying on intuition when you have little expertise in assessments tends to result in poor decisions.

This warning pertains even to top-level executives. In their research on executive selection, the Center for Creative Leadership noted that many of the top-level executives they interviewed were not experts at selection. In fact, 20 percent of those they interviewed had *never* been involved in the selection of top-level executives.[21] Relying on intuition in these cases can be very risky, indeed!

Once you become more experienced, though, you *should* listen more to your own intuition, because it will incorporate the learnings from your past people decisions. Yes, check the facts behind that intuition—and also listen to it.

My Biggest Embarrassment

I remember asking myself, *How can this be happening? Is this a nightmare?* I wished I could wake up, but unfortunately, I couldn't.

I was meeting with a very unhappy client, who with my professional help had hired a marketing manager a few months earlier. It had been a disaster. The hired candidate had an impeccable background on paper, which included an MBA degree from one of the best business schools in the States and an impressive previous career. Now, though, he not only had a poor relationship with his team, but also was behaving in a way that was absolutely countercultural and apparently even unethical.

I don't remember being so embarrassed professionally in my whole life. How could this happen to me? By that time I had some 15 years of executive search experience. My track record was strong: In more than 90 percent of the hundreds of searches I had conducted, the candidates hired had been highly successful. I had never had a failure like *this*.

What went wrong? The reason this happened to me, I finally realized, was *complacency*. Too late, I remembered the warning of our firm's founder, Egon Zehnder, who used to say that complacency is a twin that grows side by side with superb performance results.

I had overlooked one of the sacrosanct policies for our professional practice, which is to *never* present a candidate without reliable reference checks conducted with individuals who have worked close to that candidate. That candidate had been referred to me by two people whom I knew well and trusted, and I had also received positive general comments from a colleague in his alumni association. A series of factors, including the client's willingness to move forward at full speed, his imminent departure on a long business trip, and yes, my own self-confidence, persuaded me to skip that crucial step.

The worst part of the story is that I could have easily checked the candidate out through people whom I knew well, and who had worked with that individual at Company X. Too late, I found out that the successful candidate had been asked to leave Company X for reasons similar to those later experienced by our client, despite Company X's statement (probably intended to head off potential litigation) that he had left on his own. I can't emphasize it enough: *Be disciplined while checking references.* Don't take any shortcuts. Make sure that the successful candidate has what it takes to succeed in the new job.

Building Organizational Strength

If you follow the recommendations above, you are likely to enjoy remarkable results while making great people decisions. In our own organization, as mentioned earlier, we hire people without any previous executive search experience. Through the right combination of general skill, motivation, and training, our people quickly become extremely proficient, as witnessed by the fact that 90 percent of the candidates we put forward are still with our clients five years down the road—not only performing successfully, but in many cases rising well beyond their original position. In addition, as mentioned earlier, our ability to predict a manager's potential for growth (through our management appraisal practice) has been up to three times as good as that of the manager's own organization, which has known him or her for years.

I repeat this not to boast, but to point out that this level of assessment accuracy can be achieved by people who have the right motivation, and are given opportunities to practice and receive proper feedback.

Developing your assessment skills will be key for your career success, as discussed in Chapter 1. Likewise, assessment skills will make a major contribution to your company's balance sheet and income statement. A better people decision can mean billions of dollars of value won or lost, when the CEO position at a large company is in the balance. And great people decisions represent a huge value at lower levels, too, especially when aggregated across the organization, and when projecting the future value of high potentials joining the organization. This is the way you can build another GE—another visionary, built-to-last company—and for the company to move from good to great.

In order to make your people decisions a key source of organizational strength (the O factor of the HOT SHOT model), there are several things that you and your organization should do.

First, *make sure that you have high-caliber individuals appraising people*. Don't delegate this crucial task to junior or unqualified individuals, or to those who may not have the right motivation (such as the direct reports).

Second, *invest in training those individuals who will frequently play assessment roles*, following proven assessment and training best practices.

Third, *make sure to review the way the assessments have been conducted, as well as the hard evidence for each key competency, before making a final decision*. Research has shown that interviewers who know that their assessments will be reviewed achieve much better appraisals, by better focusing on job-related information and avoiding the most frequent biases.[22]

Fourth, *make sure to review the assessments not only just before making the decision, but also one or two years down the road*. Learning about the consequences of people decisions is useful feedback for the assessors, helps you assess your own organization's appraisal skills, and gives you guidance for selecting the best assessors in the future.

Finally, *objectively assess your results sometime down the road, and be willing to undo a bad decision*. When Jim Collins was asked how the top leaders of the great companies he had analyzed went about deciding who were the right people to be "on the bus," he responded as follows:

> They adopted the approach: "Let's take the time to make rigorous A+ selections right up front. If we get it right, we'll do everything we can to try to keep them on board for a long time. If we make a mistake, then we'll confront the fact, so that we can get on with our work and they can get on with their lives."[23]

You won't get it right every time—and you don't *have* to get it right every time. Early-career assessment mechanisms turn out to be as important as hiring mechanisms, since the only way to know for certain about a person is to work with that person. Meanwhile, though, you can work on getting the pipeline filled with great people, through great assessments.

Figure 7.7 summarizes the key points covered in this chapter.

Improving appraisals is key
- Current practice is very poor.
- Improving appraisals is even more valuable than generating more candidates or reducing their expected compensation.
- Powerful research has proven that assessments can be significantly improved.

The best techniques for assessments include a combination of
- Structured interviews
- Rigorous reference checks

Other key issues, however, can be even more important than the assessment techniques, including
- High-caliber assessors, with the right level of competence and motivation
- The right composition of the selection team
- A disciplined process, from the initial confirmation of the key competencies all the way to the final decision

You can significantly increase your organizational capability in this critical area by
- Selecting the right assessors
- Training them following proven practices
- Reviewing assessments before confirming the hiring or promotion decision
- Following up over time the results of these decisions, for individual as well as organizational feedback purposes

FIGURE 7.7   How to Appraise People

■ ■ ■

If you follow the principles examined in this chapter, you will achieve valid and reliable assessments and be ready to hire or promote the very best people in the world. Since you are dealing with mutual choices, though, the next issue is how to attract and motivate those great people, which is the subject of Chapter 8.

CHAPTER EIGHT

How to Attract and Motivate the Best People

If you have followed each of the steps from the preceding chapters, congratulations: You have identified the best potential candidate for your job. But be careful! At this juncture, you can successfully hire that person or you can go back to Square One by failing to hire him or her.

Up to this point, we have been focusing primarily on finding and assessing the very best people for *your* needs. Now we return to the issue of mutual choices, and the key challenge of getting the other person to accept your offer—in other words, *their* needs. This is a stage full of uncertainty and risk for both sides, where motivational and money issues come into play, and where the most powerful combination of rationality and passion must be displayed.

Let's start this chapter with two scenarios from the real world:

Scenario 1: In March 1988, I started working on a complex search for the operations manager for the startup of an oil company in Argentina. The client was an extremely bright and successful young executive, who knew perfectly well what he was looking for, both in terms of performance expectations and candidate profile. He expected a series of opportunities to open up in the market over the following years, as a result of the privatization of some of the production areas of YPF, which at that point was still a state-owned company. He would lead the startup,

229

but he wanted to complement his own general management, strategic, commercial, and financial skills with a very strong operations manager. This new manager would have extensive responsibilities: helping my client identify and assess various investment opportunities, providing technical input while bidding for different areas, effectively taking control of the production areas awarded, building up the respective teams in each place, and properly controlling costs in order to achieve high production efficiency.

We worked together very effectively as a team, conducting a thorough executive search effort that enabled us to identify and investigate 49 potential candidates for the position. Following deep assessments of a large subgroup, through proper interviewing and reference-checking processes, we were both convinced that there was just one outstanding prospect. Compensation didn't appear to be an issue, since that candidate was already working for YPF, which at that time had very low compensation levels. In addition, many at YPF were anxious about the future, thanks to the privatization rumors that were swirling around. For all these reasons, we were confident that we could "land" our prospect, especially when we put a very attractive offer in front of him.

Imagine our surprise when he rejected the offer outright, and completely withdrew from the search. It turned out that it wasn't a matter of money. He just was not at all convinced about the project, and didn't want to go forward with it.

Scenario 2: Some eight years later, I was having a crucial meeting with the president and CEO of a major consumer goods company—in fact, the worldwide leader in its segment. He was making the offer to the finalist for the CFO position, who in our collective view had a unique set of skills for the challenges ahead. It was an in-person meeting, which I attended. When the offer was made, the candidate elegantly thanked us for it, and said that it was just too low. Despite being without a job at that time, he could not accept that offer. Stunned by this unexpected setback, the president and CEO (who would have been the hired candidate's boss) asked whether his compensation expectations were very far away from the offer. The candidate replied that, yes, they were definitely far away; in fact, he was expecting exactly *twice* as much. Both of them stood up to shake hands and depart.

I will come back to both stories and their endings later in the chapter. The point I want to make now is that while every job search finally ends, *it doesn't always end in the way one would have hoped.* Many of the best candidates melt away when the focus of a hiring process shifts from evaluation to recruitment—in some cases because the job is sold to them badly (or not at all), and in others because the right mix of rationality and passion just isn't there.

Is This the Best for the Candidate?

It is at delicate junctures like the two described earlier when our emotions can overtake us—by persuading us either to give up prematurely, or to go through hoops to win the reluctant candidate over with unrealistic promises or conditions, which can only create further trouble down the road. So it's at times like these when we need to control ourselves, put ourselves in the candidate's shoes, and ask ourselves whether this proposed change is *truly the best thing for him or her.*

Obviously, I've seen many cases of satisfaction, success, and happiness that have grown out of the right job change. (That's one reason why I enjoy my work so much.) At the same time, I've also seen some very unhappy scenarios unfold, which ended up in frustration and firings. I've even seen a few cases that ended in stress-related illness, or suicide. "One of the best hiring [practices]," as Harvard Professor Howard Stevenson recently said to me, "is to think not only about what the person can contribute to the job, but also about what could *destroy* the person in that job."[1]

I've already pointed out that many candidates—particularly those without a job, or frustrated in their current ones—are tempted to present themselves in the best possible light. Unfortunately, the same holds true for many corporations. They sell an *ideal* job, rather than the real one.

Then, inevitably, they lose credibility, either at the offer stage or, even worse, when the hired candidate confronts the hard reality.

All too often, the company makes little or no effort to understand the candidate's circumstances and motivations. They prematurely float an offer, and sometimes even a second offer (in effect, bidding against themselves), trying to make up with money for either a lack of motivation on the candidate's part or significant uncertainties that have not been properly addressed.

The first critical step of selling a job is understanding the main motives and the primary concerns of the candidate, and checking for alignment between that reality and the reality of the job. Some people are motivated by money; others are motivated by challenge. Still others want to work with a great group of colleagues. Professionals typically have a significant need for achievement, and managers and leaders tend to be driven by a significant need for power or influence. But each person is different, and you have to get to know the specifics of that person.

Many years ago, I interviewed a brilliant individual who was the CEO of a nongovernmental organization (NGO). Toward the end of the interview, he revealed how much money he was then earning. I asked him whether he was aware that in a for-profit environment, he would be making at least three times as much. He looked me straight in the eye and said something like the following:

> Claudio, I am fully aware that in other organizations I could make at least three times as much money as I do. However, I tell myself that I make three times as much money, and I consciously decide to spend two-thirds out of that total making sure that I do what I truly enjoy, what makes my life meaningful, and what makes me truly happy. Luckily, with the remaining third of that total I can live a reasonable life and properly provide for my family.

I have always been very impressed with that man. Several years after that interview, he came back to my memory when I came across his obituary in the newspaper—a long article about his outstanding contributions to society. He led a life of impact and significance, made an outstanding social contribution, and doubtless died a very happy man. Yes, he needed money to provide for his family, but beyond a certain point, money had absolutely no weight in his career choices and job decisions.

For other people, obviously, money and other types of compensation are far more important. So you have to understand the candidate's interests and motivations, while making your best effort to try to genuinely understand his or her career alternatives. *Only if you become convinced that what you are offering is the best for the candidate will you be able to attract that candidate.*

Sharing Your Passion

Nothing convinces like conviction. If you have done your homework, understand the candidate's motivation, and are convinced that what you are offering is the best for her, (almost) nothing will stop you. In most cases, you *will* be able to hire the best.

Let's go back to Scenario 1, the search for the operations manager for the oil company: After the candidate rejected the offer, we met with our client and conducted a very detailed analysis about the alternative candidates, and also about the reasons why the offer had been rejected. We came to the conclusion that the candidate was so superior to any other alternative that we would be willing to invest as much time and effort as needed to persuade him, even if it required several months. We decided that the only way to succeed was to let the candidate get to know the project and the client so well that any concerns would surface, be dealt with, and vanish.

We then embarked upon an amazing process of "wooing and winning." Over the following months, I traveled three times to his home in the middle of the remote Patagonia region in the south of Argentina. For me, this meant taking a plane and driving some 200 kilometers. I developed a relationship with him, his wife, and even his Doberman. My wife María and I spent a delightful New Year's Eve with the candidate and his wife in the beautiful Patagonian town of San Martín de los Andes, high in the mountains, a thousand miles from our home. Shortly thereafter, our client himself went to visit them during their vacation by the sea.

As a result of this effort to get to know each other well, the candidate finally decided to join in March 1989, exactly *one year* after the search project had started. His subsequent performance on the job was absolutely spectacular. He had a unique knowledge of each of the oil areas in the whole country, which made him invaluable when YPF started privatizing their production. He and our client together made a wonderful team: assessing each area from the technical point of view, and deciding strategically, financially, and from a competitive standpoint how much to bid for it. And after a few areas had been awarded to this company, the man displayed a genius for setting up operations very fast, with very high levels of productivity. Last but surely not least, he proved very skilled at quickly building up a wonderful team, largely due to his great market knowledge, competence, credibility, and reputation.

Yes, this is an *extreme* case! But I can't emphasize enough the importance of going out of your way to understand the candidates and their motivation, address their concerns, and *share your passion* about your company, your projects, and the job you are offering.

Anyone can hire average people. Anyone can hire people who are on the market, and are hungry. But hiring the *best* people, especially those who aren't looking for a job, demands your best rational and passionate effort.

Money Talks

While passion sings, money talks. When I asked Jack Welch about his strategies for attracting top players who were not looking for a change, he replied, "Give them lots of money, and a picture. Paint a picture for them. If they are successful, they are the big men. And do it with full integrity. It's money and picture."[2] So, sharing your passion is key to "painting the picture," but the money has to come along, as well.

The current public debates about senior executive compensation are fraught with emotion, and passionate voices can be heard at both ends of the spectrum. Critics point out that between 1970 and 1999, the average real compensation of the top 100 U.S. CEOs went from $1.3 million to $37.5 million.[3] In 1979, the average compensation of the top 100 CEOs was 39 times that of the average worker; 20 years later, it was *1,000 times as large.*[4] Some compensation figures are absolutely unbelievable, such as the *$1.6 billion* option package offered to UnitedHealth Group CEO William McGuire—this at a time, as a Wharton School report points out, "when more than 40 million Americans lack health insurance."[5]

But observers at the other end of the spectrum believe that the *typical* CEO's pay is not excessive. As Wharton Professor Wayne Guay puts it, "The egregious pay packages that attract so much attention from the press—of, say, $20 million plus—only apply to a handful of CEOs." In fact, says Guay, the median CEO in the S&P 1500 makes about $2.5 million a year.[6]

Let's face it: We all expect to be rewarded in a way that is somehow proportional to our efforts and our results. This point can't be overemphasized. We calculate our risks versus our returns. It is not just part of human nature; it is even part of our *animal* nature. A lynx chasing a snow rabbit only pursues it for about 200 yards. Then it gives up, because the food gained if the prey is caught can't compensate for the lost energy. But the lynx, calculating the potential returns, chases a deer much longer.

Primatologists Sarah F. Brosnan and Frans B.M. de Waal have shown that monkeys are offended by unfair reward systems. In a fascinating experiment conducted with female capuchin monkeys, Brosnan created a market in which monkeys were trained to give her a pebble in exchange for a slice of cucumber. The experiment was set up so that the monkeys worked in pairs, and when they were both awarded cucumbers, they exchanged pebbles for food 95 percent of the time. But when the experimenter changed the rules—giving one monkey a grape as a reward (a much preferred option, from a monkey's point of view), while still giving the other a cucumber slice—the monkeys got so frustrated that 40 percent of the time they just stopped trading, even if the deal of a rock for food was still a good one. And when one monkey was given a grape for nothing, the other monkey got so frustrated that she often tossed away her pebble. Only 20 percent of the monkeys continued to trade in that most unfair world![7]

No, we're not lynxes or monkeys, but we know where our interests lie, and we want fair compensation in a fair game.

Assessing Retention Priorities

We'll return to the subject of designing the right compensation package to attract the best candidate. First, though, I want to highlight how important it is to make sure that *your compensation packages are aligned with your retention priorities*. It makes little sense to develop the best compensation package to attract an external candidate, while at the same time losing invaluable resources due to uncompetitive internal compensation practices.

This becomes particularly important in times of change, as in the case of the telecommunications company (described in Chapter 4) that was facing a new set of challenges, including service deregulation and increased competition in local markets. In addition to assessing their management team in terms of competence and potential, we helped them assess their retention priorities. Besides assessing the criticality of each *manager* (as a function of his or her competence and potential), we assessed as well the criticality of each *job*, and compared that with the potential market demand following deregulation. The result of this analysis is summarized in Figure 8.1.

Whenever significant changes happen in an industry, compensa-

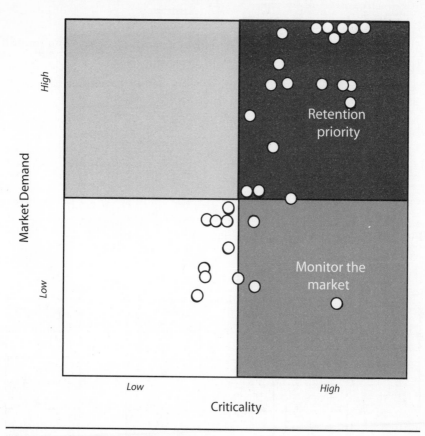

FIGURE 8.1 Retention Priorities

tion packages are at risk of becoming badly misaligned with the critical-ity of the most senior resources. This proved true in the case of this telecommunications company. Figure 8.2 compares for each key manager his or her criticality with the market competitiveness of the compensa-tion package. While the competitiveness of the compensation packages should have been aligned with the managers' respective criticalities, there was almost no correlation whatsoever, putting the company at real risk of losing some of its most critical resources over the coming years.

Given this situation, we analyzed the retention risk for each of the

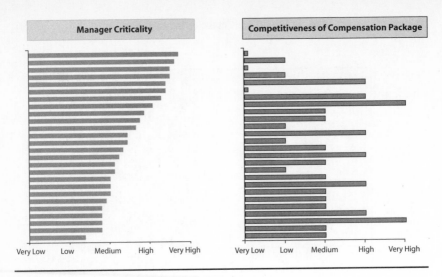

FIGURE 8.2   Critically vs. Compensation

	Job Criticality	Market Demand	Compensation Risk		Retention Risk
Manager A	●	○	○		○
Manager B	◐	●	●		●
Manager C	○	○	○		○
Manager D	●	○	○		○
Manager E	●	●	●		●
Manager F	◐	●	◐		◐
Manager G	◐	◐	◐		◐
Manager H	●	●	●		●
Manager I	○	◐	◐		◐
Manager J	◐	●	○		◐
Manager K	◐	◐	○		◐

● High   ◐ Med.   ○ Low

FIGURE 8.3   Retention Risk

strategic resources, in light of their criticality, the potential market demand, and the compensation risk (which was obviously inversely proportional to the competitiveness of their respective packages). The simple analysis summarized in Figure 8.3 proved very helpful in introducing some objectivity into a series of retention actions including, but not limited to, adjusting compensation packages, which otherwise might have been highly emotional and controversial.

The Problems with Incentives

Type the word "compensation" into the Google search engine, and you'll get close to 240 million hits. Type in the word "rewards," and you'll get more than 5.6 million hits. Clearly, mountains of literature exist on these topics. But while money is indeed important, the evidence about the inherent power of "pay for performance" is surprisingly inconclusive. According to Stanford professors Jeffrey Pfeffer and Robert Sutton, "The use of financial incentives is a subject filled with ideology and belief— and where many of those beliefs have little or no evidence to support them."[8] As a result, they conclude, a careful analysis should be made before setting up financial incentives.

To start with, a reasonably high level of total compensation is needed to *attract* the best. This is particularly true for senior positions for which, as I emphasized in earlier chapters, the spread in performance is so large that it pays to attract a top performer. What is "reasonably high," of course, depends on each market at the given point in time.

The second objective of compensation is to *motivate* the best. From this point of view, *how* you pay can be as important as *how much* you pay. *Motivating for objectivity* argues for some form of long-term incentive, ideally along the lines of restricted shares (or some equivalent) rather than stock options, which have a very strong upside but limited downside. *Motivating for performance* in most cases argues for some form of short-term, variable pay component, such as a yearly bonus.

Meanwhile, you need to take special care to properly structure your offer to avoid creating the *wrong* incentives. First, exaggerated incentives, particularly short-term ones, can put an excessive emphasis on short-term results. In addition, exaggerated incentives can actually bring a person way beyond the tipping point of performance. Yes, we need some level of stress to operate effectively, and clear objectives and proper incentives are powerful up to a certain level. This derives, in part, from brain chemistry: The right level of stress increases the activity of the glucocorticoid system, with a moderate level of secretion of cortisol, which is associated with engagement, performance, and learning. But when the level of stress becomes too high, a second neural system kicks in, where the brain secretes high levels of cortisol and norepinephrine. These secretions, associated with a state of outright fear, dramatically *limit* our rational abilities, our effectiveness at work, and even our memory and learning ability.[9]

While our brains have been shaped to focus our attention on a target (probably a survival mechanism for our hunter ancestors, who needed to focus fully on their prey), excessive target-fixation can make us lose perspective, become insensitive, and even make fatal errors. The crash of the entire Thunderbirds acrobatic team of the U.S. Air Force in 1982 provides a tragic illustration. All the pilots were killed just because they were focused only on exactly following the previous plane a few feet away. When the leader's plane suffered a mechanical malfunction and plunged earthward, everyone else followed.[10]

Second, it is very hard to construct proper incentive systems, and any purely quantitative formula can suffer from either rewarding results not attributable to the manager or, at the other end, not properly recognizing efforts and contribution when external factors may have produced poor results. Thus, if you want to develop significant incentive components in your package, make sure to analyze them carefully, possibly with the help of specialists.

Third, most complex jobs require collaboration, and therefore individual incentives can be extremely negative, motivating individuals to compete rather than to collaborate. Several years ago, while I was attending an executive program for professional services firms at Harvard, the professor asked how many in the room had individual financial incentives within their firms, and something like 70 out of the 80 participants raised their hands. Out of the 10 who did *not* have individual financial incentives, there wasn't a single U.S. firm represented, despite the fact that the vast majority of the participants were Americans. Individual financial incentives are in fact the norm for professional services firms, particularly in the United States—a type of incentive that usually goes by the name "eat what you kill." The opposite type of system is often called the "lockstep," in which individual compensation does not depend on individual performance, but rather on the firm's overall profits and some measure of seniority, typically tenure.

While most firms feature some version of an eat-what-you-kill system, in every single domain of professional services there are typically a few firms with a lockstep system. Somewhat surprisingly, these few firms are usually the most profitable ones and those with the best reputation, as in the case of Wachtell, Lipton, Rosen & Katz among law firms, McKinsey & Company in management consulting (technically a "modified lockstep"), or our own firm in executive search.[11] In fact, Professor Marshall W. Van Alstyne, who teaches Information Economics at Boston University and conducts research at MIT, has recently published an article demonstrating that firms with collective incentives share much more knowledge, and are indeed far more profitable, than those that reward individual performance.[12]

Dealing with Risks and Incentives

Let's summarize where we've been so far: To attract and motivate the best people, you need to put yourself in the candidate's shoes, candidly assess whether your opportunity is truly the best for him or her, share your passion, and then prepare an attractive compensation package (without overdoing it, and in light of your retention policies).

It really helps at this stage to follow a disciplined process, particularly for a very senior position such as a CEO, where the compensation components should be the natural outgrowth of the key performance measures aligned with the major objectives for the new manager.

Before structuring your offer and confirming the right incentives, you also need to try to *assess the main sources of risk* as objectively as possible. External managers are frequently hired for high-risk situations, such as startups, mergers and acquisitions, and major change efforts including turnarounds.[13]

My first recommendation for dealing with risk is *to invest enough time to share very openly the true sources of risk.* When discussing this point with clients and candidates, I frequently use the analogy of statistics, where inevitably you run into two types of error: either rejecting a true hypothesis, or accepting a false one. If you reduce the risk of one of these types of error, you inevitably increase the other. From the point of view of the candidate, he or she can make two types of mistakes: getting into the wrong job, or not jumping at a unique opportunity. For him or her, the only strategy to simultaneously reduce both risks is to have more information about you, your company, and the job—including its risks.

There are two classic risk-related mistakes that are often made at this stage. The first, as indicated above, is to ignore risks as the candidate sees them. (By so doing, you miss the chance to confront and correct the candidate's misperceptions.)

The second mistake is to compensate for these risks with lots of money in the absence of proper analysis. The negative consequences include leaving money on the table, and (in many cases) creating exactly the wrong incentive. The best example is the "golden parachute," which creates a perverse incentive to promote conflict and get fired. But the signing bonus is nearly as bad, because it pays reluctant candidates to suspend their judgment—which is exactly the capacity you're hiring them for!

In more than 300 executive search assignments, I have recommended golden parachutes and signing bonuses only in exceptional cases. And I would *never* recommend them to overcome a lack of trust on the part of the candidate. Nobody should work for someone they don't trust. While special situations actually demand for these types of components, they should be the exception rather than the rule. A manager should join a new company feeling confident that both sides will deliver, and that they will feel mutually comfortable with each other. If these two conditions are met, these types of incentives shouldn't be needed.

Again, objectively analyze the major risks, and deal with them by sharing information very openly and eventually making sure that your contract properly addresses them.

Figure 8.4 illustrates the conceptual analysis of the package put to-

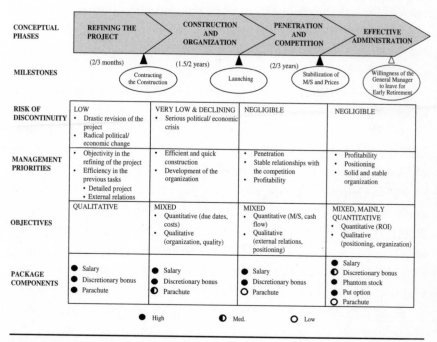

FIGURE 8.4   Package Engineering

gether when a consumer goods company was hiring a local country manager to launch a startup for the first time in a new country. As his initial job, the hired manager would have to reconfirm whether they should definitely go ahead with the proposed launch in the target country. While there was a low risk of pulling the plug entirely, we agreed with the client that we wanted the candidate to be objective, and not recommend a major investment if he became convinced that it was not worthwhile to invest. A special protection was engineered into the contract that was (1) fair enough to compensate the manager if he "talked himself out of a job" after just a few months, but (2) not so strong as to create an incentive against the investment, if it was indeed justified.

As can be seen in Figure 8.4, the different phases of the startup included, sequentially: refining the project; constructing the facilities and setting up the organization; launching their product to fight the former monopolistic competitor; and finally maintaining an effective administration. For each of these phases, clear management priorities were confirmed, with a series of qualitative and quantitative objectives, which helped define the different package components along the life of the project.

While the details of the complex contract exceed the scope of this chapter, my point here is to highlight a series of incentives for each phase—and even a different type of parachute for each, tied to the specific risks of that phase—which declined over time. In order to achieve alignment with the shareholders, there was a very significant long-term incentive that took the form of phantom stock with a put option that could be exercised after the company had stabilized its penetration in the market. Given all the uncertainties in the interim periods, there was a significant-yet-discretionary bonus, together with a competitive salary.

As it turned out, the hired candidate was highly successful for several years. At the right time (from his perspective and the company's), he decided to exercise his put option and leave, at which point a different type of manager was recruited.

It's All About the Right People

One of the searches I conducted many years ago was for the controller of a not-for-profit organization. The finalist received an offer that was for about *half* the compensation he was then earning. To my surprise, he accepted, and performed exceedingly well for many years. Furthermore, he stayed in that job despite the fact that he had to take the initiative to fight a very high level of internal corruption, as a result of which he and his family were repeatedly threatened. He had to change his phone number twice in order to be able to get through the night without frightening calls.

I must confess that when the client made the offer to the candidate without discussing it with me in advance (I was present at the meeting) I was surprised, concerned, and even disappointed. I later on acknowledged that the offer represented a true test of the candidate's commitment to the organization's noble mission, which was a key condition for success and continuity.

This may sound naïve or idealistic, but it's simply true: In more than 20 years of executive-search experience, I have found that what candidates look for, first and foremost, is not more money, but a job where they can do their best, with a challenge that perfectly matches their skill level, in a place where they will grow and develop, in an organization they like, with a good boss and a great group of peers. Conversely, most people don't leave jobs because of money issues; they leave bad bosses and frustrating situations. If there is a good challenge, a good fit, and a good boss, the right candidate will be motivated.

From the candidate's point of view, research about happiness consistently shows that the two driving circumstances are a meaningful job and rich relationships, while money (past a certain minimum level) is more of a hygiene factor. From the organization's point of view, you want the right candidate, one who really cares about the job and the organization. As Stanford Professor James Baron has discovered in his

MBA course on Human Resources Management, even MBAs (who arguably are more oriented toward financial incentives than most people) prefer a doctor who has entered medicine because he or she was interested in the subject matter, and had a desire to serve people, much rather than one who has entered medicine primarily to make a lot of money.[14]

When asked how important executive compensation and incentive decisions are for building a great company, Jim Collins gives the following answer:

> To our surprise, executive compensation appears to play no significant role in determining which companies become great. After 112 analyses looking for a strong link between executive compensation and corporate results, our research found no pattern. We learned that making a company great has very little to do with how you compensate executives, and everything to do with which executives you have to compensate in the first place.
>
> If you have the right people, they will do everything in their power to make the company great. The purpose of compensation is not to "motivate" the right behaviors from the wrong people, but to attract and retain the right people in the first place. This is not to say that we should entirely ignore the compensation question. Certainly, many corporate boards have failed in their responsibility to shareholders by granting compensation packages that have huge upside and little downside. Still, the most important decision a board makes is not how it pays, but whom it pays.[15]

In the end, if you want to build a great company, it is all about having the best people. For them, money is important, but not disproportionately so. As Collins observes, it's more about *whom* you pay, rather than *how much* or *how* you pay.

A Matter of Courage

Now let's go back to Scenario 2, my meeting 10 years ago with the president and CEO of the large consumer goods company, where the finalist had rejected the offer, confessing that his compensation expectation was twice as high. He and the CEO were on the verge of shaking hands and saying good-bye. I was sitting at the head of the table, with my client on my right and the candidate on my left.

What I did next surprised even me. I stood up and said, "Please don't say good-bye!" Looking at the client, I said, "Quite frankly, I admire what you have done with your company, and I am absolutely convinced that you just can't let this opportunity go."

Then I turned to the candidate and said, "Likewise, I have followed you for the last ten years, and I am absolutely convinced not only that you will be able to add huge value to this company, but also that this is the best opportunity that's available to you. You will achieve great success, and you will enjoy your job immensely. You simply can't let this opportunity pass."

I escorted the candidate to another meeting room, asked him to wait a minute, and went back to my client. We both sat down. After a few seconds of silence, I shared with him with full candor that his offer was too low for the reality of the market and the caliber of that CFO candidate. Even if this candidate had accepted the offer, he would have presented a retention risk the minute he sat down at his desk. I pointed out how negligible the CFO's package would be compared with the potential value he represented to the company. If there were doubts about the candidate's capabilities or fit, I plunged ahead, of *course* we should not proceed. But if there were no doubts, we should not accept a "no," at least without another effort.

It was, without exaggeration, a turning point in the history of the company. This CEO had never paid that level of compensation to any subordinates, and yet, he was well aware that several other candidates whom we had investigated were earning compensation packages very similar to, and in some cases even larger than, that expected by the finalist.

I left him to reflect on our exchange, and went back to meet the candidate, still waiting in the other room. I noted that he was sitting on the edge of his chair—a clue that he also perceived a potential turning point.

We talked. I knew that he had been unemployed for a full year. What I *didn't* know (and was astounded to learn) was that during that tough period he had the guts to turn down *seven* offers. He told me, in so many words, that he just couldn't bring himself to take a job that didn't convince him. He said, candidly, that he was fully convinced about this opportunity, except for the money. I checked whether there were any other issues, but he convinced me that there were none. I told him to sit tight.

Then I went back to the client, and expressed my absolute conviction about the candidate's motivations, as well as the reasonableness of the compensation package that the candidate expected. Finally, the CEO acquiesced. Within 20 minutes they were shaking hands again— but this time in the spirit of beginning a wonderful professional relationship. The final conditions, as negotiated, were much closer to the candidate's expectations (and the market rate) than the original offer. The CEO and his new CFO worked together for almost a decade. The new CFO provided enormous financial value to the company, playing an invaluable role not only in the day-to-day management but also in very special financial restructuring, acquisitions, and crisis-management situations. Over that decade, he received not only generous compensation, but also rich nonmonetary rewards.

The lesson I took away from that meeting was that the critical element at these crucial instances is to *have enough courage.* You have to have the courage to depart from traditions and self-imposed constraints when there is a compelling reason to do so. How does the old saying go? *Stupid people have no rules. Clever people have rules and follow them. Geniuses know when to make an exception.*

If you have done your homework in finding and assessing the best candidates, if the order of magnitude of the compensation package is reasonable against the market, if you have confirmed the right motivation and dealt with the potential risks properly, then it is the time to *move*: from candor, concern, and rational analysis to straight courage. You need to go the extra distance to close the deal.

Getting the Right Kind of Help

Maybe you were surprised at my audacity in deciding to bridge the gap between the CEO and CFO described above. Well, so was I. But I was emboldened because my client and I had worked together closely over a number of years, and we knew and understood each other.

This leads me to raise the subject of getting outside help in your people searches. I once asked Jack Welch whether, in the unusual cases in which GE went outside for leaders, he employed executive search firms. If so, what advice might he offer to others in his shoes? His response:

> Yes, I used search firms. I can't speak for GE's criteria for picking and using search firms. But for me, I just have one criterion. I choose someone I trust. And this only comes with time, with years. Someone you have a good personal relation with. Who is in the game, who is a good player. Who is always interested in getting the right person, rather than in collecting the fee.[16]

"Trust" has several components, in this context. Obviously, it grows out of a client's perception of the consultant's personal competence. But it also grows out of the client's faith in the consultant's firm, and how that firm is structured. These observations lead to two prescriptions.

First, *select an individual consultant*, rather than just a firm. Picking a search firm based only on its literature is like hiring an executive based only on his resume. Like many other professional services firms, some executive search firms use seasoned partners to land assignments, and then use less experienced people (including newly minted MBAs) to conduct the searches. *So make sure that you meet the consultants who will actually be handling each step of your search.* You need to assess their experience and technical competence, and get a read on their availability, affability, and candor. Integrity is critical, so strong and reliable references are a prerequisite.

Second, *explore the stability of the firm's professional staff, and the mechanisms it uses to enhance collaboration.* This is key, because the value of executive search firms grows directly out of their knowledge-sharing abilities. A good search firm will provide you first with insight about positions and candidates, and subsequently with access to them. Both tasks, clearly, will depend on the consultants' abilities to collaborate and share knowledge. A recent article by Boston University economist Marshall W. Van Alstyne demonstrated how the incentives (or *lack* of incentives) for collaboration within recruiting firms drastically influenced internal communications among consultants, and thereby affected client service.[17] Firms with stable teams that share their knowledge are much more likely to have amassed, and made available to their whole staff, a unique store of information about:

- Potential candidates, sources, and references
- The specific needs of different positions
- The most powerful ways to properly find, assess, motivate, and integrate the best candidates

In the spirit of full disclosure, the executive search profession was born with deep conflicts of interest, and sadly, this circumstance still persists today. As Pfeffer and Sutton point out in their most recent book, several of the largest executive search firms *still* have the wrong incentives, since the fees they charge their corporate clients are based on a percentage of the executive's compensation (typically, one-third of the first year's cash compensation). "The more senior executives make," they point out, "the more the search firms make."[18] Obviously, this percentage-fee arrangement creates an unholy incentive for the search consultant to present the *most expensive* candidates, who may or may not be the *best* candidates.

Another closely related structural source of conflicts arises when search firms are paid on a contingency, in whole or in part. A contingency arrangement is one in which the firm will be paid only if a candidate (and usually an external one) is finally hired. If contingencies are in place, either or both of two problems are likely to arise. First, the search consultant has an incentive to evaluate candidates more gently. (Otherwise, the contingent fee may not be forthcoming!) But no candidate is ever perfect, and advisors should be motivated to candidly share with their clients their honest perspective regarding each of them. In addition, a contingent fee builds pressure for recommending an outside candidate, rather than objectively considering both internal and external candidates.

A fixed flat fee and a retainer arrangement can sidestep all of these fee-related structural problems. It can reinforce *personal* trust with *structural* integrity.

Getting the Deal Done

To sum up, in the end, all of the preparation, identification, and assessment work will be wasted if the best candidate declines to join the company. You have to get the deal done.

Consider the case of a major foreign retail organization that conducted a North American search in a context of mounting business difficulties and growing competitive threats. Top U.S. talent was brought to the table, and a finalist was identified. But the company balked at the

$2 million compensation package that the person wanted, and it ulti-mately hired an internal candidate who wasn't as strong. That decision turned out to be penny-wise but pound-foolish, as the company eventu-ally went bankrupt.

In contrast, consider the effort made by the global dairy company introduced in earlier chapters. Once they confirmed the decision to hire an outstanding candidate who had been identified, they resolved to *get the deal done*. In that case, the courtship was not mainly about compensa-tion; instead, it comprised both significant gestures—including an exten-sive relocation trip for the person's spouse—and a host of small touches. This latter category included everything from not assuming the candi-date's wife had the same last name as the candidate (she didn't); to hav-ing mountain bikes available for them on their arrival, and maps of suggested paths to explore; to a casual and down-to-earth dinner with the chairman and his wife; to access to a special school, which was criti-cal to a family that would have to move halfway across the world; to ex-tensive housing tours, advice, and information. In my experience, small touches like this have frequently kept alive deals that otherwise would never have closed.

There are two final comments to make about this crucial juncture, in which all the previous effort either can pay off or can turn into a huge waste of time and effort:

First, just as high-caliber individuals are needed for assessing, high-caliber people are also critical in motivating the right candidate.

Second, as indicated earlier, having an intermediate advisor often can be valuable in helping each party openly express his or her interests and concerns, while at the same time bridging and presenting creative alternatives for mutual accommodation. Certainly when it comes to get-ting the deal done, executive search firms can play a key role in attract-ing and motivating the best candidates.

Figure 8.5 summarizes the key points covered in this chapter:

Moving from assessment to recruiting is a critical step
- The whole opportunity can materialize or vanish all of a sudden, for both parties.
- Expectations, doubts, anxiety, and concerns reach the limit.
- The best combination of reason and emotion needs to be displayed.

Classic mistakes at this stage include
- Failing to understand the other side
- Underinvesting in your selling efforts
- Giving up too early when the best candidate has doubts
- Focusing only on money issues
- Paying too much or too little
- Setting up the wrong incentives

Best practices for attracting and motivating the best people include
- First, understanding the candidate's motivation, concerns, and alternatives
- Sharing your passion about the opportunity
- Paying competitively for the relevant market, without overdoing it
- Setting up the right incentives, with great care in their design
- Properly dealing with any special risks
- Having enough courage to do exceptional things in exceptional cases

FIGURE 8.5   How to Attract and Motivate the Best People

■ ■ ■

Following the practices set forth in this chapter, you will be able to close the deal and hire the best candidate.

But your job is not done yet! By properly planning and supporting the integration process, you can significantly enhance the new hire's chances of success, as well as his or her expected performance. This is the subject of our next chapter.

CHAPTER NINE

How to Integrate the Best People

In June 1997, I participated in one of our firm's global conferences, attended by our consultants and their spouses, who had flown into Washington D.C. from all around the world. The theme of that conference was *collaboration*, and one of our keynote speakers was Captain James Lovell, the commander of the famed and ill-fated Apollo 13 mission.

As you may recall, two days after its April 1970 launch, Apollo 13 was crippled by a catastrophic failure of its cryogenic oxygen system. The planned lunar landing was aborted, and Mission Control in Houston decided to use the moon's gravity to "slingshot" the wounded spacecraft back to Earth. Lovell and his crew, working with their counterparts in Houston, successfully modified their Lunar Excursion Module (LEM) into an improvised "lifeboat." This required enormous ingenuity: The lunar module was designed to sustain only two people for two days; now it would be required to sustain three people for four days. There was only limited energy available, moreover, so there was almost no room for error—on the ground, or in space. If the returning spacecraft's trajectory was even slightly off, it would skip off the Earth's atmosphere like a stone off the surface of a pond. The world held its breath, following the drama on TV, as the three astronauts struggled against long odds to make their way home.[1]

Reflecting later on Lovell's presentation, which included a series of videos and clips from the Hollywood epic about the mission, I was struck by an analogy between bringing a spacecraft safely back to Earth and integrating a successful candidate into a new job. If the process is not properly managed, the candidate may very well "bounce off the atmosphere"—in this case, the culture of the organization—and be lost to the organization forever.

Apollo 13 made it home as the result of careful planning and collaboration, both among the returning astronauts and between the spacecraft and Houston.

Integrating a new manager into a workplace is challenging, and entails risks. But if the right candidate has been hired, a well planned process, based on effective collaboration between the manager and the organization, not only can help minimize these risks, but also can accelerate the integration process and position the new hire for far stronger performance.

What Are the Integration Risks?

New hires must learn a new job. If they come from outside the organization, they must figure out a new corporate culture (almost never an easy assignment!). They must develop new or revised relationships with key people.

All the while, they are being observed closely. Their surefootedness (or lack of it) as they make their initial moves will create indelible perceptions about their potential effectiveness. *The jury is out, and the verdict will be delivered.*

Despite this situation, most companies provide very little support, if any, to newly hired candidates. Studies conducted by the Center for Creative Leadership have shown that *fewer than one-third of newly hired executives receive any sort of integration or development for their new position at all,* while fewer than one in four receive support from their superiors.[2]

Because the risks of integration grow exponentially when it comes to senior positions (due to their complexity, visibility, and importance), I will focus in this chapter on integration at the top. But my analysis and prescriptions also apply to more junior positions, and I encourage readers to think about the possible broader implications of integration.

Integration into a new job is always challenging, but for a variety of reasons it's particularly daunting for candidates hired from outside. First, as previously discussed, outsiders are typically hired for challenging and risky assignments, including turnarounds, startups, and major change efforts. Outsiders usually lack the knowledge about how things are done in the new company, and don't have any social networks to orient them rapidly. Furthermore, while in many cases internal candidates are promoted with a development purpose in mind, external candidates are usually expected to hit the ground running. External candidates are less well known, and so there's often less awareness on the part of the hiring organization about specific weaknesses in the new hire that should be compensated for.

In addition to all of these challenges, individuals hired from outside typically confront a much higher level of organizational resistance than do insiders. First, internal candidates who aspired to the position have been frustrated. Second, while most promoted insiders start with a foundation of mutual trust, developed over years of working with their colleagues, external hires start with almost no such foundation—just a few hours of interviews, and perhaps some favorable internal PR. To make things even worse, external candidates are often recruited through higher compensation packages (the details of which generally flash around the workplace with amazing speed), and this, too, creates jealousy and resentment.

The Three Waves of Integration

Some 18 years ago, a few years after starting my career as an executive search consultant, I was wondering whether there was something else that we could do to help our clients, in addition to finding, assessing, and attracting the best potential candidates. This was before the days of on-line book vendors, so I tended to spend hours in the best bookstores whenever I visited the United States.

On one of those sojourns, I stumbled across a book called *The Dynamics of Taking Charge*, by a Harvard professor named John J. Gabarro. I thumbed through the book with growing interest. It presented a comparative study of 17 managerial transitions of division presidents, general managers, and functional managers. It described the very predictable stages that incoming managers pass through when taking on their new responsibilities, and delved into the kinds of organizational and interpersonal work that characterizes successful transitions.

I read the entire book on the plane going back home (one of the few benefits of long plane flights!), and as soon as I got into the office the following morning, I got in touch with my colleagues who were helping organize our upcoming firm conference in Vienna. I described Gabarro's book, and we decided to invite him to join us in Vienna as a guest speaker and share his insights with us. He subsequently made a powerful presentation to our assembled consultants, and I think it's fair to say his ideas have exerted a strong influence on our firm ever since.

I personally have gone back to that book regularly. I've given it as a present to dozens of new managers and clients. It's still the best book ever written on the integration of new managers, probably because Gabarro studied his 17 subjects in great depth over the course of eight years, conducting rich and deep personal interviews with each of them. It details successful and failed successions, in companies of different sizes and industry sectors, at turnarounds and non-turnarounds, analyzing the integration of both insiders and outsiders.

Gabarro opens the book with remarks from a division general manager who was then 18 months into his new assignment:

> The longer you're in the new job, the more you develop a personal sense of comfort. You go from a period when you're on the edge of

your seat all the time—it feels like you have no knowledge base whatsoever about anything. You have to learn the product, the people, the situation, and the problems. It takes a period of time before you develop a comfortable feeling. It just plain takes awhile. You go through an early period of first trying like hell to learn about the organization. You're faced with a set of problems that are foreign to you. You have to learn about the people and their capabilities awfully fast and that's the trickiest thing to do. At first you're afraid to do anything for fear of upsetting the apple cart. The problem is you have to keep the business *running* while you *learn* about it.[3]

This excerpt illustrates the challenge, uncertainty, and excitement that managers feel when they take charge of a new assignment. Significantly, those comments weren't the observations of a young manager being tested for the first time, but those of a seasoned veteran who had spent over 20 years in executive assignments in sales, marketing, and manufacturing, both in consumer and industrial products. Integration is *hard*, even for the pros!

Gabarro argues that the process of taking charge comprises a series of highly predictable stages of learning and action, which he summarizes as the "Three Wave Phenomenon." The phrase refers to the average number of significant organizational changes made by a new manager in the first three years of his tenure. It is depicted in Figure 9.1.

Newly installed managers begin by going through a "taking-hold" stage, during which, after some initial diagnosis, they implement a series of changes, usually in the realm of basic corrective actions (Wave #1). Then comes the "immersion" stage, in which the new manager acquires a deeper knowledge of the organization and precipitates less change. Next comes the "reshaping" stage, which involves more profound and strategic changes (Wave #2). Finally, a third and smaller wave of change comes with the "consolidation" stage, which makes adjustments based on the outcomes of the reshaping period.

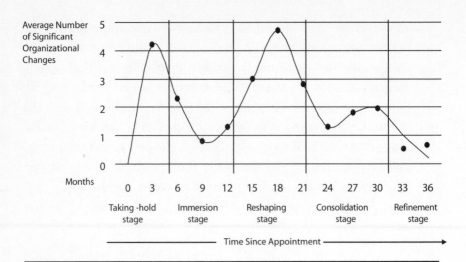

FIGURE 9.1   The Three-Wave Phenomenon

Source: Reproduced from *The Dynamics of Taking Charge*, by John J. Gabarro, with permission from HBSP.

Two important points grow out of this Three Wave model. First, *taking charge takes time.* Yes, time is money, and we would all like to accelerate these processes, but particularly for senior positions, acceleration is just not feasible. Building the right diagnosis, establishing trust, clarifying mutual expectations, and achieving influence—all of this takes significant time. Most of the managers in Gabarro's study expected a faster integration, but they were disappointed. The three-year integration period seemed to pertain across very different industries, and even across a range of industry outsiders and insiders. (It should be noted, however, that industry insiders typically achieved more change in each of the waves.) Likewise, the duration of the process was relatively similar for turnarounds and normal successions (although turnarounds involved greater change in each wave, reflecting the higher pressure to improve performance).

A second conclusion I draw from Gabarro's findings is that new managers face a dilemma: *how quickly to take action.* On the one hand, if they act too quickly, they may do so based on the wrong diagnosis, and fail. On the other hand, if they take too long to complete their diagnosis, they will frustrate the organization. Especially when the barn is on fire, *people want action.*

This brings us back to the subject of competencies, introduced in earlier chapters. One of the surest paths to a successful integration is to hire (or promote) emotionally and socially intelligent managers who can *get others to help them in the diagnostic phase,* accelerating it without sacrificing its quality. The manager most likely to fail at integration is the "Lone Ranger" (Gabarro's label), who can't involve others in the learning and action stages.

Accelerated Transitions

Given the ever-accelerating pace of business, you may wonder whether the long integration periods described by Gabarro still hold. Based on my experience, they do, and especially for senior positions in large organizations. Major change in the context of large companies still takes some three years, and the Three Waves still show up.

Having said that, there are other contexts, particularly in small, emerging companies, where new managers simply have to get integrated and make their mark within the first few months.

Our firm has conducted several studies of the integration of CEOs in different sectors. One interesting sector is the biotechs, where new managers are usually appointed as the result of initiatives by new investors (including venture capitalists). Typically, these companies have gone through a successful product-development phase under the guidance of a founder with a technical background. Now, as the new investors look for significant growth, they also look for leadership with new skill sets.

Our 2005 "Biotech CEO Survey" focused on the first 100 days of CEOs hired by a biotech or emerging healthcare company. We found significant action happening in those first 100 days, as illustrated in Figure 9.2. As can be seen in the figure, one-quarter of the CEOs decided within the first three months or so to restructure the company, cutting costs and eliminating fat. A second early step involved rearranging the team, with nearly one CEO in five taking this kind of action.[4]

In 2006, we conducted a similar study of the first three months on the job of 70 top managers working in the financial sector in Europe, Australia, Asia, and the United States. While in some cases there was significant action in the first three months (consistent with Gabarro's findings), on average it took about five months for these managers to feel comfortable in their roles, and this was true both for internal and external candidates. In this sector, the focus in the first months was mainly internal (structural and people decisions), while an external focus in the

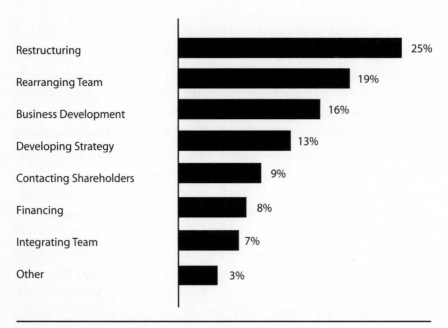

FIGURE 9.2 **Activities in the First 100 Days of Biotech CEOs**
Source: Biotech CEO Survey 2005: The First 100 Days, Egon Zehnder International.
© Egon Zehnder International.

first few months (with clients, shareholders, and other stakeholders including creditors) tended to arise only in crisis situations.

So yes, there are industries and circumstances in which accelerated integrations are the norm. If you find yourself in such a situation, either as the new hire or the receiving organization, you have my sympathy and best wishes. Beyond a certain point, I believe, integration can't be compressed, and change can't be shortchanged. Recently I read an article about "the first 100 days," in which a specialist in "onboarding services" was claiming that a new boss should have his new team picked and a communications strategy in place on his *first day* on the job![5] I don't buy it. Precipitous actions during the integration phase—actions that cut short the diagnosis, and cut out relevant people—are highly unlikely to produce the desired results.

The Six Deadly Integration Traps

Based on my experience, there are deadly traps that tend to get sprung during the integration phase, unless you guard against them. First, there is a natural tendency on the part of the company to minimize the challenge, in part to facilitate recruiting. This is a mistake. "Managing a new company is like riding a wild horse," the CEO of one of the biotechs described earlier told us, "but luckily, I have a wife who has a career and a good income." The mistake is compounded, in many cases, by the candidate's inclination to exaggerate his or her capabilities. Superman (or Superwoman) takes on a simple challenge: What could be easier?

A second trap is becoming "kidnapped" by the stress of the situation. As noted earlier, there is an ideal level of stress at which we humans achieve maximum performance. Below that level, we are bored; above that level, we become distressed. At high levels of stress, a series of neural systems kick in that interfere with learning and memory, and we become increasingly defensive and aggressive.[6] New managers (and their employers!) have to remember that they are running a marathon, rather than a sprint. They have to maintain a balanced life, if they want to operate at maximum effectiveness and efficiency.

A third problem I have seen quite frequently is a mismatch between the new manager's style and that of the working team, particularly in the area of control and delegation. This is a combination of both sides' expectation of what's right and normal. If the manager is (or is perceived to be) overly controlling, the team gets frustrated, and rebels by either resisting or withdrawing. In either case, the result is underperformance.

A fourth typical trap arises when the new manager fails to invest in developing strong relations with key people. This requires a 360° perspective, extending to bosses, peers, and subordinates. All of the relevant research shows that most managers actually spend most of their time relating to others; the question is, *how well do they do it?*[7] Gabarro argues that the ability to develop proper relationships with key people is the best predictor of success or failure:

> Perhaps the most salient difference between the successful and the failed transitions was the quality of a new manager's working relationships at the end of his first year. Three of four managers in the failed successions had poor working relationships with two or more of their key subordinates by the end of twelve months.[8]

Likewise, research from the Center for Creative Leadership indicates that top-level executives define executive "success" according to two measures:

1. Bottom-line organizational results achieved during those individuals' tenure
2. The relationships they maintained with others, and in particular, their subordinates[9]

Another frequent integration trap grows out of the legacy actions of the predecessor. This is particularly serious in the case of outgoing

CEOs, who may succumb to various types of temptation over the last few years of their tenure (especially if they have stayed on a little too long). These run the gamut from procrastinating on pressing problems to deciding to end their career with a "big bang" (e.g., a major acquisition or merger), which may not be in the organization's best interest over the long run.[10]

Finally, a trap that very often manifests itself in the integration phase is a lack of organizational support. Because this sixth trap is such a serious problem, and because it arises so frequently, I'll consider it at length in the next section.

Managing the Integration Process

In order to increase the chances of a new manager's success, accelerate the integration process, and maximize his or her contribution, companies should approach the integration proactively. They should prepare for the integration and follow it up. Let's look at each of these steps in turn.

First, *companies should be proactive*. In the case of the dairy company referred to in previous chapters, a very visible search for a new CEO of this company (actually the largest in its home country) led to the hiring of a foreigner who was literally on the other side of the world. Within hours of the final contract being signed and the successful candidate resigning from his former CEO role, the board proactively staged a series of private and public announcements of the hiring. The communications began at 6:00 P.M. with a call to the country's prime minister. They continued the next morning with a videoconference hookup in the company's boardroom, so that the new CEO could meet his team, at least in a virtual sense, and have an initial session with the local media. Then came a series of individual phone calls from the new CEO to each of his direct reports.

In addition to skillful communication, being proactive means maximizing preparation before taking charge. Consider the case of a company that hired a foreigner to be its CEO. The newcomer experienced a huge cultural shock in his new setting, and lasted only six weeks. The chairman of the board, understandably upset, and concluding that the search firm they had used up to that point didn't adequately understand the company's culture, dumped that search firm and retained a new one.

But the new search firm, sizing up the situation, concluded that it wasn't simply a matter of paying more attention to culture: The company and its internal politics were far more complex than first met the eye. The consultants informed the chairman that he personally needed to make an extra effort to prepare the next CEO. When the new person was finally hired, both executives attended a "boot camp," spending two days on a university campus with the search firm and a carefully planned-out series of professors and advisors. The process helped the two individuals confirm their priorities and mandates, discuss cultural and people issues, and get to know each other on a more personal basis.

The second thing companies should do is to properly *prepare the integration*. A couple of years ago, a good friend and client—the president and CEO of a very successful durable goods company, which I'll call "DuraGoods"—paid me a visit. He represented the fourth generation of his family to run the business. He told me that he was about to turn 50, and he had made the decision to retire from an executive role. For the first time in a century, he confided, there were no family members who were qualified to take over DuraGoods, nor were there other strong internal candidates. As a result, he had decided to conduct an external search, in which he wanted our help.

It was clear to me and my colleagues that for this family business to bring in an external CEO for the first time in its long history would be a major challenge. But we worked with the retiring CEO (and another board member who was on the search committee) to plan and implement a series of integration actions. These included:

- Communicating to all key internal stakeholders, in a consistent and regular way, the reasons for the search, and ultimately for their choice

- Coming up with a very explicit mandate for the new CEO
- Spending time with the new CEO to review the company's history and culture in an intensive way
- Presenting the new CEO to relevant leaders and managers
- Reviewing with him successful examples of integration, highlighting what had actually worked in other relevant contexts
- Setting up a plan to provide feedback "early and often" during the integration process
- Agreeing on a realistic timetable for objectives, including learning, building relationships, and scoring some "early wins"

The right search, together with the right integration support, allowed for an extremely successful integration, which was followed by a record performance, despite the newness of the manager.

Particularly for very senior positions, the *minimum* preparation for an integration should include:

- An explicit understanding of the governance, structure, and key processes of the organization
- Key agreements about immediate priorities and action steps
- A shared understanding of long-term aspirations
- A clear plan to spend enough time together with the key stakeholders, to help build trust-based relationships

In the case of internal promotions to CEO positions, the board should insist on a longer and properly structured transition process, in which the heir apparent is given the chance to learn, prepare, and develop the right type of organizational network and support. At the same time, the board should continually monitor the outgoing CEO's engagement with the business as he approaches retirement to ensure that there is still a hand on the tiller, and that the retiring executive is not tempted to make a counterproductive "last gasp" grand gesture.

The third thing that companies can do to support the integration is to *follow it up closely*. Every few months, the organization should formally analyze progress against expectations, by trying to answer at least four basic questions:

1. *Has the organization been providing the proper support to the hired candidate?* Potential issues to consider include the clarity of mandate, a proper briefing on the company's history and culture, the right level of early feedback, as well as the availability of some clear internal sponsor.

2. *Is the new manager developing proper relationships in the organization?* Networking, working closely with peers, understanding the corporate culture, and securing the trust of her own team, boss, and peers all should be counted as signs of appropriate progress.

3. Is the business model being properly worked by the new manager? This means, for example, understanding the fundamental processes, products, services, and business requirements, and putting assets to work in appropriate (initial) ways.

4. *Is there evidence of progress?* There's no point in asking this question too soon. On the other hand, it's fair to look for clear statements of priorities and milestones, and (at some point) evidence for progress toward those milestones.

There's one more thing that companies have to be prepared to do during the integration phase, if and when it becomes clear that the integration simply isn't working: *Pull the plug*. This is never easy. Significant amounts of time and money have been spent in finding, recruiting, and integrating the newcomer. But sometimes it just doesn't work, and the parties involved have to have the courage to face that fact, and *act*, uncomfortable as that may be.

I remember being impressed by a colleague who had conducted a search for a country manager for a consumer goods company in a major strategic market, far away from headquarters. The best available candidate was signed up, and took over. But there were danger signals almost immediately. The client and my colleague decided to assess the integration after three months. They met individually with the new manager, and also with some 20 insiders, trying to get a sense of where things were heading. The lights were definitely flashing yellow.

The new manager received in-depth feedback and mentoring. After another three months, a similar interview was conducted. Both the client and my colleague reluctantly concluded that the new country manager was not going to make it, and that it would be better for all concerned to acknowledge that. A new search began, in a way that would not unnecessarily embarrass the failed incumbent, and another candidate who was previously unavailable was hired.

"Saving face" can be a trap and a sign of weakness. You do no one a favor by keeping him or her in an untenable situation. If the integration can't work, have the strength of character to end it.

From the Successful Candidate's Perspective

When I was in the early stages of writing this book, I had a long meeting with Jack Welch. In the course of that discussion, I asked him about the best way to integrate a new manager in a senior position, particularly if he or she is coming in from a different business. His response:

> He'll need to have a sponsor! I will advise *no one* to move when he or she is not hired by someone with real authority, real clout, who would support him, who would bet on him through thick and thin. This is the key. It's essential for success.

I agree. First: If you're the successful candidate for a challenging post, and there's no "champion" in sight, *don't take the job.*

The second thing that candidates should keep in mind is that the work is almost certain to be harder than expected. We asked the CEOs of biotechs how they would spend their first 100 days differently, if they had it to do again. Their answers are summarized in Figure 9.3. Most thought that they should have done more of just about everything. *Acting* and *learning* at the same time is almost always a tough challenge!

The third thing that hired candidates should keep is mind is that they can and should demand the kinds of organizational support outlined in the previous section. Most companies provide only minimal integration support. It's not because they're cheap or malevolent, but simply because they don't know any better. Asking for this support and helping the company plan for it can make a big difference.

Fourth, new hires should start by focusing on a few key areas, rather than being pulled in every direction at once. A recent study by McKinsey & Co., written as a guide for the CEO-elect, highlighted three essential areas:

1. Understanding the organization and its other leaders more fully

2. Diagnosing and addressing their own weaknesses

3. Identifying resources that can smooth the transition, including the right advisors[11]

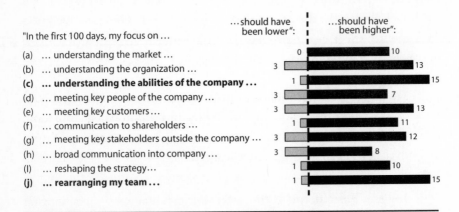

FIGURE 9.3   Attention in the First 100 Days—Revisited

Source: Biotech CEO Survey 2005: The First 100 Days, Egon Zehnder International. © Egon Zehnder International.

Yes, life at the top can be lonely, but you can work against that outcome. A key strategy for success is to find the right type of personal advisor, which more than 80 percent of the managers we studied in the financial sector cited as one of their key strategies. The most frequent advisor in that sample set was a colleague from the executive committee, followed by the company's president (mainly among external candidates) as well as external sources, including a variety of consultants (to gain insights either about the sector or about the integration process itself).[12]

Eventually, the new manager must also make the critical decision about which expectations to honor and which to abandon.[13] The expectations defined at the outset are very likely to include conflicting, or even impossible, goals. This problem may be aggravated by the implicit or explicit promises that have been made by predecessors. Expansion plans, job security, promotion prospects, career trajectories, compensation expectations, and working conditions—all are grounds for expectations, which may or may not be met (or even "meetable"). The new leader has to surface and deal with these expectations, which otherwise may translate into "broken promises."

Meanwhile, of course, the new manager has to confirm his or her team. The initial months are a very difficult period, because the new manager has to judge the competence and attitude of team members while still working with them. Each side is sizing up the other, wondering if the other will "make the cut." At the same time, someone has to be making and shipping the widgets.

When we asked the financial institutions' CEOs what they should have done differently during their first three months in charge, the most common response was they should have paid more attention to *analyzing* and *managing* the company's senior leaders. The biotech CEOs said that they should have developed a better understanding of the abilities of the company, and spent more time diagnosing and redeploying their team members.

Finally, from Day One all the way through Year Three and beyond, the new manager has to make a special effort to seek out and spend personal time with representatives of all relevant stakeholders. If I had to make just one recommendation, based on my experience, this would be it. There is no substitute for your personal presence, and personal touch.

The Human Element

The power of "personal touch" can't be overemphasized. Stated negatively, the failure to develop strong personal relationships with key players is the most telling indicator of integration failure. Stated positively, if you can find allies who will go to the wall for you, you can compensate for almost any other shortcoming.

Developing relationships with key people is essential for many reasons. First, as noted, allies (in the form of experienced organizational insiders) can help the new manager succeed. They can help accelerate the learning process, shortening the diagnostic period without sacrificing its quality. And good relationships are the basis of *trust*, which in turn is a critical underpinning of leadership and "followership."

In this Age of the BlackBerry, I can't emphasize enough the critical importance of spending enough time person to person, eyeball to eyeball, in order to develop trust. Trust grows out of character (including integrity, motives, consistency of behavior, and openness) and competence. But assuming that you have the right character and competence, as well as the minimum level of formal authority, your ability to cultivate trust will depend critically on the amount of quality personal time that you spend eyeball to eyeball with your boss, your key team members, and other relevant peers and stakeholders.

This commonsense observation has recently been confirmed by discoveries in the field of neuroscience, focusing on brain cells called "mirror neurons." These cells apparently help us sense the movements another person is about to make, and prepare us (on an unconscious level) to imitate that movement. Simply stated, we are prepared to smile the instant the other person smiles. An emerging notion in the philosophy of mind, moreover, argues that we understand others not by observing them and thinking about them, but by "translating their actions into the neural language that prepares us for the same actions and lets us experience alike."[14] I'll take the liberty of putting these two ideas in the same sentence: When we spend time with others, we experience them through the work of our mirror neurons, and by experiencing them, we understand them and bond with them.

Face time—eyeball to eyeball—is important. The development of bonding relationships is bound up with the eyes, which contain nerve projections that lead directly to a key brain structure for empathy and matching emotions.[15] When we are interacting with a person, that structure—again, accessed through the eyes—reminds us whether we love or loathe that person.[16]

There's simply no substitute for one-on-one sessions. If you could do only one thing in service to integration, this would be it.

How to Beat the Odds

A couple of weeks ago, I received a research brief from the *McKinsey Quarterly* on the subject of who should and shouldn't run the family business.[17]

The report showed that family-owned companies run by outsiders appear to be better managed than other companies, while family-owned companies run by eldest sons tend to be managed relatively poorly. This last correlation seemed particularly strong. The authors asserted that family-owned companies run by eldest sons accounted for 43 percent of the gap in managerial quality they identified between companies in France (where almost half of family companies are run by the eldest son as CEO) and those in the United States.

When I read that article, however, I was reminded of a case

that I witnessed that clearly overcame those odds. Several years ago, I received a phone call from a client. He was the executive chairman of a very successful company that had been founded at the beginning of the previous century, in which he represented the third generation of family leadership.

The man, then in his seventies, asked me for an urgent meeting to discuss an important issue. I replied to him that I was about to take a plane from Buenos Aires to New York within just a few hours, but that I would be more than happy to meet with him upon my return in two days.

He had always struck me as a very calm and patient individual. I was therefore extremely surprised when he asked me if I could stop by his house on the way to the airport. He really needed me to spend at least half an hour with him, *now*, he said, because the matter was so important and time sensitive.

Perplexed, I went to his house in La Isla, one of the nicest neighborhoods in town. I was greeted first by his wife, who served us tea and promptly vanished, leaving us alone. I sensed that something special was up.

"I will get straight to the point," he began. "I have a bad cancer, and my days are numbered. I want to ask you whether you think that my eldest son would be the best CEO for our company. I have asked you to come here because I want to look into your eyes when you answer that question. I don't want an answer out of compassion. I want the best for my company and my family, long after I'm gone. So I beg you to give me your most professional and honest answer."

I don't think my eyes left his more than once or twice during the whole hour we spent together. I wanted him to know that I was being as honest as I possibly could be, in that critical circumstance. Luckily, the situation was made easier for me because I genuinely believed that the son was probably the best potential candidate to run that company. Extremely competent, hardworking, and responsible, he had an impeccable education and all his career had prepared him for that challenge. He was in his early forties. He would have the advantage of knowing the company, the business, and the relevant people, and of course would be the fourth generation to run the business.

I told the father this, in so many words. And yet, he spent at least half an hour probing me, quizzing me about potential external candidates whom I could identify off the top of my head given my experience in the Argentine market, asking about his son's shortcomings, and grilling me on the pros and cons of external solutions.

Even after he finally became convinced about my own conviction, he still wouldn't let me go. We spent another half hour planning various integration issues at increasing levels of detail.

Finally, he also wanted my candid advice on the compensation level and structure for his son in the new CEO role. He wanted to be fair both to him and to the company, and he didn't want to create any problems with the rest of the shareholders and family members, several of whom were brothers and cousins of the would-be CEO.

His son did indeed become the CEO of the company, and shortly after that, the father died. The company turned in an outstanding performance in terms of growth, profitability, and diversification by product, service, and geography.

After almost a decade of service as the CEO, the son came to visit me at my office. He explained that he felt that the time was coming for him to retire from his executive responsibilities. Although still a young man (about to turn 50), he was convinced that leaders should step down after a decade or so. Companies need new blood, he told me.

But there was more. Remember "DuraGoods," the successful durable goods company I referred to earlier, where the soon-to-retire CEO of a family business decided that it was time to step down, and that there were no qualified successors within the family? That CEO was actually the son of this brave father. We worked with him to hire an outsider, with whom we worked closely to plan and implement a successful integration process.

Why do I close this chapter with this story? Because unlike most companies in the McKinsey study, this family-owned company managed to achieve the best of both worlds. They maintained their long-term strategic perspective, but gave up the pressures of delivering quarterly results to investors, and hitting short-term earnings targets.

Integration of a new manager is a critical step
- The process is long and risky.
- Most organizations don't provide the right type of support.

Several traps can sabotage this process, including
- Minimizing the challenges of acting and learning
- Becoming kidnapped by stress
- Mismatches of management styles
- Underinvesting in the development of strong relations with key people
- Legacy actions of the predecessor
- Wrong hiring decisions
- Lack of proper organizational support

Companies can do several things to support integration
- Being proactive at internal communication and candidate preparation
- Properly preparing the ground within the organization
- Closely following up the process at regular intervals, monitoring the level of organizational support, relationship building, working of the business model, and setting the stage for early wins

Candidates should also take charge of their successful integration
- Ensuring the right sponsor
- Realizing that the integration work is harder than expected
- Asking up front for the type of organizational support required
- Focusing on a few key areas
- Properly managing expectations
- Confirming the new team
- Spending enough personal time with all relevant stakeholders

---

FIGURE 9.4   How to Integrate the Best People

Meanwhile, they played an active role in finding and mentoring the best possible leaders for the company, whether a son, or an unknown outsider.

In my view, both father and son displayed an amazing level of self-awareness and anticipation: the former in confronting his death, and the latter in acknowledging the need to pass the baton while still in peak form. Neither procrastinated. Both precipitated the change that was needed. Both insisted on the strongest possible integration, although the two integration processes were dramatically different.

Both generations demonstrated as well a remarkable level of discipline and objectivity in assessing candidates—even when father assessed son. Both showed courage and compassion.

In my estimation, that's how they beat the odds cited in the McKinsey study. And the lessons are more broadly applicable, I think. If you want to aim at great performance, and if you want to make great people decisions surely and consistently, do what this family did: Be self-aware, look down the road, be disciplined, and be courageous.

Figure 9.4 summarizes the key points covered in this chapter.

■ ■ ■

Following the practices described in this chapter, you will be able to successfully integrate the best candidate.

In our final chapter, I explain why mastering great people decisions is important on a larger scale.

CHAPTER TEN

The Bigger Picture

As I write this final chapter, I have in front of me a recent issue of *The Economist*, which features a 15-page cover article called "The Search for Talent (Why It's Getting Harder to Find)."[1] The report makes the central point that today's economy places an enormous premium on talent, and that there isn't enough of that commodity to go around. It underscores the critical importance of "intangible" assets, which have ballooned from something like 20 percent of the value of the typical S&P 500 company in 1980 to something like 70 percent today. Finally, it points to the various structural factors behind this challenge, including demographics, the collapse of loyalty (both to and from the employer), and various forms of skills mismatches.

But because you've read this far in *Great People Decisions*, none of this surprises you. In fact, *The Economist*'s report only confirms that making great people decisions represents a major challenge, as well as a unique opportunity, for those able to master them. And because you've read this far, you are probably convinced that mastering great people decisions not only can help drive organizational performance, but also can enhance your chances of personal career success.

Now it's time to adopt a bigger frame. In this final chapter, I explain why making great people decisions is important on a *much larger scale*.

Every Day, All the Time

Because you've internalized the lessons of *Great People Decisions* up to this point, you have the skills you need to hire someone for your team, promote a team member, and participate in other key people decisions in your organization. But there's more: *You also possess a set of tools, processes, and concepts that should be invaluable in your leadership role every day, all the time.* Why is this so? There are several answers. The first is that the lessons in the previous chapters apply not only to major people decisions, but also to every single *delegation* decision.

In every day of your life as a leader, when you're deciding who's going to do what, you can follow the principles outlined in this book. Is there anything you are planning to do that you could delegate to someone else? If so, what should you be looking for, in terms of competencies? Where will you look for the right person to perform that task—whether on your team, within the larger organization, or perhaps even outside, through some form of outsourcing? How are you going to motivate him or her to do the job? How will you facilitate his or her initial actions? How will you monitor or assess his or her performance over the longer term?

Just like great hiring and promotion, delegating more often and more effectively improves your organization's results, and helps ensure your own career success. By being a better delegator, moreover, you build the larger organization by helping others grow. For knowledge workers, the best way to develop is not through traditional training, but rather through on-the-job experience in appropriate, increasingly challenging settings. Great *delegation* decisions are therefore a win-win solution, both for you and your people.

How about Yourself?

For most of the preceding pages, we've looked at principles and practices from the employer's point of view. Well, the other great thing about great people decisions is that they apply equally to *you* and *your own career decisions.*

By now, you're better equipped to recognize when a change is needed—whether that need has arisen because you don't have the required competencies or because you don't have the right motivation. You are better prepared to sidestep crippling psychological biases, including procrastination and an exaggerated sense of your own capabilities. You are in a good position to develop increased self-awareness about your capabilities and preferences, and to capitalize on the opportunities inherent in different jobs, either inside or outside your current organization.

At the same time, I'm confident, you'll stay out of the other common traps of job-change decisions: making snap judgments, falling victim to emotional anchoring, or sticking with the familiar. You'll avoid tactical mistakes, such as giving up your current job before you've prepared the ground for that next position.

But in this final chapter, I don't want to focus too much on traps and mistakes. I want to accentuate the positive. Sometimes people tease me about being relentlessly optimistic, and I usually own up to that. But think about the amazing opportunities we have before us, in these miraculous times! In the 1800s, almost everyone was a farmer. In the late nineteenth century, almost everyone was either a farmer or a factory worker. Today, a little over a century later, there's an astounding profusion of job opportunities out there—including the jobs we invent for ourselves. And far more people are allowed to participate: In the last two decades, literally billions of people who were formerly oppressed by centralized state economies have joined the *world* market.

Today, we live longer, and stay active far longer. We aren't limited to one career; we can pursue several careers in our lifetimes, serially or concurrently. (I was an executive search consultant; now I'm an executive search consultant, a lecturer, and an author!) Except in extreme circumstances, we don't have to do what we don't *want* to do. As Herman Miller's former CEO, Max DePree, is fond of saying, *everyone in the workplace is a volunteer.*

So if you don't like what you're doing, *stop volunteering for it*. Take the necessary steps to make a change. Get to know yourself. Source and network to generate better opportunities for yourself. Act on the knowledge that we live in a small world (the six degrees of separation, described in Chapter 6) and that your persistence will pay off if you search in a smart and systematic way.

And finally, consider whether it's time for you to get off the organizational track entirely. Have you made the greatest contributions that you're going to make, as a leader inside a traditional organization? Maybe your corporate legacy is already in place. Maybe you can move on to other rich ways of contributing to society, and perhaps enjoy your life and your loved ones all the more in the process.

Making Others Happy

In addition to fueling the high-performance organization and advancing your own career, making great people decisions will also help you make others very happy.

Think of the worst boss you ever worked for, and how miserable he or she made you and your colleagues. Ultimately, terrible leaders bring themselves down, but they can create a lot of heartaches for others along their paths. They can steal the happiness, even the health and well-being, of all those around them.[2]

Again, let's turn to the bright side. Mastering great people decisions will help you choose the right bosses for your team. They in turn will create the conditions of meaningful work and rich relationships that foster happiness. Having the right boss and the right working environment allows us to achieve a state of flow in which we are fully engaged in what we do and our productivity is maximized. This is a virtuous circle in which happiness fuels productivity and vice versa. And our positive emotions, which tend to be highly contagious, spread to those around us, as well.

Great people decisions will also promote health and happiness across your entire team, from the corner offices down to the front lines.

The Great Hidden Scandal

We are all thoroughly familiar with the outrageous corporate scandals that in recent years have had such a dramatic impact on society, and on the way business will be done for the foreseeable future. In fact, we have been practically drowned in the details of these sordid stories: tens of thousands of jobs lost, billions of dollars in losses for investors, life savings wiped out, and the wholesale squandering of trust in our businesses and their leaders. We're aware of the negative consequences for investment, job creation, economic growth, and ultimately our standard of living.

It's not hard to get a bead on the causes of these train wrecks. An ineffective board falls under the sway of a dominant leader. That leader—influenced to a great extent by greed and hubris, but also hemmed in by the expectations of Wall Street—devises short-term (or even corrupt) strategies, which often hinge on doomed acquisitions and overexpansions. The pressure to cook the books builds inexorably, and weak internal controls help seal the company's fate.

This may seem all too familiar. But as it turns out, the Enrons, WorldComs, Global Crossings, Adelphias, and Tycos—companies that more or less fit the profile delineated at the beginning of this section— are extremely rare cases. The *Wall Street Journal* reports that of the tens of millions of businesspeople in the United States, only about 1,000 have been convicted of corporate crimes since July 2002: a tiny fraction.[3] Most of the time, it turns out, business plays by the rules. When business leaders complain about the unnecessary strictures of Sarbanes-Oxley and other similar legislation, they have a legitimate beef: The great mass of businesses are being punished for the sins of a very few.

So there I go again, the relentless optimist? In this case, no; I believe the picture is *far worse than we know*. There is a huge scandal lurking out there, one that is orders of magnitude larger than the collective misdeeds of the companies cited above, and about which almost nobody speaks.

This hidden scandal involves the multitude of cases where organizations not embroiled in any scandals whatsoever have made appointments to senior positions, which have led in turn to mediocre individual and corporate performance. Think back to the dramatic spreads in senior management performance that I described in earlier chapters. Now aggregate this mediocrity across the multitude of organizations that make bad people decisions. This is the real scandal that is hidden right before our eyes.

And I am not speaking only about the "dogs" of the corporate world. Even in organizations with strong reputations, I've seen absolutely *huge* opportunity costs. And I'm certainly not speaking only about for-profit organizations. I recently talked to a medical researcher who told me that, for some key procedures in university hospitals in the United States, *mortality differs by 1,000 percent* across identical procedures, employing identical equipment! The difference, of course, is the *people* involved.

Let's switch back to positive mode. Can great people decisions even save your life? Obviously, the answer is yes!

Educating for Great People Decisions

An obvious way to capitalize on the lessons of *Great People Decisions* is to get yourself and the others around you in your organization educated. In my trade, there's an old truism: *Those who have the power don't have the knowledge, while those who have the knowledge don't have the power.* The solution, then, is to educate the powerful.

Consider the way that organizations today make their financial decisions: with rigor, professionalism, and the application of advanced knowledge. Now consider how people decisions get made. Most often, they are distinguished by a lack of rigor at every step: from figuring out when a change is needed all the way to the integration of the candidate. And this contrast holds true consistently, across all business functions. Manufacturing, product design, even marketing—all are approached far more professionally than people decisions.

Yes, *even* marketing; not so long ago, advertising was considered an *art*—an intuitive activity that didn't lend itself to professionalization. As Charles Revson, the founder of Revlon, used to say, "I know half the money I spend on advertising is wasted, but I can never find out which half." In much the same vein, Fred Allen once quipped, "An advertising agency is 85 percent confusion and 15 percent commission."

Obviously, marketing has changed for the better. Today, Revson could have far more confidence that he wasn't wasting every other dollar.

People decisions are made today the way advertising decisions were made a half-century ago. I believe that this will change, and *change fast*. And, as always, those who move first will reap the greatest benefits.

I recently had the pleasure of spending a day with business author Jim Collins discussing a wide range of topics, including the ideas that I was thinking through for this book. At one point, I mentioned how strange it is that in the years that we are preparing ourselves to become managers, whether in college or MBA programs, we study finance, accounting, marketing, and other key subjects in depth—and yet most of us spend literally *no time* learning how to make great people decisions.

Collins readily agreed with my implied point. "Business schools should have courses on how to make people decisions," he said. "They have courses about strategy, but people come before strategy."

In other words, the right people will come up with the right strategy. But the right strategy without the right people is doomed from the outset.

Looking to History

One way to assess the importance of great people decisions is to look to history. We see great leaders in the light of their own accomplishments, and sometimes also in the gaps they left by failing to groom an appropriate successor.

Alexander the Great and Napoleon are, at once, among the best and worst examples. Under their leadership, Macedonia and France respectively achieved things that would have been impossible without their leadership. (In this context, I won't speak to the sometimes objectionable *methods* of their leadership.) And yet, despite their huge historical footprints, much of what they accomplished proved unsustainable as soon as they were unavailable to exert their personal leadership.

Could anyone else have prosecuted the Civil War with the determination of Abraham Lincoln? He had plans for a forgiving and generous reconstruction of the Southern states. But his assassination scuttled those plans, and the weak and vindictive leaders who followed him set the healing process back a hundred years.

Winston Churchill presents an interesting example of competency and "fit." As a peacetime politician in the years between World Wars I and II, Churchill's career was far from distinguished. When it came to prosecuting World War II, however, the British counted themselves incredibly lucky to have him available to lead them. But the worm continued to turn. Immediately after the war, the British electorate threw Churchill out of office in favor of a Labour Government, which they presumed to be better prepared to deal with the complex social issues caused by six years of war.

Perhaps it's unrealistic to expect national leaders to do all that they have to do, especially in times of war, and also set the stage for their successors. But I'd phrase the question a different way: If business leaders have the power and tools at hand to manage succession properly, do they *ever* have any excuse for not ensuring that qualified successors are in place?

Bad Collective Processes; Bad Collective Results

I recently sent my colleagues globally an e-mail asking for dramatic examples of bad people decisions. While I was looking for *corporate* examples, I also received a flood of "nominations" of allegedly inept presidents or prime ministers who have led the most advanced countries in the world.

Think about it: How many of the presidents or prime ministers in office today, even in the most developed countries, are the best possible people to hold those posts? How many of them are outstanding, and how many are just good enough, in terms of their competence, credibility, and even integrity? Clearly, bad people decisions are being made in the public sector, as well—and precisely where they matter the most! Without strong political leadership, we can't begin to address the pressing challenges that are bearing down on our societies: genocides, terrorism, economic disparities, social injustices, and so on.

Perhaps you're thinking that the analogy between corporate leadership and political leadership is stretched. After all, aren't the challenges very different? And even if they can be seen as similar, aren't the ways we pick our leaders very different in the public and private sectors?

As for the first question, my answer is a qualified "yes." In fundamental ways, leading a nation is different from leading a company. And yet there *are* key overlaps, especially in areas like agenda-setting, resource allocation, and winning the hearts and minds of your constituents.

As for the second question—the way we go about picking leaders in these two arenas—it's clear that electoral choices are very different from corporate hiring choices. But once again, I think the overlaps are compelling. Consider the psychological biases and emotional traps that I described in Chapter 3. While always voting for candidates from our own party, aren't we perhaps sticking with the familiar? Aren't we engaging in the public-sector equivalent of branding or herding?

Have we even done the most basic homework regarding what to look for—that is, what the competencies should be based on the specific priorities and circumstances facing the country? How else can we possibly know what to look for? Do we appraise candidates properly, or are we just giving away our votes based on TV debates—events that are dominated by the image consultants, and which push us toward snap judgments that are very much like those arrived at through speed-dating?

When deciding how to vote, are we trying to be objective and dispassionate in our choice? Or are we simply seeking confirmatory evidence to justify a thoughtless choice?

What are we doing to broaden the pools of potential candidates for these key positions? What are we doing to attract and motivate the very best people to serve in those critical roles? Why do we take for granted the idea that civil servants and key government officials should earn only a fraction of what their counterparts in the private sector make? If we accept these pay disparities as a given, can we honestly say at the same time that we want to "attract the very best" to public service? Why do great leaders and managers from the private sector so rarely jump the chasm and run for office?

What are we doing to properly integrate the talent we may be able to attract? Does it make sense to have fixed terms of office? What if a change is needed, due either to new challenges, or the fact that we have made a mistake, or the fact that the elected incumbent has lost his or her competence? I'm thinking, for example, of the final year of Woodrow Wilson's administration in the United States, after the President had been disabled by a stroke, and the government was effectively paralyzed until the next administration took office.

Would shareholders stand for such a circumstance? (I hope not!) Should citizens stand for such a circumstance?

I realize that these are provocative questions, and I also am fully aware that there can be no easy answers. Good political systems are conservative by their nature and design, and the overlay of partisan politics makes it all that much harder to effect real change. And certainly, the law of unintended consequences has to be considered at every turn. But shall we not at least ask ourselves these questions? Shall we not ask what it would take to make better people decisions in government and thereby reward ourselves with better leaders?

Great People Decisions on the World Scale

Again, I'm an optimist, and just as often, an idealist. But what's our alternative? If one country has inept leaders and another one has outstanding leaders, the first one will be at a competitive disadvantage. Its citizens will be at greater risk of economic, political, and social turmoil.

This is not an abstract notion. Consider the case of Singapore, which in the last Global Competitiveness Report of the World Economic Forum came in at #5, putting it just ahead of the United States. How can Singapore—a tiny nation, with no natural resources—emerge as the world's fifth most competitive country? How has Singapore achieved annual growth rates of between 7 and 10 percent in recent years?

Obviously, the answer is complex. Way back in the 1960s, the country embraced a vision of long-term economic growth as its central goal. At the same time, it resolved to share the benefits of that anticipated growth broadly across its population. This was to be achieved not through wealth- and income-redistribution policies (which almost always impede economic growth), but by equipping all of its men and women with the means and opportunities to earn a living and acquire assets.

But how did they *get* there, some four decades later? I argue that a big factor was the nation's explicit decision to attract the *very best talent* to the public sector, and pay those outstanding individuals fully competitive wages and benefits.

One of the most impressive statements that I have read in recent years was an address to Singapore's Parliament on June 30, 2000, by its then Prime Minister, Goh Chok Tong. On that occasion, he was presenting his recommendations for public-sector salaries. He spoke eloquently about the relatively low cost of good government, and the staggeringly high cost of bad government. He declared flatly that the most important factor behind the country's stellar economic performance and its high (and rising) standard of living was the quality of its political leaders.

A few years ago, I was visited by the advisors to a presidential candidate who ultimately was successful in his quest for his nation's highest office. When I mentioned the case of Singapore and its highly professional administration, they immediately responded that the case was irrelevant, because Singapore didn't have a "normal" democratic government. I responded that I wasn't speaking to the pros and cons of Singapore's particular version of democracy—which not everyone in the world would embrace—but rather to the *great people decisions* that Singapore has made in the process of moving into the very front economic ranks. In fact, I continued, the example of Singapore only underscores on a national level what has also been discovered repeatedly at the corporate board level: It's not particular rules or regulations, or a particular governance system, that makes a great board. Rather, it's the caliber of the directors, and the ways they work together. Singapore's example, I concluded, begs the obvious question: Why can't we have the best of *both* worlds, in terms of a governmental system and people decisions?

Let's be both idealistic *and* realistic. In an ideal world, Aristotle said, enlightened one-man rule would be the best form of government, followed by oligarchy, and then followed by democracy. But in the *real* world, Aristotle said, the order is reversed. Given human nature and the corrosive potential of power, democracy is the least bad alternative, and a perverted dictatorship the worst. In the end, Aristotle voted for democracy. So do I—especially when that democracy is run by the *best possible* public servants, identified and selected through great people decisions.

And if we can make great people decisions at the national level, can we also look one level up, and make them on an international level? I hope so, since this is obviously a prerequisite for achieving sustainable development, justice, stability, and peace on a global scale.

How could this be accomplished? Here, I'm clearly out of my depth, but I'd like to point to at least two promising directions. First, it's clear that *on a global scale*, we need to educate people about the impact of great people decisions. I remember observing a discussion between a former country president and a renowned economist. The president stated that he wanted to eradicate poverty from the country. The economist told him, respectfully, that he would never be able to achieve and sustain that lofty goal, because the minute he had achieved it, he would start importing poverty from neighboring countries.

Our global village is getting smaller every day. Even if altruism isn't reason enough to worry about the world beyond our national boundaries, then certainly enlightened self-interest is. We need to educate ourselves on a global scale.

Second, and certainly far more audacious, we should consider appraising and rating people who put themselves forward for public service—and we should do so on a global scale. Does it sound too fantastical, too political, or too risky? Maybe it is all of those, and more. But the World Economic Forum, as noted, issues its Global Competitiveness Report, which attempts to capture key findings in an objective way. The U.S. State Department rates the relative safety of countries for U.S. travelers. The problem with these useful but relatively unambitious measures is that they speak to *outputs*—that is, the results of past decisions. What I'm proposing is to focus on the *inputs*: the people who make the decisions that will shape our lives. Bond rating agencies tell us where it's wise, and not wise, to put our money. Why not politician rating agencies, telling us who's good at what?

I can practically hear the politicians howling. No matter! Through education and information, we can make great people decisions even as we cast our votes. The world can only get better as a result.

■ ■ ■

Writing this book has been one of the great experiences of my life. I hope that it will be useful to you. I wish you the best as you make your great people decisions, and as you help yourself succeed along with your organization.

I'll close by quoting from Dr. Seuss's last book, *Oh, the Places You'll Go!*,[4] which contains great wisdom about life and its challenges. The first page reads:

> Congratulations!
> Today is your day.
> You're off to Great Places!
> You're off and away!

Good luck in your great people decisions!

The Value of Investing in People Decisions

A few decades ago, a number of consumer goods companies realized that larger and better investments in creating and assessing advertising appeals would boost their profitability. At that time, mathematical models were already in place to quantify the expected value of such investments. These same models can be applied to calculate the expected value of investing in the search, assessment, and attraction of the best potential candidates for a senior executive position. The formula given here indicates that, in order to maximize the value of this key investment, a sufficient number of potential candidates should be generated, and the assessment should have very high levels of validity and reliability. This formula also shows that, the more complex the job, the higher the expected value of investing in people decisions. Finally, it demonstrates that, given the low frequency and high specialization needed, professional help is usually highly cost-effective for senior levels, although in order to maximize value some usual conflicts should be avoided (such as percentage fees for search services).

$$\text{Expected Value} = e_n \cdot \sigma \cdot V \cdot \rho - C_n - X_c$$

Factor	Definition	Implication
e_n	Expected value of the maximum of a random sample of size n from a standardized normal population	A large number of potential candidates should be generated.
σ	Standard deviation of the candidate's performance	The more complex the job, the higher is the expected value of investing in people decisions.
V	Validity of the assessment criteria	Understanding the competencies required for unique jobs becomes critical.
ρ	Reliability of the assessment of candidates	For senior positions, highly competent evaluators need to be involved, in a process of high integrity, including reliable reference checking.
C_n	Cost of generating, assessing, and hiring the best candidates	Given the low frequency and high specialization needed, professional help is usually highly cost effective for senior levels.
X_c	Extra cost of the hired candidate compared with the average candidate	In order to maximize value, conflicts should be avoided (such as percentage fees for search services).

Example

An investment C_n is made to generate a number of candidates n, assess them, and hire the best.

Company Values and Assumptions

Average profitability in the sector (ROA) = 5%

Company's assets = $1 billion

Standard deviation of ROA = 10 percentage points

Leader effect = 25% of standard deviation

Company valuation = 20 × Profit After Taxes

Assumptions about Yearly Costs of Search and Extra Cost of Hired Manager

Average manager cost = $3 million

Extra cost of hired manager = 50%

Cost of the search (1 time, assuming 7 years turnover) = $1 million every 7 years

10 candidates generated, which implies that $e_n = 1.54$

Assumptions about Assessment Quality

Assessment validity = 0.7

Assessment reliability = 0.7

Values for the Formula

$e_n = 1.54$

$\sigma = 0.25 \times \$100$ million = $25 million

$V = 0.7$

$\rho = 0.7$

$C_n = (\$1$ million$/7) = \$0.14$ million

$X_c = 0.5 \times \$3$ million = $1.5 million

Expected yearly profit increase = $1.54 \times 25M \times 0.7 \times 0.7 - 0.14M - 1.5M$

Expected yearly profit increase = $17 million = 34%

Increase in company value = $20 \times \$17$ million = $340 million = 34%

■ ■ ■

Further References and Background for This Formula

Irwin Gross, "The Creative Aspects of Advertising," *Sloan Management Review* 14, no. 1 (fall 1972): 83–109.

R.Y. Darmon, "Sales Force Management: Optimizing the Recruiting Process," *Sloan Management Review* 20, no. 1 (fall 1978): 47–59.

APPENDIX B

Selected Bibliography on Assessment Methods

There are hundreds of books available on assessment techniques, as well as some excellent advanced research papers. The most relevant pieces of research for those who want to dig further into the recommendations from Chapter 7 are included as end notes to that chapter.

This appendix includes three types of additional resources on the topic of assessment:

1. The introductory notes describe an overview of the main steps and process of assessment at a general level, without incorporating all the best practices described in the chapter.

2. The introductory books are accessible publications that can be useful for improving your practice of interviewing and checking references. While you won't achieve mastery by reading "how-to" books (this can be done only through disciplined practice, together with proper training and feedback), these resources can help you identify some further useful do's and don'ts.

3. The more advanced book references are likely to be of interest mainly to specialists.

1. Introductory Notes

Hattersley, Michael (1997). Conducting a Great Job Interview. *Harvard Management Update*, article reprint no. U9703C.

Jenks, James M. and Brian L.P. Zevnik (1989). ABCs of Job Interviewing. *Harvard Business Review*, reprint no. 89408.

Roberts, Michael J. (1993). Note on the Hiring and Selection Process. Harvard Business School.

2. Introductory Books

Andler, Edward C. (1998). *The Complete Reference Checking Handbook: Smart, Fast, Legal Ways to Check Out Job Applicants.* AMACOM/ American Management Association.

Arthur, Diane (2006). *Recruiting, Interviewing, Selecting & Orienting New Employees*, 4th ed. AMACOM/American Management Association.

Beatty, Richard H. (1994). *Interviewing and Selecting High Performers: Every Manager's Guide to Effective Interviewing Techniques.* New York: John Wiley & Sons.

Bell, Arthur H. (1989). *The Complete Manager's Guide to Interviewing: How to Hire the Best.* Dow Jones–Irwin.

Berman, Jeffrey A. (1997). *Competence-Based Employment Interviewing.* Quorum Books.

Camp, Richaurd, Mary E. Vielhaber, and Jack L. Simonetti (2001). *Strategic Interviewing: How to Hire Good People.* University of Michigan Business School Management Series. San Francisco: Jossey-Bass.

DeMey, Dennis L. and James R. Flowers, Jr. (1999). *Don't Hire a Crook! How to Avoid Common Hiring (and Firing) Mistakes.* Facts on Demands Press.

Fear, Richard A. and Robert J. Chiron (1990). *The Evaluation Interview, Featuring Richard Fear's Time-Tested Interview Methods, Applied to: Strategic Visioning, Team Building, Appraisal Feedback*, 4th ed. New York: McGraw-Hill.

Harvard Business Essentials (2002). *Hiring and Keeping the Best People: Your Mentor and Guide to Doing Business Effectively*. Boston: Harvard Business School Press.

Janz, Tom, Lowell Hellervik, and David C. Gilmore (1986). *Behavior Description Interviewing: New, Accurate, Cost Effective*. Prentice-Hall/Simon & Schuster.

Kanter, Arnold B. (1995). *The Essential Book of Interviewing: Everything You Need to Know from Both Sides of the Table*. New York: Times Books/Random House.

Sachs, Randi Toler (1994). *How to Become a Skillful Interviewer*. AMACOM/American Management Association.

Rae, Leslie (1988). *The Skills of Interviewing: A Guide for Managers and Trainers*. Gower Publishing.

Sessa, Valerie I. and Richard J. Campbell (1997). *Selection at the Top: An Annotated Bibliography*. Center for Creative Leadership.

Uris, Auren (1988). 88 *Mistakes Interviewers Make and How to Avoid Them: Recruiting, Performance Evaluation, Problem Solving*. AMACOM/American Management Association.

Veruki, Peter (1999). *The 250 Job Interview Questions You'll Most Likely Be Asked . . . and the Answers That Will Get You Hired!* Adams Media Corporation.

Wilson, Robert F. (1997). *Conducting Better Job Interviews*, 2nd ed. Barron's Educational Series.

Wood, Robert, and Tim Payne (1998). *Competency-Based Recruitment and Selection: A Practical Guide*. New York: John Wiley & Sons.

3. Advanced Book References

Anderson, Neil, and Vivian Shackleton (1993). *Successful Selection Interviewing*. Blackwell Business.

Deal, Jennifer, Valerie I. Sessa, and Jodi J. Taylor (1999). *Choosing Executives: A Research Report on the Peak Selection Simulation*. Center for Creative Leadership.

Dipboye, Robert (1992) *Selection Interviews: Process Perspectives.* South-Western Publishing.

Eder, Robert W. and Gerald R. Ferris (1989). *The Employment Interview: Theory, Research, and Practice.* Sage Publications.

Eder, Robert W. and Michael M. Harris (1999). *The Employment Interview Handbook.* Sage Publications.

Ekman, Paul (2001, 1992, 1985). *Telling Lies: Clues to Deceit in the Marketplace, Politics, and Marriage.* New York: W.W. Norton.

Gatewood, Robert D. and Hubert S. Field (1998, 1994, 1990, 1987). *Human Resource Selection,* 4th ed. Dryden Press/Harcourt Brace College Publishers.

Hollenbeck, George P. (1994). *CEO Selection: A Street-Smart Review.* Center for Creative Leadership.

Jeanneret, Richard and Rob Silzer (1998). *Individual Psychological Assessment: Predicting Behavior in Organizational Settings.* San Francisco: Jossey-Bass.

Kehoe, Jerard F. (2000). *Managing Selection in Changing Organizations.* San Francisco: Jossey-Bass.

London, Manuel and Valerie I. Sessa (1999). *Selecting International Executives: A Suggested Framework and Annotated Bibliography.* Center for Creative Leadership.

Murphy, Kevin R. (1996). *Individual Differences and Behavior in Organizations.* San Francisco: Jossey-Bass.

Nunnally, Jum C. and Ira H. Bernstein (1994, 1978, 1967). *Psychometric Theory.* New York: McGraw-Hill.

Schmitt, Neal and Walter C. Borman and Associates (1993). *Personnel Selection in Organizations.* San Francisco: Jossey-Bass.

Schneider, Benjamin and Neal Schmitt (1986, 1976). *Staffing Organizations.* Waveland Press.

Notes

Chapter 1

1. Matt Ridley, *Nature Via Nurture: Genes, Experience, and What Makes Us Human* (HarperCollins, 2003).
2. A good discussion about the effect of size findings of different human resources management interventions on performance can be found in *The Emotionally Intelligent Workplace*, edited by Cary Cherniss and Daniel Goleman, specifically in Chapter 4 by Lyle M. Spencer, "The Economic Value of Emotional Intelligence Competencies and EIC Based HR Programs" (Jossey-Bass, 2001), p. 45.
3. Monica C. Higgins, *Career Imprints: Creating Leaders Across an Industry* (Jossey-Bass, 2005).
4. I should clarify here that Zehnder is now retired, and no longer exerts any influence over my own career—even if he were inclined to do so.
5. "The Awards for Alumni Achievement" (Harvard Business School, 2002).
6. James M. Kouzes and Barry Z. Posner, *The Leadership Challenge* (Jossey-Bass, 2002), pp. 62, 256–257, 397.
7. Egon Zehnder, "A Simpler Way to Pay," *Harvard Business Review*, April 2001: 53–61.
8. See "Strategic Review at Egon Zehnder International," Cases A, B and C (Harvard Business School, August 2, 2004). Zehnder completed

his job by pointing toward an outstanding successor, Dan Meiland, who in turn later appointed John Grumbar as his CEO. Meiland and Grumbar projected the firm to even higher levels of professional client services and success, following Zehnder's retirement.

9. Valerie I. Sessa and Jodi J. Taylor, *Executive Selection, Strategies for Success* (Jossey-Bass, 2000), pp. 19–26.

10. Marcus Buckingham and Curt Coffman, *First Break All The Rules: What the World's Greatest Managers Do Differently* (Simon & Schuster, 1999), p. 57.

11. Marcus Buckingham, *The One Thing You Need to Know . . . About Great Managing, Great Leading, and Sustained Individual Success* (Free Press, 2005), pp. 73, 83.

12. See, for example, "Drivers Rate Themselves Above Average," at www.ambulancedriving.com/research/WP65-rateaboveav.html, accessed September 15, 2005.

13. T.R. Zenger, "Why Do Employers Only Reward Extreme Performance? Examining the Relationships among Performance, Pay, and Turnover," *Administrative Science Quarterly* 37, 1992: 198–219.

14. B.M. DePaulo, K. Charlton, H. Cooper, J.J. Lindsay, and L. Muhlenbruck, "The Accuracy-Confidence Correlation in the Detection of Deception," *Personality and Social Psychology Review* 1, 1997: 346–357.

15. Robert W. Eder and Michael M. Harris, *The Employment Interview Handbook* (Sage Publications, 1999), Chapter 14, "Are Some Interviewers Better Than Others?," Laura M. Graves and Ronald J. Karren, pp. 243–258.

16. Malcolm Gladwell, *Blink: The Power of Thinking Without Thinking* (Little, Brown, January 2005), pp. 21–22.

17. Larry Bossidy and Ram Charan, *Execution, The Discipline of Getting Things Done* (Crown Business, 2002), Chapter 5, p. 109.

18. Malcolm Gladwell, *Blink: The Power of Thinking Without Thinking* (Little, Brown, January 2005), pp. 134–136.

19. Ibid., p. 182.

20. Ibid., p. 47.

21. Jack Welch and Suzy Welch, *Winning* (HarperCollins, 2005), p. 95.

22. "Strategic Review at Egon Zehnder International," Cases A, B and C (Harvard Business School, August 2, 2004).

23. Daniel Goleman, *Working with Emotional Intelligence: A Discussion about Egon Zehnder International and Its Hiring Criteria* (Bloomsbury, 1998), pp. 303–311.

24. Linda A. Hill, *Becoming a Manager: Mastery of a New Identity* (Harvard Business School Press, 1992), p. 93.

25. P.A. Mabe, III and S.G. West, "Validity of Self-Evaluation of Ability: A Review and Meta-Analysis," *Journal of Applied Psychology* 67, 1982: 280–286.

26. Professor Mihaly Csikszentmihalyi; see, for example, the book *Good Business: Leadership, Flow, and the Making of Meaning* (Coronet Books, Hodder & Stoughton, 2003), or his classic best-selling *Flow: The Psychology of Optimal Experience* (Harper & Row, 1990).

27. Dan Baker and Cameron Stauth, *What Happy People Know: How the New Science of Happiness Can Change Your Life for the Better* (St. Martin's Griffin, 2003).

28. Martin E.P. Seligman, *Authentic Happiness: Using the New Positive Psychology to Realize Your Potential for Lasting Fulfillment* (Free Press, 2002).

Chapter 2

1. Julia Kirby, "Toward a Theory of High Performance," *Harvard Business Review*, July–August 2005: 30–38.

2. James C. Collins and Jerry I. Porras, *Built to Last: Successful Habits of Visionary Companies* (HarperBusiness, 1994, 1997).

3. Jim Collins, *Good to Great* (HarperCollins, 2001).

4. THE FOCUS online (http://www.ezifocus.com/content/thefocus/issue/article.php/article/54300471), vol. X/1, 2006. Keynote topic by

Jim Collins: "Filling the Seats: How People Decisions Help Build a Great Company." This quote and several others in the book are an excerpt of some of Collins's answers to a series of questions I prepared for him for this Question and Answer article in our firm's institutional publication.

5. Ibid.

6. William Joyce, Nitin Nohria, and Bruce Roberson, *What Really Works* (HarperCollins, 2003), p. 200.

7. Ed Michaels, Helen Handfield-Jones, and Beth Axelrod, *The War for Talent* (Harvard Business School Press, 2001).

8. Tsun-yan Hsieh and Sara Yik, "Leadership as the Starting Point of Strategy," *McKinsey Quarterly* 1, 2005: 66–73.

9. While he topped the list on most surveys while active, even after retiring, Jack Welch continued to be considered at the very top. In the November 2005 *Financial Times* Global Survey of Chief Executives, Jack Welch was still ranked as one of the two most respected business leaders, and one of the two most influential business writers or management gurus (in the august company of Peter Drucker).

10. Ram Charan and Geoffrey Colvin, "Why CEOs Fail," *Fortune*, June 21, 1999.

11. Sydney Finkelstein, *Why Smart Executives Fail, and What You Can Learn from Their Mistakes* (Penguin Group, Portfolio, 2003).

12. Peter Drucker, "How to Make People Decisions," *Harvard Business Review*, July–August 1985: 27.

13. Margarethe Wiersema, "Holes at the Top: Why CEO Firings Backfire," *Harvard Business Review*, December 2002: 70–79.

14. Chuck Lucier, Rob Schuyt, and Edward Tse, "The World's Most Prominent Temp Workers," Booz Allen Hamilton, *Strategy + Business*, issue 39, summer 2005.

15. Claudio Fernández-Aráoz, "Managing CEO Succession," *Global Agenda 2005* (official publication of the World Economic Forum in Davos).

16. Ram Charan, "Ending the CEO Succession Crisis," *Harvard Business Review*, February 2005: 72–81.

17. Claudio Fernández-Aráoz, "Getting the Right People at the Top," *MIT Sloan Management Review* 46(4), summer 2005. For further discussion about this topic, refer to *The Emotionally Intelligent Workplace*, Cary Cherniss and Daniel Goleman (Jossey-Bass), Chapter 4 by Lyle M. Spencer.

18. N. Wasserman, N. Nohria, and B. Anand, "When Does Leadership Matter? The Contingent Opportunities View of CEO Leadership," working paper no. 01-063 (Boston: Harvard Business School, April 2001).

19. Irwin Gross, "The Creative Aspects of Advertising," *Sloan Management Review* 14(1), fall 1972: 83–109.

20. R.Y. Darmon, "Sales Force Management: Optimizing the Recruiting Process," *Sloan Management Review* 20(1), fall 1978: 47–59.

21. For a further elaboration on the value of good people decisions, refer to my article, "Getting the Right People at the Top," *MIT Sloan Management Review* 46(4), summer 2005: 67–72.

22. William A. Sahlman, "How to Write a Great Business Plan," *Harvard Business Review*, July–August 1997: 98–108.

23. "Private Equity Gets Personal," *Financial Times Europe*, June 20, 2005.

24. Sir Adrian Cadbury was Chairman of Cadbury Schweppes between 1974 and 1989, and Director of the Bank of England from 1970 to 1994. He was Chairman of the Committee on the Financial Aspects of Corporate Governance from 1991 to 1995, and is a member of the OECD Working Party on Corporate Governance and the Panel of Conciliators of the International Centre for the Settlement of Investment Disputes. The Cadbury Report is considered one of the first and best codes of best practice in corporate governance. It can be found in several publications, including *Keeping Good Company*, a study of corporate governance in five major countries, by Jonathan Charkham, published by Oxford, 1994.

25. Jeffrey A. Sonnenfeld, "What Makes Great Boards Great," *Harvard Business Review*, September 2002: 106–113.

26. Richard Leblanc and James Gillies, *Inside the Boardroom* (John Wiley & Sons, 2005).

27. Ram Charan, *Boards that Deliver: Advancing Corporate Governance from Compliance to Competitive Advantage* (Jossey-Bass, 2005), p. 184.

28. Colin B. Carter and Jay W. Lorsch, *Back to the Drawing Board* (Harvard Business School, 2004), p. 113.

29. Jeffrey Pfeffer, *The Human Equation: Building Profits by Putting People First* (Harvard Business School Press, 1998).

30. Jeffrey Pfeffer, *Competitive Advantage Through People* (Harvard Business School Press, 1994).

31. Steven C. Brandt, *Entrepreneuring* (Addison-Wesley, 1982), pp. 1, 52.

32. Alfred P. Sloan, *My Years with General Motors* (Doubleday, 1963).

33. Geoffrey Colvin, "What Makes GE Great," *Fortune* (Europe edition) 153(4), March 13, 2006.

34. James C. Collins and Jerry I. Porras, *Built to Last* (HarperBusiness, 1997), Chapter 8 on "Home-Grown Management."

35. Peter Drucker, "Managing Oneself," *Harvard Business Review*, special issue, January 2005: 100–109.

36. Jon R. Katzenbach and Douglas K. Smith, *The Wisdom of Teams: Creating the High-Performance Organization* (Harvard Business School Press, 1993).

37. Henry Chesbrough, *Open Innovation: The New Imperative for Creating and Profiting from Technology* (Harvard Business School Press, 2003), Chapter 5, p. 93.

Chapter 3

1. Claudio Fernández-Aráoz, "Hiring Without Firing," *Harvard Business Review*, July–August 1999: 109–120. This chapter reproduces several concepts and examples from that article.

2. Claudio Fernández-Aráoz, "Getting the Right People at the Top," *MIT Sloan Management Review*, summer 2005: 67–72. This chapter reproduces several concepts and examples from that article.

3. William Poundstone, *How Would You Move Mount Fuji?* (Boston: Little, Brown, 2003).

4. Nathan Bennett and Stephen A. Miles, "Second in Command: The Misunderstood Role of the Chief Operating Officer," *Harvard Business Review*, May 2006: 70–78.

5. David Dunning, Chip Heath, and Jerry M. Suls, "Flawed Self-Assessment: Implications for Health, Education, and the Workplace," *American Psychological Society* 5(3), 2004.

6. Nigel Nicholson, *Managing the Human Animal* (Texere Publishing, 2000).

7. Peter L. Bernstein, *Against the Gods* (New York: John Wiley & Sons, 1996); and Hersh Shefrin, *Beyond Greed and Fear* (Harvard Business School Press, 1996).

8. Timothy D. Wilson, *Strangers to Ourselves* (Belknap Press of Harvard University Press, 2002), p. 17.

9. Chuck Lucier, Rob Schuyt, and Eric Spiegel, "CEO Succession 2002: Deliver or Depart," *Strategy + Business* 31, 2003.

10. Claudio Fernández-Aráoz, "Managing CEO Succession," *Global Agenda* 2005, pp. 182–184.

11. David Dunning, Chip Heath, and Jerry M. Suls, "Flawed Self-Assessment: Implications for Health, Education, and the Workplace," *American Psychological Society* 5(3), 2004.

12. Private conversation with Jack Welch, Boston, February 2006.

13. Boris Groysberg, Andrew N. McLean, and Nitin Nohria, "Are Leaders Portable?," *Harvard Business Review*, May 2006: 92–100.

14. Max H. Bazerman, *Judgment in Managerial Decision Making* (Hoboken, NJ: John Wiley & Sons, 2002).

15. Chris Argyris, *Teaching Smart People How to Learn* (Harvard Business School Press, 2004).

16. Paul Ekman, *Telling Lies* (W.W. Norton, 2001, 1992, 1985), pp. 329–330.
17. David Callahan, *The Cheating Culture* (Harcourt Books, A Harvest Book, 2004), p. 220.
18. Malcolm Gladwell, *The Tipping Point* (Little, Brown, 2002, 2000), p. 155.
19. Timothy D. Wilson, *Strangers to Ourselves* (Harvard University Press/Belknap Press, 2002), p. 137.
20. Jack Welch, "How to Win: An Exclusive Excerpt from the New Book by the Legendary CEO," *Newsweek*, April 4, 2005: 41.
21. THE FOCUS online (http://www.ezifocus.com/content/thefocus/issue/article.php/article/54300471), vol. X/1, 2006. Keynote topic by Jim Collins: "Filling the Seats: How People Decisions Help Build a Great Company."

Chapter 4

1. Valerie I. Sessa and Jodi J. Taylor, *Executive Selection: Strategies for Success* (Jossey-Bass: Center for Creative Leadership, 2000), p. 47.
2. The numbers add up to more than 100 percent because multiple people were consulted in most cases.
3. Valerie I. Sessa, Robert Kaiser, Jodi J. Taylor, and Richard J. Campbell, "Executive Selection: A Research Report on What Works and What Doesn't" (Center for Creative Leadership, 1998), p. 42. Again, the numbers add up to more than 100 percent due to multiple inputs into the decisions being scrutinized.
4. Annita Florou and Martin J. Conyon, *Top Executive Dismissal, Ownership and Corporate Performance* (The Wharton School, University of Pennsylvania, and London Business School, February 2002), revised.
5. Rachel M. Hayes, Paul Oyer, and Scott Schaefer, "Co-Worker Complementarity and the Stability of Top Management Teams," research

paper no. 1846 (R) (Stanford Graduate School of Business, January 2005).

6. McKinsey & Co., Egon Zehnder International Talent Management Survey, 2004.

7. Jack Welch with Suzy Welch, *Winning* (HarperCollins, 2005), p. 65.

8. Jeffrey Pfeffer and Robert I. Sutton, *Hard Facts, Dangerous Half-Truths and Total Nonsense* (Harvard Business School Press, 2006), p. 191.

9. Michael Y. Yoshino and Karin-Isabel Knoop, "Argentina's YPF Sociedad Anónima," Cases A to E (Harvard Business School Publishing, 1995, 1998, 1999).

10. "The Toughest Jobs in Business," *Fortune*, February 20, 2006: 54.

11. Noam Wasserman, Bharat Anand, and Nitin Nohria, "When Does Leadership Matter? The Contingent Opportunities View of CEO Leadership," working paper no. 01-063 (Harvard Business School, 2001).

12. Private conversation with Jack Welch, Boston, February 2006.

13. Boris Groysberg, Andrew N. McLean, and Nitin Nohria, "Are Leaders Portable?," *Harvard Business Review*, May 2006: 92.

14. David A. Light, "Who Goes, Who Stays?," *Harvard Business Review*, January 2001: 35–44.

15. Michael Beer and Nitin Nohria, *Breaking the Code of Change* (Harvard Business School Press, 2000).

16. Marc Gerstein and Heather Reisman, "Strategic Selection: Matching Executives to Business Conditions," from *The Art of Managing Human Resources*, edited by Edgar H. Schein, *Sloan Management Review* 24(2), winter 1983.

17. Charles O'Reilly, David F. Caldwell, and Jennifer A. Chatman, *How Leadership Matters: The Effects of Leadership Alignment on Strategic Execution* (Stanford University, Santa Clara University, and the University of California, June 2005).

18. Neal Schmitt and Walter C. Borman and Associates, *Personnel Selection in Organizations* (Jossey-Bass, 1993), Chapter 14.

19. Jim Collins, *Good to Great* (HarperCollins, 2001), p. 41.

20. Kathleen A. Farrell (University of Nebraska) and David A. Whidbee (Washington State University), "The Impact of Firm Performance Expectations on CEO Turnover and Replacement Decisions" (May 2003). JAE Boston Conference, October 2002. Available at SSRN: http://ssrn.com/abstract=318968.

21. Rakesh Khurana and Nitin Nohria, "The Performance Consequences of CEO Turnover" (March 15, 2000). Available at SSRN (http://ssrn.com/abstract=219129) or DOI (10.2139/ssrn.219129).

22. Noam Wasserman, "Founder-CEO Succession and the Paradox of Entrepreneurial Success," *Organization Science* 14(2), March–April 2003: 149–172 (winner of the 2003 Aage Sorensen Memorial Award for sociological research).

23. George S. Day and Paul J.H. Schoemaker, *Peripheral Vision: Detecting the Weak Signals That Will Make or Break Our Company* (Harvard Business School Press, 2006), pp. 22–23.

24. David Maister, "Strategy and the Fat Smoker" (this article can be accessed at David Maister's web site: http://davidmaister.com).

25. Keith Epstein, "Crisis Mentality," *Stanford Social Innovation Review* 4(1), spring 2006.

26. Jack Welch and Suzy Welch, *Winning* (HarperCollins, 2005), pp. 72–73.

27. Ibid., p. 35.

28. Frederick F. Reichheld, *Loyalty Rules: How Today's Leaders Build Lasting Relationships* (Bain & Company, 2001), p. 7.

29. Frederick F. Reichheld, ed. *The Quest for Loyalty: Creating Value through Partnership* (Boston: Harvard Business School Press, 1990), Part II, Chapter 3, pp. 67–72.

30. James M. Kouzes and Barry Z. Posner, *The Leadership Challenge*, 3rd ed. (Jossey-Bass, 2002), p. 25.

31. John T. Horn, Dan P. Lovallo, and S. Patrick Viguerie, "Learning to Let Go: Making Better Exit Decisions," *The McKinsey Quarterly* 2, 2006: 64–75.

32. THE FOCUS online (http://www.ezifocus.com/content/thefocus/issue/article.php/article/54300471), vol. X/1, 2006. Keynote topic by Jim Collins: "Filling the Seats: How People Decisions Help Build a Great Company."

Chapter 5

1. Frank L. Schmidt and John E. Hunter, "The Validity and Utility of Selection Methods in Personnel Psychology: Practical and Theoretical Implications of 85 Years of Research Findings," *Psychological Bulletin* 124(2), 1998: 262–274.

2. Boris Groysberg, Andrew N. McLean, and Nitin Nohria, "Are Leaders Portable?," *Harvard Business Review*, May 2006: 92–100.

3. Neil Anderson and Vivian Shackleton, *Successful Selection Interviewing* (Blackwell Publishers, 1993), p. 30.

4. "Conscientiousness" has a very low validity coefficient (close to 0.20). To understand the implications of this validity score, one needs to raise the validity coefficient to the square power to determine the percentage of variance in performance explained by this measure. Raising 0.20 to the square power produces 0.04, which means that only about 4 percent of the variance in performance on the job can be explained by this predictor. In other words, it is of extremely limited utility.

5. This case is well argued by Annie Murphy Paul in *The Cult of Personality* (Free Press/Simon & Schuster, 2004).

6. Daniel Goleman, *Emotional Intelligence: Why It Can Matter More Than IQ* (Bantam Books, October 1995).

7. David C. McClelland, "Testing for Competence Rather Than for 'Intelligence,'" *American Psychologist*, January 1973.

8. Richard E. Boyatzis, *The Competent Manager: A Model for Effective Performance* (New York: John Wiley & Sons, 1982).

9. Lyle M. Spencer, Jr. and Signe M. Spencer, *Competence at Work* (New York: John Wiley & Sons, 1993).

10. Cary Cherniss and Daniel Goleman, *The Emotionally Intelligent Workplace: How to Select for, Measure, and Improve Emotional Intelligence in Individuals, Groups and Organizations* (Jossey-Bass, 2001), pp. 182–206.

11. The CREIO web site (http://www.eiconsortium.org/) presents a rich list of references that support this point, as well as its "Emotional Competence Framework" and several relevant papers and pieces of research that can be accessed and downloaded.

12. Richard E. Boyatzis, Elizabeth D. Stubbs, and Scott N. Taylor, "Learning Cognitive and Emotional Intelligence Competencies through Graduate Management Education" (Case Western Reserve University, Academy of Management Learning and Education, 2002), vol. 1, no. 2, pp. 150–162.

13. Richard E. Boyatzis, "Competencies Can Be Developed, But Not in the Way We Thought," *HEC Journal*, Capability volume 2(2), 1996.

14. Daniel Goleman, Richard Boyatzis, and Annie McKee, *Primal Leadership: Realizing the Power of Emotional Intelligence* (Harvard Business School Press, 2002), pp. 111–112.

15. David C. McClelland and David H. Burnham, "Power Is the Great Motivator," *Harvard Business Review*, January 2003: 117–126.

16. See, for example, Gretchen M. Spreizer, Morgan W. McCall, Jr., and Joan D. Mahoney, "Early Identification of International Executive Potential," *Journal of Applied Psychology* 82(1), 1997: 6–29.

17. Jack Welch and Suzy Welch, *Winning* (HarperCollins, 2005), p. 83.

18. THE FOCUS online (http://www.ezifocus.com/content/thefocus/issue/article.php/article/54300471), vol. X/1, 2006. Keynote topic by Jim Collins: "Filling the Seats: How People Decisions Help Build a Great Company."

19. Boris Groysberg, Ashish Nanda, and Nitin Nohria, "The Risky Business of Hiring Stars," *Harvard Business Review*, May 2004: 92–100.

20. R. Meredith Belbin, *Management Teams* (Butterworth Heinemann, 1996), pp. 9–18.

21. Boris Groysberg, Jeffrey T. Polzer, and Hillary Anger Elfenbein, "Too Many Cooks Spoil the Broth: How Too Many High Status Individuals Decrease Group Effectiveness," Harvard Business School Working Paper Series No. 06-002, 2005.

22. Boris Groysberg, Andrew N. McLean, and Nitin Nohria, "Are Leaders Portable?," *Harvard Business Review*, May 2006: 93–100.

23. For a more detailed discussion about the process of confirming the key competencies relevant for a search, see my "Hiring Without Firing" in the July–August 1999 issue of *Harvard Business Review*, pp. 109–120.

Chapter 6

1. The story about Kepler is told in Gerd Gigerenzer and Peter M. Todd, *Simple Heuristics That Make Us Smart* (Oxford University Press, 2000). See the chapter entitled "From Pride and Prejudice to Persuasion," p. 287.

2. Valerie I. Sessa, and Jodi J. Taylor, *The Executive Selection: Strategies for Success* (Center for Creative Leadership, Jossey-Bass/Wiley, 2000), p. 65.

3. "The War for Talent," *The McKinsey Quarterly* 3, 1998: 47.

4. This is not self-serving: Our fees are independent of whether the candidate who is finally nominated for a position is an internal or an external one.

5. "The Performance Impact of New CEOs," *MIT Sloan Management Review*, winter 2001, p. 14.

6. Ibid.

7. "Leadership and Change," *Knowledge Wharton*, March 23–April 5, 2006.

8. This story is derived from Robert Iger's entry in Wikipedia, accessed August 2006.

9. Valerie I. Sessa and Jodi J. Taylor, *The Executive Selection: Strategies for Success* (Center for Creative Leadership, Jossey-Bass, 2000), pp. 73–74.

10. Barry Jaruzelski, Ken Dehoff, and Rakesh Bordia, "Money Isn't Everything," Booz Allen Hamilton Inc, *Resilience Report*, 2005: 3.

11. Alexander Kandybin and Martin Kihn, "Raising Your Return on Innovation Investment," *Strategy + Business*, May 11, 2004, 35.

12. Henry Chesbrough, *Open Innovation: The New Imperative for Creating and Profiting from Technology* (Harvard Business School Press, 2003).

13. Keld Laursen and Ammon Salter, "Open for Innovation: The Role of Openness in Explaining Innovation Performance among UK Manufacturing Firms," *Strategic Management Journal* 27(2), 2006, 131–150.

14. John S. Hammond, Ralph L. Keeney, and Howard Raiffa, *Smart Choices: A Practical Guide to Making Better Decisions* (Harvard Business School Press, 1999), p. 47.

15. Rakesh Khurana, "Finding the Right CEO: Why Boards Often Make Poor Choices," *MIT Sloan Management Review*, fall 2001.

16. Gerd Gigerenzer and Peter M. Todd, *Simple Heuristics That Make Us Smart* (Oxford University Press, 2000). See the chapter entitled "From Pride and Prejudice to Persuasion," pp. 287–308.

17. Ibid.

18. Valerie I. Sessa, Robert Kaiser, Jodi J. Taylor, and Richard J. Campbell, "Executive Selection: A Research Report on What Works and What Doesn't" (Center for Creative Leadership, 1998), p. 42.

19. Allen I. Kraut, "A Powerful and Simple Way to Predict Executive Success: Results from a 25-Year Study of Peer Evaluations," presented at the Society for Industrial and Organizational Psychology's Leading Edge Consortium, St. Louis, Missouri, October 28, 2005 (http://www.siop.org/lec/kraut.htm).

20. Mark Granovetter, *Getting a Job: A Study of Contacts and Careers* (University of Chicago Press, 1995, 1974), pp. 11–16.

21. Regarding traditional recruitment sources, those interested in the relative advantages and disadvantages can take a look at Chapter 2 of Diane Arthur's *Recruiting, Interviewing, Selecting and Orienting New Employees* (American Management Association) to find a list of basic qualitative advantages and disadvantages of a large number of traditional sources, including advertising.

22. Patricia Nakache, "Finding Talent on the Internet," *Harvard Business Review*, April 1997.

23. Theodore Levitt, *The Marketing Imagination* (Free Press, 1986, 1983), p. 129.

24. Duncan J. Watts, *Six Degrees: The Science of a Connected Age* (W.W. Norton, 2003), pp. 37–39.

25. Ibid., p. 95.

26. Rakesh Khurana, "Market Triads: A Theoretical and Empirical Analysis of Market Intermediation," *Journal for the Theory of Social Behavior* 32(2), June 2002: p. 253.

Chapter 7

1. Valerie I. Sessa, Robert Kaiser, Jodi J. Taylor, and Richard J. Campbell. "Executive Selection: A Research Report on What Works and What Doesn't" (Center for Creative Leadership, 1998), p. 42.

2. Allen I. Huffcutt, Philip L. Roth, and Michael A. McDaniel, "A Meta-Analytic Investigation of Cognitive Ability in Employment Interview Evaluations: Moderating Characteristics and Implications for Incremental Validity," *Journal of Applied Psychology* 81(5), 1996: 459–473.

3. James Tapper, "Is This Britain's Most Brazen Conwoman?," *The Mail on Sunday*, November 27, 2005.

4. James B. Mintz, "Résumé Fraud Starts at the Top," *Across the Board*, July–August 2006: 45–47.

5. T.W. Dougherty and D.B. Turban, "Behavioral Confirmation of Interviewer Expectations," in *The Employment Interview Handbook*, edited by R.W. Eder and M.M. Harris (Thousand Oaks, CA: Sage, 1999).

6. Malcolm Gladwell, *Blink: The Power of Thinking Without Thinking*. (Little, Brown, January 2005), pp. 73–74.

7. Ibid., p. 64.

8. Daniel Goleman, *Social Intelligence: The New Science of Human Relationships* (Bantam Books, 2006), p. 67.

9. T.W. Dougherty, D.B. Turban, and J.C. Callender, "Confirming First Impressions in the Employment Interview: A Field Study of Interviewer Behavior," *Journal of Applied Psychology* 79, 1994: 659–665.

10. David C. McClelland, "Identifying Competencies with Behavioral-Event Interviews," *Psychological Science* 9(5), September 1998.

11. Richard E. Boyatzis, "Using Tipping Points of Emotional Intelligence and Cognitive Competencies to Predict Financial Performance of Leaders" (Case Western Reserve University, Psicothema 2006), vol. 18, suppl., pp. 124–131.

12. Frank L. Schmidt and John E. Hunter, "The Validity and Utility of Selection Methods in Personnel Psychology: Practical and Theoretical Implications of 85 Years of Research Findings," *Psychological Bulletin* 124(2), 1998: 262–274.

13. Claudio Fernández-Aráoz, "Hiring Without Firing," *Harvard Business Review*, July–August 1999: 109–120.

14. Allen I. Huffcutt and David J. Woehr, "Further Analysis of Employment Interview Validity: A Quantitative Evaluation of Interviewer-Related Structuring Methods," *Journal of Organizational Behavior* 20(4), 1999: 549–560.

15. Daniel Goleman, *Social Intelligence: The New Science of Human Relationships* (Bantam Books, 2006), p. 98.

16. Robert W. Eder and Michael M. Harris, *The Employment Interview Handbook* (Sage Publications, 1999). See Chapter 14, "Are Some Interviewers Better Than Others?," by Laura M. Graves and Ronald J. Karren, pp. 243–258.

17. E.D. Pulakos, N. Schmitt, D. Whitney, and M. Smith, "Individual Differences in Interviewer Ratings: The Impact of Standardization, Consensus Discussion, and Sampling Error on the Validity of a Structured Interview," *Personnel Psychology* 49, 1996: 85–102.

18. Robert L. Dipboye and Kenneth E. Podratz, "Estimating Validity at the Level of the Interviewer: The Case for Individual Differences," Rice University, PowerPoint presentation accessed through Google, August 2006.

19. R. Taft, "The Ability to Judge People," *Psychological Bulletin* 52, 1955.

20. P.M. Rowe, "Unfavorable Information and Interviewer Decisions," in *The Employment Interview: Theory, Research and Practice*, edited by R.W. Eder and G.R. Ferris (Thousand Oaks, CA: Sage, 1989).

21. Valerie I. Sessa and Jodi J. Taylor, *Executive Selection: Strategies for Success* (Center for Creative Leadership, Jossey-Bass/Wiley, 2000), p. 88.

22. R.W. Eder and M.R. Buckley, "The Employment Interview: An Interactionist Perspective," in *Research in Personnel and Human Resource Management*, 6th ed., edited by G.R. Ferris and K.M. Rowland (Greenwich, CT: JAI Press, 1988).

23. THE FOCUS online (http://www.ezifocus.com/content/thefocus/issue/article.php/article/54300471), vol. X/1, 2006. Keynote topic by Jim Collins: "Filling the Seats: How People Decisions Help Build a Great Company."

Chapter 8

1. Private conversation with Howard Stevenson, Buenos Aires, June 2006.

2. Private conversation with Jack Welch, Boston, February 2006.

3. Jerry Useem, "Have They No Shame?," *Fortune*, April 14, 2003: 57.

4. Laura Nash and Howard Stevenson, *Just Enough* (Hoboken, NJ: John Wiley & Sons, 2004), p. 45.

5. "CEO Pay: A Window into Corporate Governance," Knowledge@ Wharton, February 8, 2006 (http://knowledge.wharton.upenn.edu/ article.cfm?articleid=1481).

6. "SEC's Spotlight on Executive Pay: Will It Make a Difference?" Knowledge@Wharton, May 17, 2006. (http://knowledge.wharton .upenn.edu/article.cfm?articleid=1481).

7. James Surowiecki, *The Wisdom of Crowds* (Doubleday, June 2004), pp. 113–114.

8. Jeffrey Pfeffer and Robert I. Sutton, *Hard Facts, Dangerous Half-Truths, and Total Nonsense* (Harvard Business School Press, 2006), p. 133.

9. Daniel Goleman, *Social Intelligence. The New Science of Human Relationships* (New York: Bantam/Dell, September 2006), p. 271.

10. Dan Baker, Cathy Greenberg, and Collins Hemingway, *What Happy Companies Know* (Pearson Prentice Hall, 2006), p. 62.

11. The description of the potential benefits of a lockstep compensation system appears in "A Simpler Way to Pay," *Harvard Business Review*, April 2001: 53–61.

12. Marshall W. Van Alstyne, "Create Colleagues, Not Competitors," *Harvard Business Review*, September 2005: 24.

13. Valerie I. Sessa and Jodi J. Taylor, *Executive Selection: Strategies for Success* (Center for Creative Leadership, Jossey-Bass/Wiley, 2000), p. 48.

14. Jeffrey Pfeffer and Robert I. Sutton, *Hard Facts, Dangerous Half-Truths, and Total Nonsense* (Harvard Business School Press, 2006), p. 123.

15. THE FOCUS online (http://www.ezifocus.com/content/thefocus/ issue/article.php/article/54300471), vol. X/1, 2006. Keynote topic by Jim Collins: "Filling the Seats: How People Decisions Help Build a Great Company."

16. Private conversation with Jack Welch, Boston, February 2006.

17. Marshall W. Van Alstyne, "Create Colleagues, Not Competitors," *Harvard Business Review*, September 2005: 28–30.
18. Jeffrey Pfeffer and Robert I. Sutton, *Hard Facts, Dangerous Half-Truths and Total Nonsense* (Harvard Business School Press, 2006), p. 196.

Chapter 9

1. The Apollo 13 mission was later celebrated in Ron Howard's 1995 movie of the same name.
2. Valerie I. Sessa and Jodi J. Taylor, *Executive Selection: Strategies for Success* (Center for Creative Leadership, Jossey-Bass/Wiley, 2000), p. 94.
3. John J. Gabarro, *The Dynamics of Taking Charge* (Harvard Business School Press, 1987), Chapter 1, Introduction, p. 1.
4. "Bio-Tech CEO Survey 2005: The First 100 Days," Egon Zehnder International.
5. "That Tricky First 100 Days: Executive Onboarding," *The Economist*, July 15, 2006.
6. Daniel Goleman, *Social Intelligence: The New Science of Human Relationships* (Bantam Books, September 2006), p. 271.
7. H. Mintzberg, "Managerial Work: Analysis from Observation," *Management Science* 18(2), 1971: B97–B110.
8. John J. Gabarro, *The Dynamics of Taking Charge* (Harvard Business School Press, 1987), p. 57.
9. Valerie I. Sessa and Jodi J. Taylor, *Executive Selection: Strategies for Success* (Center for Creative Leadership, Jossey-Bass/Wiley, 2000), Preface, p. xiv.
10. Jay A. Conger and David A. Nadler, "When CEOs Step Up to Fail," *MIT Sloan Management Review* 45(3), spring 2004.
11. Kevin P. Coyne and Bobby S.Y. Rao, "A Guide for the CEO-Elect," *The McKinsey Quarterly* 3, 2005: 47–53.

12. "Financial Services 2005 Survey: The First Three Months of CEOs," Egon Zehnder International, unpublished work.

13. Tsun-Yan Hsieh and Stephen Beat, "Managing CEO Transitions," *The McKinsey Quarterly* 2, 1994.

14. Daniel Goleman, *Social Intelligence: The New Science of Human Relationships* (Bantam Books, September 2006), p. 43.

15. Ibid., p. 63.

16. Ibid., p. 64.

17. Stephen J. Dorgan, John J. Dowdy, and Thomas M. Rippin, "Who Should and Shouldn't Run the Family Business," *The McKinsey Quarterly* 3, summer 2006: 13–15.

Chapter 10

1. Bill Frymire, "The Search for Talent (Why It's Getting Harder to Find)," *The Economist*, October 7, 2006.

2. Maybe this sounds like so much hyperbole, but actually it's not. Living under constant tension excessively stimulates our right prefrontal brain cortex, which (through a series of complex mechanisms) prompts our sympathetic nervous system to promote high blood pressure and the excessive secretion of cortisol and adrenaline, weakening our immune system and increasing the risk of cardiovascular diseases, diabetes, and even cancer.

3. Jack Welch and Suzy Welch, "Ideas—The Welch Way: The Real Verdict on Business," *BusinessWeek*, June 12, 2006.

4. Dr. Seuss [Theodor Seuss Geisel], *Oh, the Places You'll Go!* (New York: Random House, 1990).

Acknowledgments

While I don't know how successful this book will be, I do know what made it possible. As always, it's all about people. I couldn't have been luckier, and I couldn't be more thankful.

The many clients I have worked with for over two decades have entrusted me with their most delicate and sensitive key people issues. I feel honored by that trust, just as I am thankful for the opportunities and the associated learning.

The many candidates who have shared with me their glories, dramas, and dreams have enabled me to consider both sides of people decisions, while they have humbled me with many of their unique life lessons.

Our firm's founding chairman, Egon Zehnder, has inspired me like no one else. With unprecedented levels of integrity and aspiration, he dove into (and helped create) a fascinating profession. His successor, Dan Meiland, now also retired, allowed me to start working and learning from our firm on a global scale shortly after I joined. Our current chairman and CEO, John Grumbar, provided me with an incredible level of support and encouragement to follow my passion and write this book. He shares my conviction about our social responsibility to help improve people decisions, with or without professional help.

Damien O'Brien, my great friend of two decades, has been an invaluable companion in our adventures to improve our executive search practice. So have Evelyne Sevin, David Kidd, and Mark Byford, with whom Damien and I worked so closely over the years to implement in our firm the best practices we found both inside and out. Steve Kelner, too, has generously shared a unique level of knowledge and insight about competencies for senior executives, and best practices for assessing competence and potential.

Many other colleagues at Egon Zehnder International have directly helped me for this book, with invaluable insights and examples. The list includes, among others, Gabriel Sánchez Zinny, Jorge Steverlynck, Juan van Peborgh, Marcelo Grimoldi, Victor Loewenstein, Horst Bröcker, Philip Vivian, Rajeev Vasudeva, Mark Hönig, Ru Jordaan, Jan Stewart, Ashley Stephenson, Chris Figgis, Chris Thomas, Tom Long, Jane Allen, Robin Roberts, Nick Chia, George Davis, Brian Reinken, Fiona Packman, Martha Josephson, YL Huang, Carl Edenhammar, Joao Aquino, Luis Garreaud, Luis Cubillos, Antonio Purón, Joe Haim, Thomas Allgäuer, Germán Herrera, Edilson Camara, Dave Harris, Frank Heckner, Ignacio Gasset, Philipp Harmer, Russell Boyle, Celeste Rodgers, Angel Gallinal, Kim Van Der Zon, Justus O'Brien, Kai Lindholdst, Fritz Boyens, Peggy Cornwell, Ian Maurice, Raimund Steiner, Elaine Yew, David Majtlis, Hélène Reltgen, Stephen Benkö, Andreas Gräf, Juan Torras, Torgny Segerberg, Andre Le Comte, Isao Sakai, Alessandro Di Fusco, Andrew Gilchrist, Norbert Sack, Jill Ader, Fred Jacobsen, Henrik Aagaard, Sikko Onnes, Bill Henderson, and Neil Waters.

Looking toward Stanford, I am highly inspired by our Graduate School of Business dean Bob Joss, and particularly grateful for the learnings from my professors Jerry Porras and David Montgomery and my classmate Henry Chesbrough.

My classmate Jim Collins deserves a very special mention for his extraordinary research and practice—which has so clearly validated the importance of great people decisions—and for even coming up with this title for the book at one of our meetings in Boulder.

Several professors at Harvard Business School have greatly advanced our understanding about the crucial importance and conditions for great people decisions, and have been very generous in meeting with me to discuss ideas and share knowledge. They include Jay Lorsch, Howard Stevenson, Jack Gabarro, Nitin Nohria, Ashish Nanda, Rakesh Khurana, and Noam Wasserman.

While working for McKinsey & Company in Europe many years ago, I learned from several masters how to be a professional consultant—and even an honest "insultant" if needed—while acting with full integrity. Rolando Polli, Marcial Campos, Paco Moreno, and Juan Hoyos were clearly in that league.

Daniel Goleman has been an inspiration first for his research on the relevance of emotional and social competencies, second for his unique gifts for communicating his message, and finally for his extraordinary passion to make our world a better place by cultivating and applying those competencies.

I am also indebted to several members of the Consortium for Research on Emotional Intelligence in Organizations, including its co-chair Cary Cherniss, as well as Richard Boyatzis, Lyle Spencer, Robert Caplan, Kathy Kram, Ruth Jacobs, Rick Price, Fabio Sala, and Marilyn Gowing, among others.

Jim Kouzes has been a wonderful discussion partner on leadership issues.

John Alexander, while president of the Center for Creative Leadership, has been also a wonderful discussion partner and a generous source of research and insight on selection practices as they happen in the real world.

Marshall W. Van Alstyne, who teaches at Boston University and conducts research at MIT, has been very generous in sharing his research on the power of collective incentives for knowledge sharing at executive search firms.

I very much appreciated my various exchanges over the past few years with Peter Lorange while president of IMD, as well as with Herminia Ibarra from INSEAD and with David Maister while researching people decisions in professional service firms. Rick Camp was a wonderful trainer at the University of Michigan in my earliest days of practicing behaviorally based interviewing.

Jack Welch deserves a very special mention for his incredible passion for the topic, as well as for the generous time he shared with me while discussing his unique insights and conviction.

Suzy Welch is one of the most intelligent persons I have ever met, and I will never be able to thank her enough for the fascinating exchanges we have had over the years, ever since working together on my *Harvard Business Review* article "Hiring Without Firing" back in 1998.

My agent Helen Rees believed in this book, and has shared my passion from the very first minute. She has become along the way a wonderful partner and very dear friend.

Laurie Harting, Senior Editor at John Wiley & Sons, has been an incredible resource and guide throughout the whole process, with her always professional, resourceful, and enthusiastic approach.

Jeff Cruikshank is an outstanding professional and exceptional writer who has added enormous value, from the book proposal stage all the way to the printer. If I ever write another book, I hope I have the chance, the pleasure, and the privilege to count on his help again.

You met my assistant Joanna Eden in Chapter 1. Throughout the process of piecing together this book, she has exceeded even her own incredible standards of excellence and commitment. She made this process so easy and so much fun.

I have of course left for the end the most important. My beloved wife María is, as mentioned in the dedication, the greatest people decision I have ever made. She contributed directly to this book in so many ways, including her constant encouragement and support, her wonderful insights, and her infinite patience. But above everything else, she has kept me full of life and enthusiasm for the past 30 years, every single day. Her love is a true reflection of God's unconditional love, and I will never be able to thank her enough for this blessing.

Index